CHINA AND IRAN

CHINA AND IRAN

Parallel History, Future Threat?

EDWARD BURMAN

First published 2009

The History Press
The Mill, Brimscombe Port
Stroud, Gloucestershire, GL5 2QG
www.thehistorypress.co.uk

British Library Cataloguing in Publication Data.
A catalogue record for this book is available from the British Library.

ISBN 978 0 7524 4854 1

Typesetting and origination by The History Press
Printed and bound in Great Britain by Athenaeum Press Limited

Contents

Introduction

Two questions recur frequently in strategic thinking about the world in the twenty-first century: first, what will be China's role as it reassumes its traditional importance in world affairs; and, second, what will be the role of Iran? Yet these questions are rarely considered in tandem.

This book will show how these apparently diverse and distant countries – actually only 700 miles apart across Afghanistan as the crow flies – are in fact profoundly similar, and how the forces that shaped their present forms were driven by a potent blend of admiration for and resentment towards Western imperialism. For each has been conditioned over the past 150 years by an on-off love-hate relationship with Western political ideologies, and in each case development and modernisation have been characterised by spurts of economic and political reform based on European and American ideas alternating with outbursts of anti-colonial and, later, anti-American sentiment. At present, despite the presence of US and EU sanctions, military expenditure and technological sophistication in each country are on the rise; in the near future, as demand-driven conflict over natural resources such as oil and gas increases, China and Iran are likely to become closer allies. The initial signs are already visible. Several key long-term deals for the development of oil and gas fields and supplies to China have been signed over the past few years, one of which alone – as we shall see later – is worth $100 billion over a twenty-five-year period; in return, there is increasing trade in Chinese-made computers, cars and domestic appliances, and several hundred Chinese companies now operate in Iran beyond the oil and gas fields. Plans for improved links by sea, road, railway and pipeline are being implemented. Yet outside specialised sources, perhaps temporarily blinded by the focus on Afghanistan and Iraq, the Western world seems oblivious to this growing partnership. This book seeks to explain the consequences of this important shift in geopolitical alliances.

China and Iran, or Persia, as it was known until 1935, are both countries whose people nurture a sense of their long and proud history. In its most ancient form, the Persian language dates to the Achaemenian Period, between 550 and 330 BC, when it appeared in cuneiform inscriptions, overlapping with the evolution of classical Chinese during the Spring and Autumn Period of the Eastern Zhou dynasty from 771 to 481 BC.[1] At that time, the area of the Persian Empire was much greater than that of China, nearly as vast as its Chinese counterpart at its territorial zenith under the Mongols over a thousand years later – when the 'Chinese' empire comprehended Persia as part of the Ilkhanate. When the Achaemenid king Cyrus the Great (r.550–529 BC) presented himself to the Babylonians as 'king of the four quarters',[2] he was enunciating a concept akin to that of the Chinese emperors who thought of the furthest extent of their central and universal kingdom in terms of the 'four seas'. Under his successor Darius the Great (r.522–485 BC), Achaemenid Persia exercised influence over the entire area between East and West, comprising north-western India, Afghanistan, much of southern Russia, and satrapies as far west as Thrace and Libya. It was Darius who organised the empire into twenty provinces each ruled over by a governor known as the *satrap*, and introduced a system of tribute remarkably similar to that of the later Chinese Empire.[3] This is something usually overlooked in discussions of the modern 'Iranians', who resent being associated with Arabs and also dislike being compared as a nation to Iraq (a *very* recent coinage as the name of a country, in 1920, deriving from the Farsi phrase *ēr āk*, meaning 'lower Iran'); after all, King of Babylon was one of Cyrus's many titles.

China vaunts a longer history, as much as five thousand years' worth, although documentary evidence dates from the ninth century BC. It is indisputable, however, that Chinese civilisation has evolved over a much longer period than that and its influence on neighbouring countries including Japan, Korea and Vietnam was profound and long-lasting. The Confucian classics which are the basis of this civilisation were composed around 500 BC, and the first empire dates from 221 BC, when the king of one of seven rival Warring States, the Qin, managed by conquest and annexation to create a single, stable polity and establish himself as the first emperor, Qin Shihuang, standardising the written script and setting up a strong central administration which informs China even today (had he heard of Darius the Great?). Thereafter it was ruled as a single empire, sometimes contracting and sometimes expanding, reaching its greatest extent as a *Chinese* empire in the eighteenth century. The political vision of the modern republic, deriving from the ideals of Emperor Qianlong (r.1735–1795) and the first president, Sun Yat-sen (1866–1925), was one of a single nation comprising the 'five peoples' of Han, Mongol, Tibetan, Hui and Manchu united within a territory much larger than that of Qin Shihuang.

Today, a much smaller but still vast Iran (nearly seven times the size of the United Kingdom) has a population of about 68 million, all Muslim save tiny minorities of Baha'i, Jews, Christians and Zoroastrians, having doubled since the last Shah's time. By contrast, China (which is in turn over six times the size of Iran) has anywhere between 100 and 150 million Muslims. Officially there are only 20 million, but this is taken to mean practising Muslims; if, however, we include what might be defined 'cultural Muslims' – that is men and women of Islamic background who accept some of the basic cultural elements of Islam in their daily lives but do not participate in public prayers in the mosques – then the number is well over 100 million.

In the ancient past, links between the two countries were strong. In one of the few detailed studies of the cross-influence of the two countries, Berthold Laufer, an early twentieth-century German-trained orientalist who knew all the relevant languages (including Chinese, Persian, Sanskrit, Mongolian and Tibetan), explained a little-known role of Persia:

> We now know that Iranian peoples once covered an immense territory, extending all over Chinese Turkistan, migrating into China, coming into contact with Chinese, and exerting a profound influence on nations of other stock, notably Turks and Chinese. The Iranians were the great mediators between the West and the East, conveying the heritage of Hellenistic ideas to central and eastern Asia and transmitting valuable plants and goods of China to the Mediterranean area.[4]

Then, as now, the inhabitants and traders of both countries were extremely pragmatic – 'utilitarian' is the word Laufer uses – in the ideas and products they decided to use or disseminate. The means of dissemination was the Silk Road linking East and West through Iran, which will be discussed below.

In the preface to the first book ever written about the Chinese Muslims, *Islam in China: A Neglected Problem* (1910), Marshall Broomhall observed that the 'accessible Moslem population of China is larger than the Moslem population of Egypt, Persia, or Arabia'.[5] This has not changed. There is, however, one important difference. In Iran the population is mostly Shi'a; only around nine per cent of the population is Sunni, and was forcibly returned to a unified religious stance by the events of the Revolution in 1978–9. In China there are wide and significant differences. Chinese Muslims do not constitute a single bloc either in time or in space. In terms of time, there have been several waves of influence and immigration, most notably the first influx as Islam spread eastwards in the early centuries of its history, and a second, mainly Sufi influx in the sixteenth and seventeenth centuries. In terms of space, there are ten different Muslim minority groups, which Sun Yat-sen conflated into the Hui in his rhetoric of the 'five peoples', mostly with a strong geographical focus. Two groups are the largest and most visible, the Hui themselves, who are found throughout China, and the Uyghurs, who are concentrated in Xinjiang, followed by the Kazakhs and seven smaller groups of Dongxiang, Kyrgyz, Salar, Tajik, Uzbek, Bonan and Tatar

Muslims. As we shall see, there are also wide variations in religious practice and language between these groups. Yet their deepest loyalty is to the Islamic faith and a sense of kinship with other Muslim peoples, and, as one of the world's leading experts on Muslims in China has expressed it, although compared with the total population of China they are relatively few 'they play a role disproportionate to their numbers in influencing relations with Central Asia.'[6] Here, Central Asia stands for a vast region of common interest and influence which extends from the strongly Muslim Chinese provinces of Gansu, Ningxia and Xinjiang to Iran, Turkmenistan and western Kazakhstan.[7] For China and Iran are physically linked by a crescent of Muslim nations with populations which correspond to the various minorities within China – one group consisting of Kazakhstan, Kygrystan, Tajikistan and Uzbekistan, together with a second group consisting of Afghanistan and Pakistan to the south – with the Uyghurs placed strategically between the groups.

In recent years, China has moved gradually but ineluctably into closer relations with the ex-Soviet nations through membership, together with Russia itself, of the Shanghai Cooperation Organisation (SCO) in a clear attempt to diminish and restrict American influence in Central Asia. Xu Jian, a foreign policy specialist at the China Institute of International Studies, argues that 'increasing regionalism is an important way to restrain American hegemonism.'[8] Observers admitted to the SCO include Pakistan (predominantly Sunni although twenty per cent of the population is Shi'a) whose relationship with China is considered to be the 'most stable and durable element of Chinese foreign relations'[9] and also India, where there are around 170 million Muslims with a dominant Persian and Sufi heritage. India and Pakistan have a common 'Persian' heritage of language shared in vocabulary and script between Farsi, Hindi, Urdu and Punjabi, the latter three of which are derived from the former and are widely spoken in both countries and also in Afghanistan (the official language of Tajikistan, Tajik, is another variant of Farsi, though now written in Cyrillic script).[10]

Iran itself also has observer status in the SCO, and could become a full member when relations with China – the main force behind the organisation – develop in future years and present controversies over its nuclear policies are overcome by effective full membership of the nuclear club. Member states and observers of the SCO share problems of economics, defence and terrorism, but especially of future energy supply and demand. They also share fears of each other: China and Russia have many good reasons to be suspicious of one another, while other members remember the very recent Soviet domination of their territories. China and Iran do not have these difficulties, but rather a common, distant background. In coming years, pressure on the supply of oil and natural gas is likely to increase rather than decrease suspicions and resentments, and also to increase rather than decrease the number of such previously unimaginable partnerships as that between China and Iran. This may sound odd, or at first sight implausible. But if we think of some of the stranger partnerships formed in opposition to American hegemony, such as those between Russia and Iran, China and Pakistan or China and Sudan, then we will see that this is not the case. In three or four decades much could change, and the aim of this book is to consider possible scenarios for the future based on an examination of past and present.

Oddly enough, there have only been two books in English dealing with China and Iran together. The first was A.H.H. Abidi's *China, Iran, and the Persian Gulf*, published in 1982, most of which deals with relations between the two countries during the reign of the last Shah and in the first two years of Ayatollah Khomeini's Islamic Republic. The second is John Garver's more recent academic study *China and Iran: Ancient Partners in a Post-Imperial World*, published in 2007. The focus of Garver's scholarly work – in spite of its title – is very much on the impact of relations between these countries on the United States and *its* foreign policy, and on such problems as China's possible response to an American attack on Iran. Neither of those books considers the future geopolitical consequences of Chinese-Persian relations per se.

This book is not only about China and Iran, for that relationship will succeed or fail against the backdrop of what one futurologist has imagined as a 'time of extremism, religious belligerence and suicidal terrorism'[11] driven by a wide range of problems such as global warming, the Islamic resurgence, terrorism, regional warfare, the depletion of oil and conflicts due to population increase.

Notes

1. Browne, *Literary History of Persia*, p. 7; Endymion Wilkinson, *Chinese History: A Manual*, Cambridge, MS: Harvard University Press, 2000, pp. 21–2.
2. Quoted in Olmstead, *History of the Persian Empire*, p. 51.
3. See the excellent summary of the conquests of Darius, in Olmstead, *History of the Persian Empire*, Chapter X (pp. 135–51).
4. Laufer, 'Sino-Iranica: Chinese contributions to the history of civilization in ancient Iran', p. 185.
5. Broomhall, *Islam in China: A Neglected Problem*, pp. ix–x.
6. Gladney, 'Central Asia and China: Transnationalization, Islamization, and Ethnicization', p. 435.
7. *The Economist* has referred to Xinjiang ironically as 'Chinastan' (4 September 2008).
8. Quoted, and translated from Chinese, by Gries, 'China Eyes the Hegemon', p. 408.
9. Garver, *Protracted Contest; Sino-Indian Rivalry in the Twentieth Century*, p. 187
10. In 1977 I had the amusing experience of travelling through the deserts of south-eastern Iran, near Zabol and the frontier with Pakistan, with a Tajik-speaking geologist: I could read aloud the consonants on road signs and guess at the pronounciation (painters of the hand-painted signs didn't bother to use vowel-signs to indicate vowels), and he then

recognised the place-names from the sound and sometimes knew the route; in fact I had already had a similar experience three years earlier in Algeria when French road signs were suddenly abolished and taxi drivers who spoke Arabic couldn't always read it.
11. Martin, *The Meaning of the 21st Century*, p. 5.

Maps

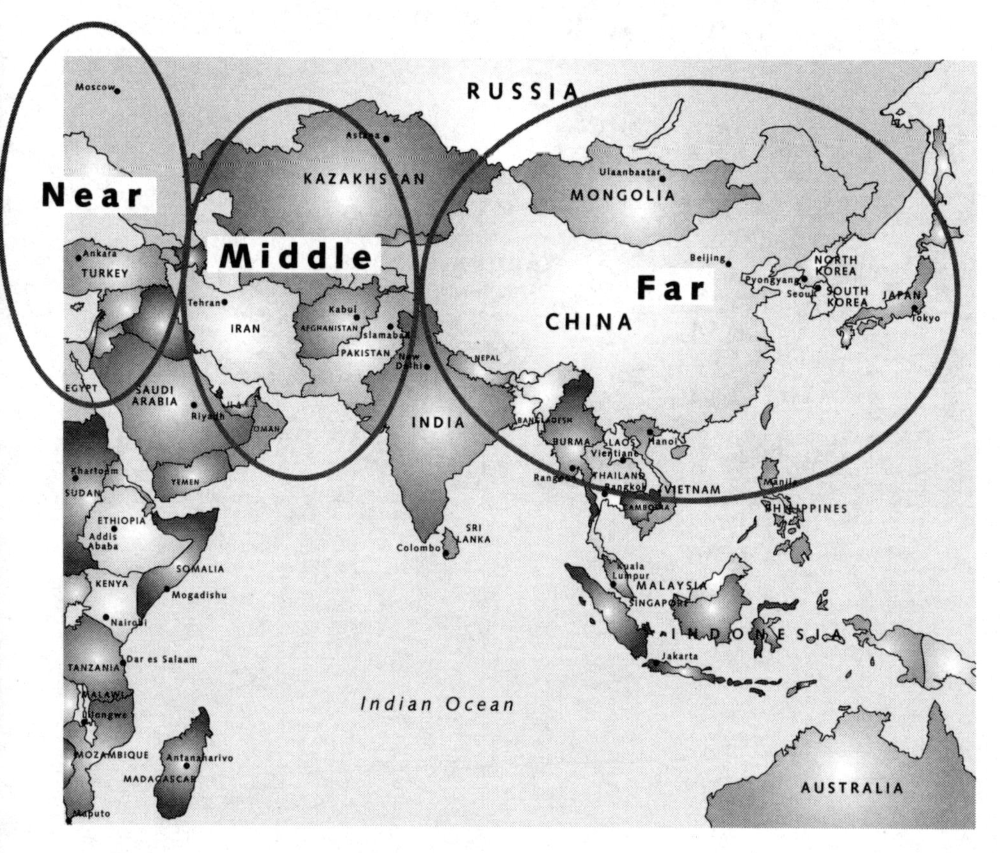

1. Near East, Middle East and Far East.

2. Turkestan: East and West.

3. Countries bordering the Caspian Sea.

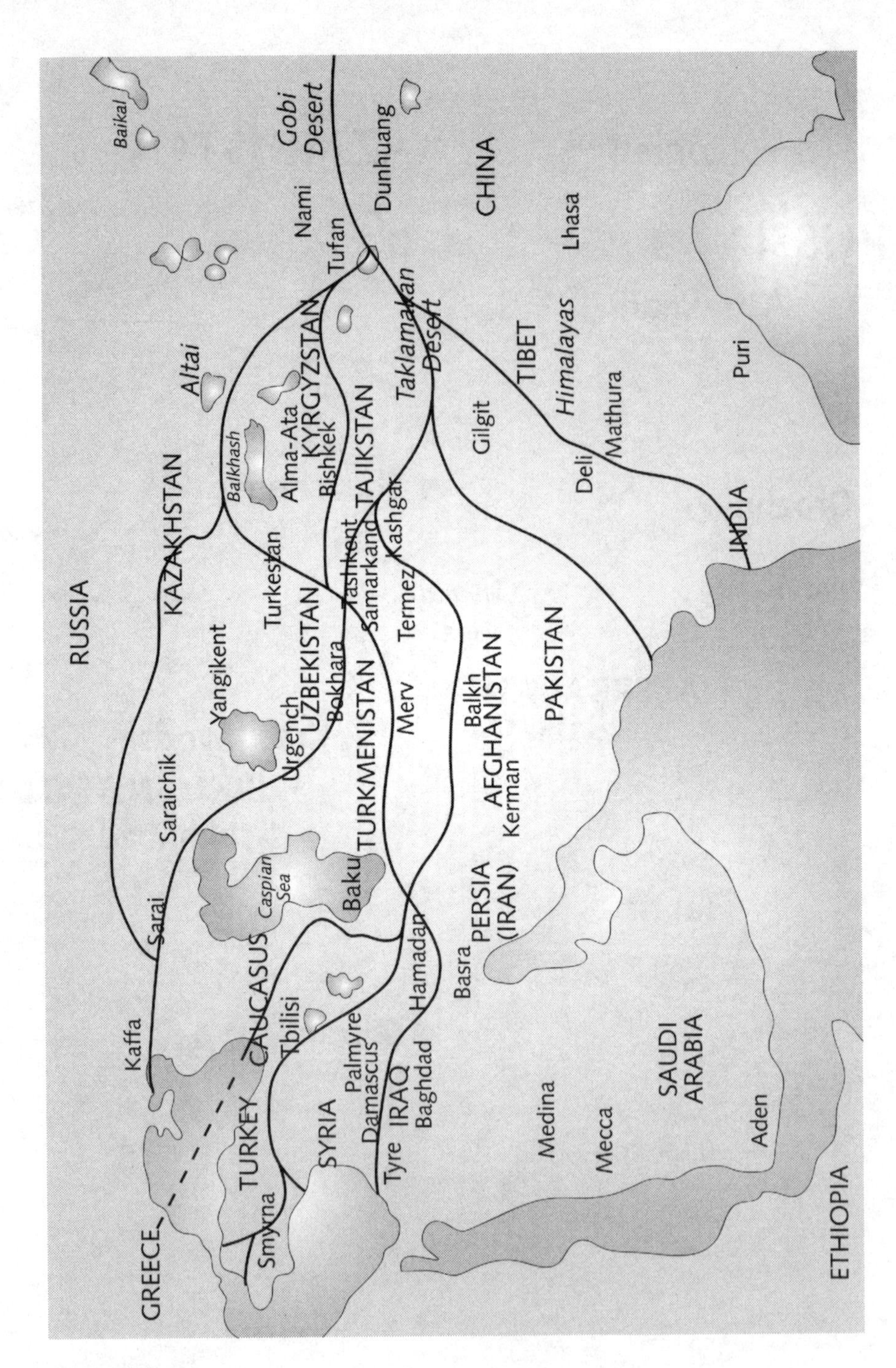

4. The Silk Road.

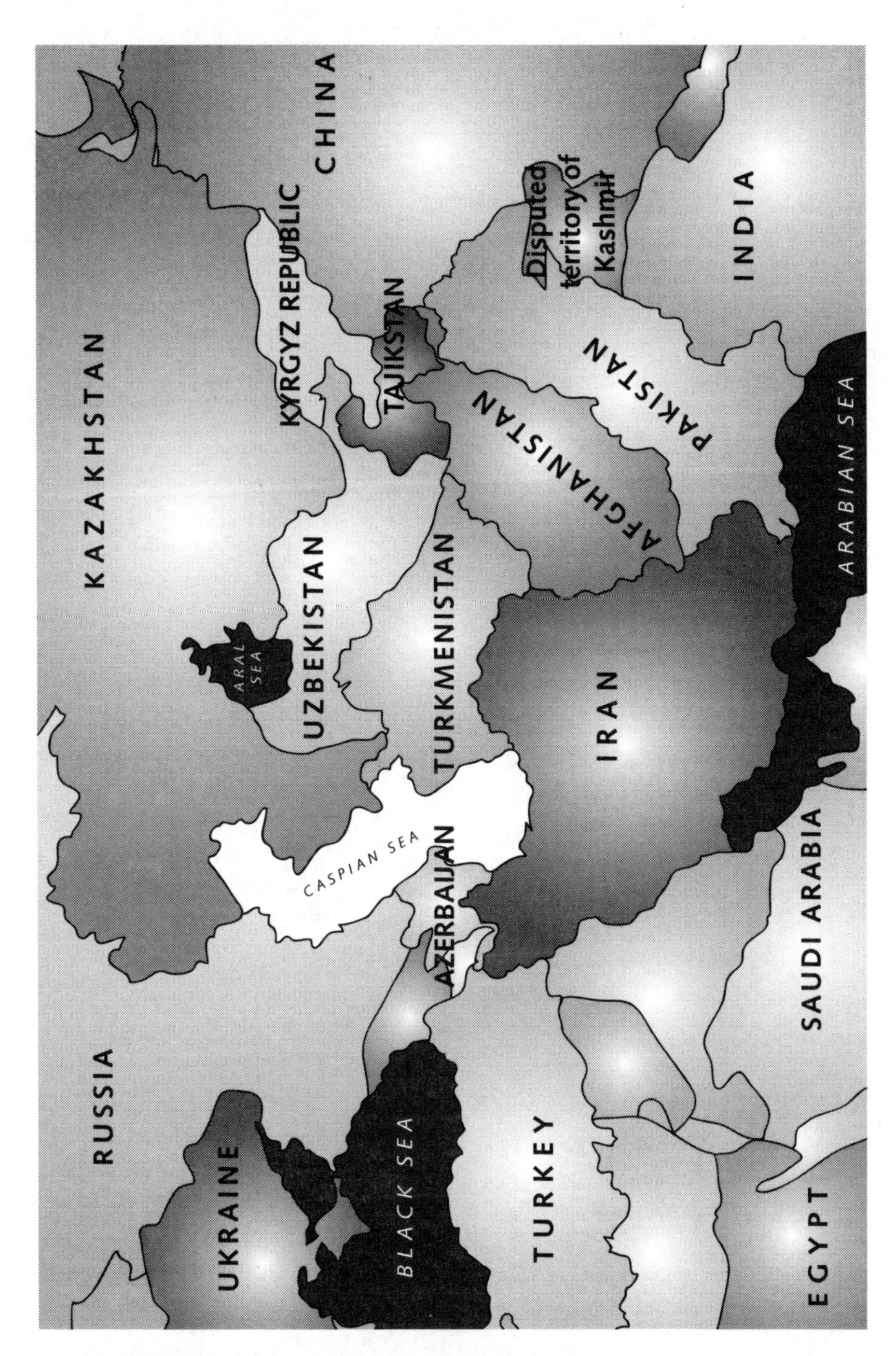

5. The member states of ECO (Economic Cooperation Organization).

PART I

The Seeds of Resentment

Resentment seems to have been given us by nature for defence, and for defence only. It is the safeguard of justice and the security of innocence. It prompts us to beat off the mischief which is attempted to be done to us, and to retaliate that which is already done;
Adam Smith, *The Theory of the Moral Sentiments*, 1759

I should like a flagstaff in front of the house, but that would be resented, for there is a tradition that this implies territorial rights.
Sir Arnold Wilson, *S. W. Persia: Letters and Diary of a Young Political Officer, 1907–1914*, 1942

Chapter 1

Iran to 'East Turkestan'

The geographical range of this book extends from the modern nation known as Iran to the Chinese province of Xinjiang. It comprises the huge, sometimes ambiguous and often misunderstood area between Europe and Asia, between West and East, which has fallen foul of modern definitions. Indeed, its cities and provinces often slip into history briefly before disappearing again, as George Curzon noted in 1889 when he wrote of the beautiful Silk Road oasis of Merv (once in Persia, and now in Turkmenistan) that it was 'difficult to realise that a place which less than a decade ago was pronounced to be the key of the Indian Empire is now an inferior wayside station on a Russian line of rail.'[1] For our purposes, it is a single area whose coherence may have an impact on the future of world power – as it has often had in the past. We will follow the wisdom of Herodotus, who over two thousand years ago questioned the need to assign the three different names Asia, Europe and Libya (i.e. Africa) to 'a tract which is in reality one', which according to the Greek historian had no obvious boundaries.[2] Instead of such simplicity we are saddled with expressions like Far East, Middle East, Central Asia and Inner Asia which sometimes obfuscate rather than clarify. Then there are even more confusing coinages such as Transcaspia, and evocative names like Oxiana and Greater Khorassan. So let us begin with some definitions.

Near East, Middle East and Far East

These geographical expressions are often used in everyday conversation and in the media in different ways. The 'Far East' is perhaps the easiest to define: in the language of the British Empire, it was used to mean all countries east of India. Today, India and its neighbours such as Bangladesh, Sri Lanka, Nepal and Myanmar are sometimes added to the core countries of China, Japan, Korea,

Thailand, Malaysia, Laos, and Cambodia, together with island nations such as Indonesia and the Philippines. More usually, it is used to refer to the countries comprising South Asia, East Asia and South-East Asia.

The 'Middle East' is a much more difficult and abused concept. Nowadays we tend to think of it in media terms of a central conflict core of Israel and the Palestinian Territories surrounded by Arab states such as Egypt, Jordan, Iraq, Syria and Lebanon which are often embroiled in the conflict. Since the expression 'Middle East' used in this way also refers more loosely to Arab and Islamic nations, it is often extended in one direction to the Gulf and occasionally in the other as far as Morocco – which is actually situated to the *west* of most European countries (Arthur Koestler noted many years ago that Marrakesh was where 'the Arabian Nights survive at 8 degrees longitude west of Greenwich'[3]). In the first sense, it is the area of reference of an influential book like Edward Said's *Orientalism*, which is rooted in memories of Arab-Israeli conflicts and the Lebanese Civil War and rarely gets further east than the literary Persia of the fourteenth-century poet Hafez (which is in any case viewed through the prism of Goethe[4]). This area, together with Turkey and the Balkans, used more accurately to be called the 'Near East', a usage which will free up part of the Middle East and make the central argument of this book more comprehensible.

For the purposes of our argument we will use the term the Near East to mean a Christian/Judaic/Islamic area comprising Egypt, Iraq, Israel, Jordan, Lebanon, Syria and Turkey. The Middle East will be used – unusually but consistently – to refer to a Muslim bloc comprising Iran, the Gulf States and Saudi Arabia, and the '-istans': Afghanistan, Turkmenistan, Tajikistan, Uzbekistan and Pakistan. One of the most striking facts for a visitor to Oman is the proximity to and affinity with Pakistan, and even Karachi, in the east, is only a ninety minute flight from Muscat. As if to prove the point, in September 2008, the Pakistan Cricket Board signed a three-year deal to play its *home* internationals in neighbouring Dubai. The Far East will be used to define the largely Buddhist area comprising Japan and South Korea, the countries of Indo-China, especially Vietnam, and China itself (see Map 1).

At the heart of this huge tripartite region sits what the Persians named Turkestan, the 'land of the Turks'. This is usually defined as extending from the Caspian Sea in the west to the eastern edge of the Tarim Basin in China, and from the Aral-Irtysh watershed in the north to the borders of Iran and Afghanistan in the south. It therefore comprises much of what has been defined above as the Middle East, to which we will add Iran and the Gulf States. Historically, Turkestan has fallen within the bounds of both the Persian Empire and the Chinese Empire: the entire territory was held by the Achaemenians around 500 BC, then by the Seleucids from 323 to 60 BC; around 200 BC it was divided into Parthia in the west and Bactria in the east. Then, during the Han dynasty, much of Turkestan fell under the sway of China, facilitating the passage of Buddhism from India through eastern Turkestan into China; with the fall of the Han, in AD 220, control swung back to Persia under the Sassanids (AD 226–651). Although with the spread of Islam much of the area came under Arab and later Turkish control, with an interregum of 'Chinese' control under the Mongols, the culture of the entire area remained predominantly Persian until the last century. Persian was one of the three official languages of the Mongol court in Peking, and many inhabitants of the Soviet Islamic Republics continued to speak it between themselves. More recently, most of the area fell within the Russian Empire, and then the Soviet Union.

Conventionally, it has been divided into Western Turkestan (also known as Russian Turkestan, comprising Kazakhstan, Kyrgyzstan, Tajikistan, Turkmenistan and Uzbekistan; collectively 4 million square kilometres) and East Turkestan (or Chinese Turkestan, now known as Xinjiang; 1.6 million square kilometres, see Map 2). Most of the countries in Western Turkestan thus defined are predominantly Muslim, with between seventy-five and ninety per cent of the population belonging to that faith, with the exception of Kazakhstan which has an almost equal balance of Muslims and Russian Orthodox at forty-seven and forty-four per cent respectively.[5] Uzbekistan is perhaps the most potentially explosive, as we shall see, with eighty-eight per cent of the largest population of these countries – nearly 28 million in 2008 – being Sunni Muslims, and with the greatest penetration of Islamic fundamentalism.[6] It is also the world's eighth biggest exporter of natural gas, and in order to avoid control of its exports by Russia's Gazprom has recently looked to another SCO partner, China, as a major market. In July 2008 construction work began on a gas pipeline which could be used to export as much as half of Uzbekistan's production to China.

The inhabitants of modern Turkey originated in this region, migrating westwards sometime before the tenth century AD, and the linguistic and cultural ties remain strong. It is a vast and wild land which has generated military giants such as Genghis Khan and Tamerlane and mythical figures like Prester John, cities of the imagination such as Xanadu, and quasi-mythical places like Samarkand and Bokhara; its size and impenetrability allowed legends recounted by medieval authors like Marco Polo and Sir John Mandeville to flourish, not to mention characters such as the more recent Borat. Kazakhstan alone is fifteen times the size of the United Kingdom, but with a quarter of its population; both Uzbekistan and Turkmenistan are roughly twice the size of the UK, with only Tajikistan being substantially smaller. Much of the landscape in all these countries consists of desert and mountains.

East Turkestan, or Xinjiang as the Chinese named it in the nineteenth century, is a land in the same mould. The sinologist Owen Lattimore, who knew it in the first half of the twentieth century as well as anyone then living, described it as a region with 'more different kinds of frontier than could be found in any area of equal size anywhere else in the world', by which he meant linguistic, cultural, religious and economic (pastoral, nomadic and industrial) as well as political frontiers.[7] A more recent scholar notes that Xinjiang has been part of Tibetan, Arab, Turkic, Mongol, Russian and Chinese empires, and that its study requires readings of texts in 'Tokharian, Türk, Soghdian, Tibetan, Mongolian, Manchu, classical Chinese, Chagatai and Persian' as well as secondary works in Chinese, Russian, Japanese, Turkish and the major European languages.[8] In short, it is a palimpsest of cultures and frontiers, and a daunting topic for scholarly research which needs to use manuscript materials and other primary sources, or even early printed books.

In its later history, with the expansion of the Russian Empire to the north and west, the Qing Empire to the east, the British Empire in Persia, and in India to the south and south-east, Turkestan became the bone of contention of what is known as the 'Great Game' for the control of Eurasia. One rather forgotten tool to understand the importance of this palimpsest is Halford John Mackinder's theory of the Eurasian 'Heartland' and its pivotal role in geopolitical power. His theories – especially the notion that whoever controls Eurasia, or the 'world island' as Mackinder calls the area stretching from the Volga to the Yangtze rivers, controls the world – influenced Hitler, which rendered them deeply unfashionable in the post-war world. But Mackinder's work contains much of interest.

The underlying theory evolved from an article entitled 'The geographical pivot of history', published in *The Geographical Journal* in 1904,[9] to its extended book-length form in *Democratic Ideals and Reality: A Study in the Politics of Reconstruction.* This was first published in 1919, and again in 1942 as the original geopolitical circumstances were repeated in another world war. After a review of the history of sea power, Mackinder explains his concept of the joint-continent of Europe, Asia and Africa as a single 'World Island',[10] a definition which was only possible with the modern discovery of the North Pole and the consequent knowledge that the sea continued around the north of this land mass. Indeed, in his view there was 'one ocean covering nine-twelfths of the globe' and 'one continent – the World Island – covering two-twelfths of the globe'.[11] Hence its immense importance and centrality. Bearing in mind his observation that this world-island is 'possessed potentially of the advantages both of insularity and of incomparably great resources',[12] and the obvious fact that the greater part of the world's population may be found there, we can see how at its heart it may consist of an area whose main axis in terms of resources is based on China and Iran – or what Mackinder refers to as the 'Iranian Upland' of Persia, Afghanistan, and Baluchistan[13] linking eastwards to the uplands of Tibet and Xinjiang. North of these uplands runs a broad belt of steppe and forest, probably the original home of the horse and the twin-humped camel, an area which was notoriously united under the empire of great horsemen like the Mongols. Together they form a heartland which offers no access to the sea, and which has been dominated briefly and in various epochs by the Persian, Mongol and Russian empires, and to a lesser extent at its eastern end by China, and at its western end by the Macedonian, Roman, Ottoman and Austro-Hungarian empires, and in its southern part by the British Empire. Not by chance, this area also comprehends the spheres of influence of the world's four great religions.[14]

Mackinder believed that problems of distance and maintaining long supply lines lay behind past failures to dominate this immense region for long periods (an idea which is confirmed in Arrian's narrative of Alexander the Great's eastern campaign), and that the new railway network he envisaged would obviate these historical difficulties. This was not in fact an entirely original notion, since Russia had built the Trans-Caspian Railway in the 1880s and 1890s for strategic purposes – it was, as Curzon tells us in his contemporary account of that railway, with fascinating historical photographs, primarily a military railway built under the command of a general and intended to overcome the 'scarcity and loss of transport animals' on earlier military campaigns.[15] Nowadays, the Registan Express (named for the square at the centre of Samarkand) links Samarkand and Tashkent in four hours.

But Mackinder went further to argue that a new, rising national power would be able to utilise the new connectivity provided by a more elaborate network to control the 'Heartland' – and by extension the 'World Island' and thus the whole world. Such a theory was, of course, attractive to the Nazis. Indeed the main focus of the book-length version was on the western end of the Heartland, and historical arguments on the specific circumstances of the First World War. Yet the 'pivot area' of his maps is clearly identifiable with the land mass which stretches from western Iran, from the line of the Zagros Mountains, to the eastern coast of China, excluding the areas south of the Himalayan range and also Indo-China.

More recently, it is interesting to see how the Gwadar Development Authority in southwest Pakistan, a port, as we shall see below, being developed together with the Chinese, presents its strategic position as a replica of the Mackinder pivot maps of a century earlier (see www.gda.gov.pk/pages/asiaregion.html). In one obvious way, it is a self-defeating map, which actually puts Iran's competing port Bandar Abbas at the centre of the entire scheme, as well as adding Turkey's European extension to link China to the West. It is, if anything, a vision of *Iran*'s future rather than that of Pakistan, and emphasises that country's role as it sets up a strong visual triangle between China, Iran and Kazakhstan. It is also noteworthy how the axis of the entire Pakistan transport network, of both highways and railways, follows a predominantly north-east - south-west line which leads directly from China to the Persian Gulf and Iran.

We should not therefore be surprised to see that in 1950 a specialist on Turkestan in its broadest sense like Lattimore could give the title *Pivot of Asia* to a book on Xinjiang, and open the first chapter by asserting that 'A new center of gravity is forming in the world.'[16] Moreover, the Anglo-American *coup d'état* against Mossadegh three years later, which placed the Shah of Iran back on his throne after a brief exile in Rome, may also be read in the context of Mackinder's thesis, as can the more recent American wars against Afghanistan and Iraq. Today, air power, especially that of long-range bombers, presents an alternative to the railways, which have not yet 'covered' Eurasia to the extent that Mackinder might have wished: USAF sorties into Afghanistan from Kyrgyzstan, Uzbekistan and Tajikistan, and into Iraq from Turkey, accord perfectly with his vision. For Turkestan is once again pregnant with military menace. Just as America sought permission for an air-base in Bishkek in 2001, so China conducted military exercises with Kyrgyzstan in 2002 and 2003, and Russia is engaged in providing military training and equipment for the member countries of CSTO (the Collective Security Treaty Organization), namely Kyrgyzstan together with Armenia, Belarus, Kazakhstan and Tajikistan. Mackinder's ideas also play an indirect role in a more recent and much discussed work, *The Clash of Civilizations* by the American political scientist Samuel P. Huntington (who does not however mention the earlier book). In the manner of his predecessor, Huntington first aired his thesis in an article in the journal *Foreign Affairs* in 1993, republished in a short book together with the comments of seven critics of the original article (1996), and then developed it into book length with the same title (again in 1996). In particular, Mackinder's ideas resurface in Huntington's notion of an Islamic-Confucian alliance against the West. Much derided both in China and in the United States and Europe on publication, in a reduced form some of the elements of Huntington's thesis are relevant here – especially because many Chinese nationalists were happy to accept his conclusions and thus implicitly accept the notion of an anti-Western alliance with Islam.[17]

In the book-length version of his argument, Huntington identified five major contemporary civilisations: Sinic (modified from Confucian in the original article), Japanese, Hindu, Islamic, Orthodox and Western, with two further possibilities of Latin American and African civilisations.[18] He defines the area of Sinic civilisation as mainland China plus the countries which have an influential population of overseas Chinese (such as Thailand, Malaysia, Indonesia, the Philippines and Singapore), together with Taiwan and non-Chinese counties which share Confucian culture like the Koreas and Vietnam. But it could also be said to include the political and economic weight of an overseas Chinese diaspora numbering around 50 million which nowadays ranges from 30,000 entrepreneurs and construction workers in Zambia to 45,000 scientists and technicians working in American universities.[19] Taken together, these countries and diffuse groups constitute what he terms a 'civilization-based world order', which in fact, although Huntington does not argue this far, is comparable to the notion of an 'Anglo-Saxon' world order in the nineteenth century – whose members retain strong local values and loyalties to a 'Motherland' wherever they happen to be in the world.[20] For these reasons, the new and developing power is a 'civilisation-based' power, as opposed to a power based on a core state.

In addition to this strictly Sinic vision, Huntington also recognises a historical 'Inner Asian Zone' which comprises 'non-Chinese Manchus, Mongols, Uighurs, Turks and Tibetans' who in the past needed for security reasons to be controlled by China.[21] These peoples, both inside and outside the core state, will still need to be controlled as China expands westwards in economic and diplomatic terms, and together with the neighbouring member states of the Shanghai Cooperation Organization, but excluding Russia, will necessarily be a part of the 'stealthy strategy toward global dominance', which integrates military, economic, and diplomatic instruments and aims to displace the United States as the world's pre-eminent power.[22]

In one of the most controversial sections of his book, Huntington wrote of a 'Tehran-Islamabad-Beijing axis' which seemed to come into being during its writing after a series of high-level visits and exchanges, with Chinese president Yang Shangkun travelling to Iran and Pakistan, President Rafsanjani of Iran travelling to Pakistan and China, and later Benazir Bhutto visiting China and Iran as soon as she became Prime Minister of Pakistan in 1993. In Huntington's words

> by the mid-1990s something like a *de facto* alliance had come into existence between the three countries rooted in opposition to the West, security concerns over India, and the desire to counter Turkish and Russian influence in Central Asia.[23]

Such an alliance, had it been formalised and had it endured, would clearly have pulled the remaining countries of Turkestan into a new version of the Great Game. But Huntington was obviously unable to take into account subsequent events in Pakistan, and the alternative Riyadh-Islamabad-Kabul axis which emerged in the early years of the new century. This geographically vertical, Sunni-inspired alliance, excluding China and Iran, was much more 'local' in the sense that it would not *necessarily* involve other countries in Turkestan.

The 'Turkestans' and the New Great Game

Yet a new version of the Great Game does exist, in which two of the great nineteenth-century powers remain – China and Russia – while Britain has been substituted in part by India and in part by the United States. One of the most powerful factors is the quest for natural resources, in particular oil and natural gas. A recent estimate, putting known oil reserves in the world at between 854 and 1,255 billion barrels, assigns to the Middle East somewhere between 362 and 678 billion barrels and to what are termed the 'transition economies' (which include the Central Asian countries) 154–190 billion barrels.[24] This means that the 'transition economies', of which Azerbaijan, Kazahkstan and Russia are the most significant in terms of oil,[25] account for between one half and one third as much as Middle Eastern reserves. In terms of natural gas, as we will see in detail in a later chapter, Russia and Iran alone possess forty-one per cent of proven global reserves (although in late 2008 it was announced that Turkmenistan might actually have more gas than Iran and nearly as much as Russia). In a period of increasing demand and diminishing reserves of oil, such data push this previously underdeveloped area of the world under a new spotlight. For Turkestan possesses more than half of known reserves of oil and gas.

Thus too a long-forgotten, misunderstood and ignored natural feature like the Caspian Sea assumes fresh importance with the discovery of oil and gas beneath its bed, and becomes a subset of the new Game in which Russia is aligned with Iran against the United States. One of the key problems is definition: forgetting its name for a moment and looking at the facts, in legal terms is the Caspian a lake or a sea? The difference is crucial. The international law of the sea guarantees such rights as navigation and overflight, and, even in a relatively limited space like the Persian Gulf, freedom of transit by ships from all states; lakes, however, may be used only by the so-called riparian states which own a section of the lake's shore.[26] But how a lake should be divided in terms of undershore assets, fishing rights or pollution control is contentious since there is no clear territorial jurisdiction as there usually is on the open ocean.

It is enough to consider the sturgeon. In the summer, it lives in the northern part of the Caspian but in winter swims to the south – migrating, as it were, from Russia and Kazahkstan to Iran. This is no minor matter, given the high market value of the fish and its eggs. Politically these questions assume even greater urgency when the riparian countries include those of such size, global economic significance and nationalistic fervour as Russia, Kazahkstan, Turkmenistan, Iran and Azerbaijan – with global powers like China and the United States vying for influence in each of them (see Map 3). For while the Friendship Treaty of 1921, reiterated in 1940, assigned an exclusive fishing zone of nineteen kilometres from the coast to Persia and the Soviet Union, it did not establish borders. So when the demise of the Soviet Union led to the creation of three new riparian nations there was no real basis for agreement. The situation is made worse by the fact that the three nations have adopted a common policy based on their belief that there is more oil and gas in their sectors than in those of Iran and Russia.[27] But on separate, specific issues they often disagree. In the recent past, Iran and Azerbaijan have tended to consider the Caspian as a sea, so that the United Nations Convention on the Law of the Sea – which allows 320 kilometres from the shore as an exclusive economic zone – could be applied, while Russia treated it as a lake where the Convention did not apply; Turkmenistan has often sided with Iran on this issue, and Kazahkstan with Russia.[28] The problem is, to ignore the oil and gas for a moment, to whom does the caviar rightfully belong?

Islam

Another factor which has led to the revival of the Great Game is the growing vitality of Islam both as a belief system and as a set of political ideologies which run the gamut from relatively liberal to revolutionary and terroristic. The resurgence began with the immense increase in oil wealth deriving from the quadrupling of prices after the 1973–4 OPEC embargo, and received new momentum from Khomeini's revolution in Iran in 1979, which emphasised a revival of traditional culture, costumes and way of life. The new Iran sought to encourage Islamic revival in the Muslim republics which emerged after the break-up of the Soviet Union, and Ayatollah Khomeini actually wrote a letter to then-President Mikhail Gorbachev offering to 'fill the ideological vacuum of your system.'[29] Although that particular overture fell on deaf ears, the increased oil wealth of Muslim nations facilitated the rise of problematic political figures such as Muammar al-Gadaffi and Saddam Hussein, and is now expressed more legitimately in some of the world's largest Sovereign Wealth Funds in states like Dubai and Abu Dhabi, providing funding for a wide range of research, propaganda and political movements.

One striking example of this resurgence and renewed pride in Muslim identity is the loosely organised group known as the al-Qaida network, a genuinely transnational movement which won widespread allegiance in spite of its terroristic ambitions. In fact the use of technology by al-Qaida, and its ability to create a transnational network, should remind us of the disturbing fact that taken together the number of Muslims in the world is about the same as the population of China, and that it therefore represents another possible 'civilisation-based world order'. For a faith-based network like al-Qaida generates transnational influence and wealth equivalent to that of the social network of the overseas Chinese, rather like the biblical multiplication of bread. Such networks are likely to be one of the causes of future disruption and conflict, no longer war between nations but war between markets – with Islam considered here as a 'religious market' pitted against the United States as a 'financial market'. In Afghanistan, in 2007, what have been described as the 'neo-Taliban' used DVDs to advocate *jihad*; these are much cheaper to copy and easier to distribute than living preachers, and also satisfy the preference of potential youthful recruits for messages in modern media format. The declared objective of these Taliban was to create a similar network, or in their words the 'mobilization of Muslim opinion worldwide as a source of funding, moral support and volunteers'.[30] With technological *jihad*, their scope of operations is no longer delimited by mountain ranges. Today, when Islam moves, even in such remote areas, the rest of the world feels it – and watches it in real time in the media. In the area we have defined as Turkestan, the collapse of the Soviet Union and the rise of Islam have led to wars and insurgencies between peoples and in places most Westerners had not heard of until a few years ago such as the Chechen Wars and the Karabakh War between Christian Armenians and Muslim Azeris (not to mention even more recondite distinctions between Karabakh, Nagorno-Karabakh and Artsakh), in addition to civil wars in Tajikistan and Afghanistan, and the Islamic insurgency in Uzbekistan.

This resurgence has had an impact on *all* Muslim societies and countries, sometimes in a subtle and profound way on the personal lives of their inhabitants and sometimes in collective manifestations of violence. It is also represented by a widespread desire to replace Western law with Islamic law, or as the global resurgence movement Hizb ut-Tahrir expresses it, to *resume* the Islamic way of life. Huntington has compared the Islamic resurgence to Marxism in the sense that it is marked by 'scriptural texts, a vision of the perfect society, commitment to fundamental change, rejection of the powers that be and the nation state.' But he finds an analogy with the Protestant Reformation of the sixteenth century more apposite, in particular as a dynamic and pure 'reaction to the stagnation and corruption of existing institutions' which requires huge and fundamental reform.[31] That may be true. Yet the resurgence must necessarily differ from the Reformation in one significant way, since it cannot be geographically limited. While the ire of Martin Luther focused on a single institution in an identifiable city, the target of the resurgents is diffused throughout the world in a multitude of institutions of global governance and cities. As the Russian Islamic scholar Aleksei Malashenko has suggested, Islam is 'the cutting edge of the resistance to the globalization process, which it cannot digest.'[32] For this process has been until now predominantly Western. Thus, in a sense, the focus on Islam and the religious aspects of resurgence and terrorism can be misleading. The French arabist Gilles Keppel, writing in October 2001 and referring to the attack on the World Trade Center, suggests that religion is only the 'crystallisation of much greater conflicts, the language in which the immense unease which exists in Muslim society is expressed for want of something better.'[33] The real issue is the simultaneously close and conflictual relationship with the Western world. In other words, in line with Malashenko, the problem is how the Islamic world can come to terms with globalisation.

In Turkestan, this problem is exacerbated by the volatile combination of newly discovered natural wealth and the fervour of Islam. Invisible to all save the 'Immanent Will' which brings together the Iceberg and the Titanic in Thomas Hardy's poem 'The Convergence of the Twain', the two elements could in the future explode in unexpected ways. Huntington summarised his section on core states and fault line conflicts as follows, considering the two forces as separate issues: 'The dynamism of Islam is the ongoing source of many relatively small fault line wars; the rise of China is the potential source of a big intercivilizational war of core states.'[34] But suppose these two sources, in the form of Iran and China, are driven together by a new catalyst at a time – to use Hardy's phrase – for now 'far and dissociate', say, between 2030 and 2050?

The Silk Road as the defining factor of Turkestan

Once, they were thus united. For many centuries, the defining factor of the Turkestan was the Silk Road, linking the Far East with Europe through the mediation of the Near East and its Mediterranean ports already during the Han dynasty (206 BC – AD 220) (see Map 4).

Chinese knowledge of the 'West' in ancient times mainly concerned the Parthians and Persians, with communications being opened up between China and the pre-Islamic Arab world by the roving ambassador Zhang Qian, who made a ten-year westward exploration in the second century BC. On subsequent journeys, however, envoys travelled as far west as Syria and on one occasion to the court of Augustus in Rome. Later, it was natural for the west-facing Tang dynasty (AD 618-907), with its partly Turkic origins, to trade with Turkestan, and knowledge of Mohammad and Islam circulated along the routes of trade soon after the Prophet's death. But even before that, from the sixth century, Persia was known in China by an approximation of its own name, '*Po ssŭ*'.[35] The walled Tang capital of Chang'an, today Xi'an, had a population of one million people in the mid-Tang period, and was the most cosmopolitan city in the world, blending its Turkic and Han inhabitants with Persians – including Persian Jews – and Indians from the west, and Japanese and Koreans from the east. In the later Song dynasty (960–1280), when the capital shifted eastwards to Kaifeng, on the Grand Canal, as many as twenty Persian embassies reached China. There were many cases of Persians serving in Chinese armies, and a significant presence of Persian engineers and astronomers in China, even before Qubilai's Mongol Empire.[36] Although most Chinese Muslims now live in the western province of Xinjiang, still today Xi'an boasts a magnificent Great Mosque and an entire Muslim quarter with ten smaller mosques, and as many as 80,000 Hui; in Kaifeng, the first synagogue in China was built in the twelfth century near the city's mosques.

There was genuine cultural exchange as well as the impact of a powerful new religion. Persian musical instruments were introduced into China, where they were developed into what are now thought of as traditional Chinese instruments: the Persian lute became the Chinese five-stringed pipa, the surnay became the vertical bamboo wind-pipe known as the bili, [37] while the Persian santur, a zither-like instrument played with hammers and introduced to China at that time, is the progenitor of the Chinese yangqing which has been described as 'the indispensable instrument of the Chinese orchestra',[38] being at the same time a plucked string instrument, a percussion instrument and a harmonising instrument. Together, these instruments of Persian origin were used to play the so-called *xiyu*, or western-style, music. It was in fact a time when the aristocracy

> indulged in a passion for Kuchean music, for Soghdian whirling dance and for exotic western goods brought by Soghdian merchants. One Tang prince chose to live in a

> yurt, and would offer guests chunks of roast mutton carved off with his own dagger. Tang music was played on the lutes, viols and percussion instruments of Central Asia and India; Tang poets sang of infatuation with western dancing girls.'[39]

The Tang were also open to Indian ideas on astronomy and calendars, and to Arabic medicine, and in their capital polo was played in the streets by Persians and other players from Central Asia.[40] Li Bai (701–62), who is often considered by the Chinese to be their greatest lyric poet, was in fact born in Suyab or Suiyeh, on the Silk Road in what is today Kyrgyzstan; this ancient trading town, now known as Ak-Beshim, was then an outpost of the Tang trading empire. Li Bai's wine-drinking poems are strikingly similar in content and tone to those of his near contemporary Abu Nuwas (750–810), who was himself half-Persian and half-Arab, especially a famous poem like 'Drinking Alone by Moonlight'.[41] They are poems in the tradition of contemplation of love and pleasure in remote desert and mountain landscapes, which could also have been written by later Persian successors of Abu Nuwas such as Hafez and Omar Khayyam. From a cultural point of view, many Chinese consider the rule of the Tang dynasty to represent the greatest period in their country's history.

But the most interesting point for our purpose is that throughout the history of the Silk Road, the Persian language, Farsi, was the lingua franca of trade. Moreover, it was one of the official languages of the Mongol Empire, known to the Chinese as the Yuan dynasty (1271–1368). China, it is true, was merely a part of the Mongol Empire, but for a while the entire area of the Four Khanates – the Kipchak Khanate or Golden Horde (Russia), the Ilkhanate (Middle East), which included Persia itself, the Chagatai Khanate (Western Asia), and the Great Khanate (Mongolia and China) – was ruled from Beijing in Mongol and Farsi. The language was used well into the Ming dynasty (1368–1644) by merchants, artisans, the educated nobility and of course the imams. In 1407, a special 'Aliens Academy' was established for official translations between Chinese and seven other languages in use within the Empire – apart from Persian, also Mongolian, Jurchen, Tibetan, Thai, Uyghur and Burmese. Many medieval Persian documents have been discovered, especially Sufi writings, and it has been argued that the language of Chinese Muslims referred to as *Huihuihua* was in fact equated with the Persian of Bokhara (then in Persia, now in Uzbekistan).[42]

Thus trade and diplomatic exchange were facilitated by the presence of an internationally recognised language, like Latin in Europe at the time, and we might argue that it was the language and culture of a Sino-Persian commercial union, together with the Turkic origins of many of its participants, which defined Turkestan. For no city was closer to the heart of Turkestan – and is today more central to the current Islamic resurgence – than Bokhara.

Islam in China

One way of viewing the history of Islam in China is to consider it in terms of three major waves or modes of influence identified by Dru Gladney among many Islamic movements which have entered China over the past 1,300 years.[43]

The first wave arrived in the early centuries of Islam with Persian and Arabic merchants and mercenaries, who arrived by sea in the south-east as well as along the Silk Road. These Muslims lived in tightly-knit groups, both in their own villages and in urban enclaves, and their descendants are known as *gedimu* from the Arabic word for 'old', *qad'm*. Their communities were built around a mosque which was overseen by an *Ahong*, or teacher, from Farsi *akhun*, which was the focus of their lives. The Arab traveller Ibn Battuta, who visited China in 1342, noted as he travelled north from Canton that 'in every Chinese city there is a quarter for Muslims in which they live by themselves, and in which they have mosques both for the Friday services and for other religious purposes.'[44] He also wrote that the Muslims are 'honoured and respected', and that in Hangzhou the 'amir', or Imperial Governor, took the trouble to have animals slaughtered according to Koranic law for his Arab guests. In Hangzhou, there were bazaars and muezzins calling the faithful to prayer from minarets, while one of the leading families was that of an Egyptian merchant who had decided to spend the rest of his life there, and had endowed the Great Mosque.[45] This suggests that there was a constant western presence in addition to the native Muslims. Today, the *gedimu* remain autonomous and often live quite separately from the Han people surrounding them, but they feel a keen sense of belonging to the worldwide Islamic community – to which they are often linked for reasons of trade.

The second wave consisted of Sufis, whose movements or orders began to arrive and establish themselves in China in the seventeeth century. This mystical variant of Islam was born from asceticism, and was developed by *shaikhs* who might be compared in their desert lifestyle and spirituality to the early Christian saints. An eminent Persian master defined Sufis as 'certain people who have turned with their inmost purpose to God, and have occupied themselves with following His path.'[46] Generally, they were either ascetics or mystics – the latter being, in the words of one Arabist, ascetics who allow themselves to be led by the joy and warmth of spiritual emotion to 'ardent fervour' and 'ecstatic experience' and thence to 'the hard discipline that is the necessary prelude to a proved theosophy.'[47] Originating in the eleventh century, by the twelfth century these mystical ascetics began to unit in brotherhoods and acknowledge the discipline and rituals of a common master. Thus they followed his 'path', *tarīqa*, or 'order'. The first of these orders was the Qādiri, named for the Persian-born Sufi 'Abd a-Qādir in the late twelfth century, which rapidly spread to the East and had a strong following in India.[48] The Qādiri is thought to have been the first Sufi order to establish itself in China, towards the end of the seventeenth century. One of the reasons for this is that Sufism had always been strong in north-eastern Persia, which under Safayid rule then included Herat and most of western Afghanistan and was therefore not distant from China. This was where great Sufi works such as Farid ud-din Attar's *Conference of the Birds* were written, together with poems like those of the Persian poets Rumi and Omar Khayyam.[49] Furthermore, there was a well-known exhortation in Sufi tradition to travel east, for while Sufism is an independent and self-fuelling sect, it can also 'pluck flowers from gardens other than its own.'

There is in fact a curious Chinese angle to this story which could have stimulated the movement of Sufism towards the east. The birds of Attar's *Conference* symbolise Sufi pilgrims seeking the 'Truth' in the form of the mythical Simurgh bird. When they hold a meeting, or conference, they choose as their leader the legendary Hoopoe (which had served as Solomon's emissary to the Queen of Sheba). The Hoopoe makes a speech in which it refers to a saying traditionally attributed to Mohammad: that his followers should seek knowledge even if it be in China. It also recounts the curious story that the Simurgh had lost a feather whilst flying over that distant country:

> An astonishing thing! The first manifestation of the Simurgh took place in China in the middle of the night. One of his feathers fell on China and his reputation filled the world. Everyone made a picture of the feather, and from it formed his own system of ideas, and so fell into a turmoil. This feather is still in the picture-gallery of that country; hence the saying, 'Seek knowledge, even in China.'[50]

This would be reason enough for Sufi orders to fan out through China in coming centuries.

Unlike the independent communities of *gedimu*, whose loyalty was to their own family and to the *ahong* of their village or urban enclave, the Sufis owed allegiance to the spiritual leader or *shaikh* of their 'order', to use a western comparison in terms of the religious orders. Their arrival revitalised traditional Chinese Islam, since these intense religionists found the 'older' Muslims to be far removed from their origins and using such un-Arabic things as Chinese texts and incense in their prayers. As we have seen the first 'order' to have a widespread influence was that of the Qādiri, or *Qadiriyya*, who are still prominent today, an order that was founded in China by Qi Jingyi, known as Qi Daozu or 'Grand Master Qi'. One reason for the lasting popularity of this movement is its ritual proximity to ancient Chinese customs, for worship is based on the tombs of ancestors rather than a mosque. Thus the Sufi can attend a normal mosque as part of his everyday life, and then participate in deeper mystical prayers at the tombs on special occasions. Their shrine is at Qi Daozu's tomb, in the Da Gongbei ('Great Tomb') mosque and tomb complex at Linxia, one of around eighty mosques in this Silk Road town in Gansu Province. The second main Sufi order in China is that of the *Naqshbandiya*, founded in the fourteenth century by Baha' ad-Din Naqshband, a native of Bokhara, which is further subdivided into the Khufiyya and Jahriyya. The Naqshbandiya, while participating in a similar form of worship at the tomb complexes, were and are more active in political- and missionary-style activities: they have important branches in Pakistan and Syria, and members of the order fought in Chechenya and Afghanistan. Just as the Taipings rebelled in the east in the mid-nineteeth century, so did the Naqshbandiya, usually referred to as Tungani or Dungani in contemporary accounts, in Yunnan and Xinjiang.[51] The nineteenth-century ruler of Kashgar, Ya'qub Beg, a notorious figure in the Great Game, only travelled to that city from Kokand in Uzbekistan to work as an aide to Buzurg Khan, a *shaykh* of the Naqshband order, who he later supplanted to make himself emir.[52] The more passive Khufiyya are today prominent in the north-west of China, but also have mosques in the south-west, in Kunming, and in Beijing. Should there ever be a concerted Muslim-led political protest movement in China, it is likely that it will be led by a member of one of these two Sufi orders.

The third wave which Gladney identifies relates to what he terms 'Scripturalist Concerns and Modernist Reforms', and began at the end of the Qing dynasty in the early-twentieth century when Chinese Muslims were able to travel to the Middle East on pilgrimage or to study in Islamic universities abroad. This led to the foundation of various associations, beginning with the Chinese Muslim Federation in Nanjing at the time of Sun Yat-sen's brief presidency in 1912, and a proliferation of newspapers and magazines. The locus of Islam shifted from Linxia to Beijing, where Muslims were much better integrated into Han society. Questions in a survey made of Muslims in Beijing and Urumqi at the turn of the twenty-first century revealed a wide divergence between the two cities: asked whether they were interested in the Olympic Games, the affirmative response was 100 per cent in the former city and 6 per cent in the latter; if they were interested in China's role in the world, 88 and 29 per cent respectively; and whether they had Han/Uyghur friends, 76 and 6 per cent (in spite of the Han now being in the majority in Urumqi).[53] At the heart of the Nujie community in Beijing stands a massive, bright green and hence highly visible Muslim theological college,and the nearby mosque is thronged on Friday morning. Yet these Muslims are far better integrated in terms of employment (in the same survey, 84 per cent in Beijing believed they had the same job opportunities as the Han, against 12 per cent in Urumqi), in accepting normal relationships between Muslim and Han, and in having a relaxed attitude towards food prescriptions in the interest of maintaining the strong Chinese tradition of hospitality. They represent a powerful but not dissident community.

Thus Muslims still represent an important minority group in China, one of the few with a significant presence throughout the country, from Xinjiang to Guangzhou and Beijing, and the potential to become a significant political force. In the past, up until the nineteenth century, they played a far greater role than now as a link between China and countries to the west of its border; in the future, it is entirely possible – perhaps even likely – that they will play an equally important role. The impact of imperial colonisation in Turkestan and what we have defined as an extended Middle East was largely negative, since no Muslim nation was sufficiently powerful to resist empires such as those of Britain, China and Russia. Resentment still simmers beneath the surface, awaiting a strong transnational leader – a Khomeini? – or a powerful common purpose. There are signs, as we shall see, of the resurgence of Islam creating the latter, with Iran as one of the focal points and potential coagulators in future decades. In order to understand how a common purpose might be forged between China and Iran, we shall now look at their remarkably similar history over the past two hundred years, and discuss how antique resentments could be a cohering factor in the future.

Notes

1. Curzon, *Russia in Central Asia in 1889 and the Anglo-Russian Question*, p. 4.
2. Herodotus, *Histories*, Book IV, Ch. 45 (*The Histories of Herodotus*, Everyman's Library, Trs. George Rawlinson, London: Dent, 1964, Volume One, pp. 304–5).
3. In *The Heel of Achilles*: Essays 1968–73, London: Hutchinson, 1974, p. 183.
4. See 'Preface', *Orientalism*, p. xvii and p. xxiv.
5. CIA *Factbook*, https://www.cia.gov/library/publications/the-world-factbook/geos/kz.html .
6. Ibid., https://www.cia.gov/library/publications/the-world-factbook/geos/uz.html .
7. In Lattimore, *Pivot of Asia: Sinkiang and the Inner Asian Frontiers of China and Russia*, pp. 3–4.
8. Millward, *Eurasian Crossroads: A History of Xinjiang*, p. xi.
9. Mackinder, Halford J., 'The geographical pivot of history', *The Geographical Journal*, Vol. XXIII, No. 4. (1904), pp. 421–44.
10. Mackinder, *Democratic Ideals and Reality: A Study in the Politics of Reconstruction*, p. 45.
11. Ibid., p. 46.
12. Ibid., p. 47.
13. Ibid., p. 55.
14. In Mackinder's terms Buddhism, Brahminism, Mahometanism, and Christianity ('Geographical pivot', p. 438).
15. Curzon, *Russia in Central Asia*, p. 38.
16. Lattimore, *Pivot of Asia*, p. 3.
17. See Gries, *China's New Nationalism: Pride, Politics, and Diplomacy*, pp. 40–1.
18. Huntington, *The Clash of Civilizations and the Remaking of World Order*, pp. 45–6. The term 'Sinic' was proposed by Toynbee as the name for the 'society upon whose past Confucius looked back with reverence' (Arnold J. Toynbee, A Study of History, Abridgement by D.C. Somervell, Oxford: OUP, 1960, p. 22).
19. See the chapter on the Overseas Chinese in my *Stealth Empire*, pp. 111–32.

20. The comparison is made by Frank Dikötter in his chapter 'Race in China', in Nyíri and Breidenbach, *China Inside Out: Contemporary Chinese Nationalism and Transnationalism*, p. 203.
21. Huntington, *The Clash of Civilizations*, p. 167.
22. Constantine C. Menges, *China: The Gathering Threat*, Nashville: Nelson Current, 2005, pp. 367–417.
23. Huntington, *The Clash of Civilizations*, p. 239.
24. The first number is that calculated by the Energy Watch Group and the second by the industry association IHS. See the report *Crude Oil: The Supply Outlook*, Energy Watch Group, October 2007 (EWG-Series No 3/2007), p. 8; available online at www.energywatchgroup.org .
25. The full list includes Albania, Armenia, Azerbaijan, Belarus, Bosnia-Herzegovina, Bulgaria, Croatia, Estonia, Yugoslavia, Macedonia, Georgia, Kazakhstan, Kyrgyzstan, Latvia, Lithuania, Moldova, Romania, Russia, Slovenia, Tajikistan, Turkmenistan, Ukraine, Uzbekistan, Cyprus and Malta (EWG, Crude Oil p. 5).
26. See the interesting legal discussion by Bernard H. Oxman, 'Caspian Sea or Lake: What Difference Does It Make?' in *Caspian Crossroads Magazine*, Volume 1, Issue No.4, Winter 1996, available at http://ourworld.compuserve.com/HOMEPAGES/USAZERB/141.htm.
27. Johnson, *Oil Islam and Conflict: Central Asia Since 1945*, p. 205.
28. See the discussion of these issues in Johnson, *Oil Islam and Conflict*, pp. 201–6.
29. Quoted by Edmund Herzig in 'Iran in the Caucasus, Caspian and Central Asia: Lessons for Western Strategy', in Whitlock (Ed), *Iran and Its Neighbours: Diverging Views on a Strategic Region*, pp. 21–28; p. 25.
30. Giustozzi, *Koran, Kalashnikov, and Laptop*, p.138.
31. Huntington, *Clash of Civilizations*, p. 111.
32. Alexey Malashenko, 'The Clash is for Real,' Moscow Carnegie Center Briefing Paper, Volume 9, Issue 4, November 2007, p. 3; http://www.carnegie.ru/en/pubs/briefings/77178.htm .
33. Gilles Keppel, *Chronique d'une guerre d'Orient* (automne 2001) *suivi de Brève chronique d'Israël et de Palestine* (avril-mai 2001), Paris: Éditions Gallimard, 2002; I quote and translate here from the Italian edition, *L'autunno della guerra santa: Viaggio nel mondo islamico dopo l'11 Settembre*, Rome: Carocci editore, 2002, pp. 13-14.
34. Huntington, *Clash*, p. 209.
35. Bretschneider, *On the Knowledge Possessed by the Ancient Chinese of the Arabs and Arabian Colonies, and Other Western Countries, Mentioned in Chinese Books*, p. 3.
36. Bretschneider, *Medieval Researches from Eastern Asiatic Sources: Fragments Towards the Knowledge of the Geography and History of Central and Western Asia from the 13th to the 17th Century*, Vol. I, pp. 265–74.
37. See Shen, *Cultural Flow Between China and Outside World Throughout History*, pp. 74–85, and Lee, Yuan-Yuan & Shen, Sin-Yan, *Chinese Musical Instruments*, Chicago: Chinese Music Society of North America, 1999, passim.
38. Lee & Shen, *Chinese Musical Instruments*, p. 131.
39. Millward, *Eurasian Crossroads: A History of Xinjiang*, p. 32.

40. Shen, *Cultural Flow*, p. 99.

41. Consider, for example, the opening stanza, in Arthur Waley's translation:
'A cup of wine, under the flowering trees;
I drink alone, for no friend is near
Raising my cup I beckon the bright moon,
For he, with my shadow, will make three men.
The moon, alas, is no drinker of wine;'.

42. See Dillon, *China's Muslim Hui Community*, pp. 156-8.

43. This definition, and the structure of the following paragraphs, was suggested by Dru Gladney in the first chapter of his book *Muslim Chinese: Ethnic Nationalism in the People's Republic*, in particular from pp. 36–64.

44. *Ibn Battuta: Travels in Asia and Africa 1325–1354*, Translated and selected by H. A. R. Gibb, London: Routledge and Kegan Paul, 1929, p. 283.

45. Ibid., pp. 294–5.

46. A. J. Arberry (Trs), *A Sufi Martyr: The Apologia of 'Ain al-Qudat al-Hamadhānī,* London: George Allen & Unwin, 1969, p. 41.

47. Arberry, *Sufism: An Account of the Mystics of Islam*, p. 45.

48. Ibid., p. 85.

49. Attar and Omar Khayyam were both born in Nishapur, not far from Afghanistan, while Rumi himself was born at Balkh inside northern Afghanistan – not too far from China.

50. Farid ud-din Attar, *The Conference of the Birds, Mantiq ut-Tair*, London: Routledge & Kegan Paul, 1954, p. 13.

51. Boulger *The Life of Yakoob Beg,* p. 93. Since he refers to the Tungani as 'fervent' (p. 94) and from Gansu he probably mean Sufis; he never refers to Uyghurs or Uighurs.

52. Soucek, *History*, p. 265.

53. Kaltman, *Under the Heel of the Dragon*, Table 2, p. 136.

Chapter 2

Parallel Modern History

The parallels between Chinese history and Persian history in the nineteenth and early-twentieth centuries are so uncannily precise that it is surprising they have attracted little or no attention. On a personal level, when I began reading books on the emergence of Chinese nationalism after moving to Beijing early in 2003, I was constantly struck by similarities in my reading of political history and travellers' accounts of Persian nationalism in Tehran during the late 1970s. A distinct sense of *déjà vu*. Often it was possible to substitute a Chinese name or event for a person or event I already knew about, and in the case of foreign military officers and travellers the men involved were often literally the same – two excellent observers and writers such as Sir Henry Pottinger and Sir Aurel Stein, for example. This chapter will consider some of these parallels, with the implicit subtext that such parallel pasts might lead to parallel futures in spite of present apparent differences.

The Negative Impact of Western Imperialism *c.*1850–1911

In the early part of the nineteenth century, China and Persia were two of the largest countries in the world, each overseen by a powerful martial dynasty. More particularly, each had recently reached a new acme of power and territorial extension under a great political and military strategist: the Emperor Qianlong in the case of China, and Shah Agha Mohammad Khan in the case of Persia.

At the inception of Qing rule in 1644, what we describe today as 'China' excluded Xinjiang, Tibet, and Qinghai in the west, while the policies of conquest and subjugation in the large provinces of Yunnan, Sichuan and Guizhou in the south-west had not yet been totally successful. The territory known as *Da Qing* – roughly 'the Qing lands', since there was no name for the country at that time

– when they came to power was just under half of that constituting the present People's Republic. From the second Qing emperor Kangxi (r.1661–1722), to his son Yongzhen (r.1723–1735), and on to the long rule of his grandson Qianlong (r.1736–1795), there was a gradual expansion of empire which reached its climax with Qianlong's campaign in Tibet. Although today the Chinese claim never to have invaded other people's lands, around the time of the beginning of republican history the Italian traveller and surveyor Filippo de Filippi described eastern Turkestan as a conquered territory ('*paese di conquista*') and compared the distance between conqueror and conquered to that between India and Britain.[1]

In 1792, Qianlong himself wrote a 'Record of Ten Perfections' in which he detailed ten military campaigns that had defined his reign. It shows that he fully understood the weaknesses of tribal organisation, and how to exploit the anarchy and divisiveness of the steppe tribes to the advantage of his own empire, through tribute and marriage alliances as well as military campaigns. Five of these campaigns in particular pushed Chinese territory to a new western frontier: two against the Mongols in north-western Xinjiang; one against the Turkic Muslims in southern Xinjiang; and one against the Gurkhas in Tibet. By means of these campaigns he conquered, assimilated, mapped and created the basis of the territory of the People's Republic today.

Thus on Qianlong's death in 1796 the Chinese Empire had reached its greatest extent. In exactly the same year, a few hundred miles to the west, Agha Mohammad Khan (1742–97), having exploited a similar understanding of tribal weaknesses, was crowned as Shah of Persia to rule over what was also the greatest extent of modern Persia.

In 1779, following the death of Mohammad Karim Khan Zand, the Zand dynasty ruler of southern Persia, Agha Mohammad, the leader of the Qajar tribe, set out to reunify Persia. By 1794 he had eliminated his rivals, including Lotf'Ali Khan, the last of the Zand dynasty, and had reasserted Persian sovereignty over former territories in Georgia and the Caucasus. He established his capital in the newly built city of Tehran, and was formally crowned as first Shah of a new Qajar dynasty. Yet his success, like that of Qianlong, was short-lived, because even as these two great men were extending their respective empires, militarily stronger Western empires, in particular those of Britain and Russia, were expanding into their territories.

Agha Mohammad's reign was particularly short-lived since he was assassinated in 1797 and succeeded by his nephew, Fath Ali Shah (r. 1797–1834), who took the fatal step of going to war with Russia in 1804. But the omens began earlier, with a Preliminary Treaty of Friendship signed between Britain and Persia in 1809, a further Treaty three years later signed by the British 'Ambassador Extraordinary and Plenipotentiary' Sir Gore Ouseley, and the Treaty of Gulistan in 1813 (arranged by Ouseley between Russia and Persia!). Disputes over these treaties ultimately led to the Russo-Persian War of 1826–8, which was concluded by the Treaty of

Turkmanchai, after which the Russians in Persia were given extraterritorial rights that were soon extended to the British. It resulted in the loss of Persian land in Armenia (including Yerevan), and parts of Azerbaijan, and took away the rights of Persian ships to sail on the Caspian Sea. Worse still, it assigned to Russia, and later to Britain, the right to establish consulates anywhere they wished to build them. For the British, Persia became a bulwark between India and ambitious European powers, and from the granting of permission to build an overland telegraph line after the Indian Mutiny of 1857, it gradually awarded important concessions to British companies. A series of concessions for mines, railways, tobacco, trade and banking – the Persian-sounding Imperial Bank of Persia was actually founded by Baron Julius de Reuter after a concession granted in 1873 – culminated with the D'Arcy oil concession in 1901 and the creation of the Anglo-Persian Oil Company eight years later. With the Anglo-Russian Convention of 1907, the grand Persian *Empire* became a smaller and divided *country*, effectively ruled by Russia in the north and by Britain in the south.

The Chinese story is perhaps better known. Briefly, as the British version has it, in 1793 an embassy arrived in China bearing gifts from King George III with three main objectives: to enter into an agreement which would help to reduce a huge trade deficit; to create better trading conditions by opening up new ports; and to create a permanent diplomatic presence in Peking. From the British point of view, the royal gifts were considered to be a normal part of diplomatic negotiations. The popular version of this episode is that the mission failed because its leader, Earl Macartney, refused to kowtow to the Emperor, who dismissed the gifts as worthless trifles, and asserted in an edict that he did not need British goods at all, so that the embassy returned to London empty-handed.[2] A further embassy in 1816 led by William Pitt, 1st Earl of Amherst (1773–1857; later Governor-General of India) attempted to achieve the same ends by diplomatic negotiation. That too failed, and clashes over trade and opium led to the First Opium War in 1839–42, which ended with the Treaty of Nanking (Nanjing) that famously ceded the island of Hong Kong to Britain 'in perpetuity' and allowed the establishment of the first batch of so-called Treaty Ports (Canton, Fuzhou, Xiamen, Ningbo and Shanghai), for the residence and commercial activities of British merchants. It also granted the right to open consulates in each of these cities, and sparked a series of similar treaties with other European imperial powers, leading to the concession system which later caused the same resentment in the Chinese as that in Persia – involving fewer foreign powers but greater privileges – did in the Persians.

Even the agents of encroachment were often the same. The diplomat Henry Ellis (1777–1855; later Sir Henry) was sent to Tehran in 1814 to finalise a new draft of the treaty negotiated by Sir Gore Ouseley. Two years later he travelled to Peking with the Amherst embassy and wrote an account of his Chinese experiences under the title *Journal of the Proceedings of the Late Embassy to China.*[3]

There were also several military figures in the Great Game who played roles in both China and India. One fascinating example was Henry Pottinger (1789-1856), who in 1810 was sent by Sir John Malcolm (1769–1833; three times envoy to Persia) as a young lieutenant in the Bombay Infantry to explore south-eastern Persia disguised as a Muslim pilgrim. Much later, as Sir Henry, he went to China as plenipotentiary in 1841 and after seizing Xiamen, Ningbo and Nanjing was the man who negotiated the terms of the Treaty of Nanking and signed it on behalf of Queen Victoria. Two years later, in recognition of his success in the negotiations, he was appointed the first Governor of Hong Kong.[4] Pottinger wrote a book about his Persian and Indian experiences, *Travels in Beloochistan and Sinde*, worth reading even now for the incredible adventure of travelling as a fake pilgrim and speaking local dialects to tribesmen as he rode through countryside which is still dangerous today. A good example is the passage in which he and his companion explain away their light complexion by claiming to be descendants of an Uzbek family which 'had been settled in Hindoostan for some generations'. It shows acceptance of the broad area of Turkestan. His acute observations on the Baluchis and their way of life are worthy of a modern work of social anthropology.[5]

The influence of Western imperialism was not entirely negative. The Persian capital itself had been transformed under French infuence. In 1867, a new wall with twelve ornamental gates was begun under the supervision of a French general to enclose an area about twice the size of the previous, sixteenth-century, walls with the *Argh* – the walled imperial complex which was the equivalent of the Forbidden City – now at the centre rather than at the northern limit. Then, after a visit to France in 1873, on the first of three royal European tours, a new impulse came as Nasir ed-Din Shah (r.1848–96) sought to imitate Haussmann's boulevards with tree-lined avenues and build a Paris of the East. Broad new avenues which still exist today albeit with different names, such as Avenue Shah, Avenue Sepah and Avenue Shahreza, were built across previously unused land to the north of the old city. In the street plan of 1890, echoes of Parisian names may be found, for example Avenue du Fossé, reminiscent of the Rue des Fossés St Jacques and Rue des Fossés St Bernard which indicate the line of Philip Augustus' thirteenth-century city walls, and modern-sounding names such as Avenue du Gaz – which was later updated to become Avenue d'Électricité.[6] Neither is this mere speculation, for the Shah met the city architect of his time and mentions Haussmann in the personal diary of the journey to Paris:

> On our arrival in the garden, M. Duval, the Prefect of Paris, together with M. Alfand, the city architect, and others, were waiting for us. The streets of Paris, thus straight, broad, and level, together with the avenues in which trees have been planted so regularly and tastefully, were all planned and laid out on the instructions and under the supervision of M. Haussman, formerly Prefect of Paris in the days of Napoleon, and of this architect.[7]

The Shah was impressed by the fact that the broad boulevards were lighted by gas, which helped to make it a 'bright, beautiful and charming city' worth emulating.[8] He was fascinated by new technologies such as photography, and introduced to his country Western innovations such as a 'House of Sciences' (*Dar al-Funun*) to teach modern science and languages for future civil servants and diplomats. In 1858, forty-two boys from this college were sent to Europe for advanced studies.[9]

In fact, already in the first decade of the twentieth century an American visitor to Persia, William Penn Cresson (1873–1932), could observe that a traveller expecting to find an *Arabian Nights* fantasy in Tehran would be disappointed because 'Persia has fallen under the spell of Western ideas, and the Persian of to-day is striving to adapt his ancient civilization to the ways and customs of Europe.'[10] Cresson noted on going to an audience with the Shah that most of the Persian officials wore European Court dress or uniforms, and that the younger ones spoke French among themselves (Cresson himself had studied at the *École des Sciences Politiques*). The Shah conversed with his visitors in French, and spoke – as his contemporaries in China did in the same years – of the importance of improving communications in the country with a railway network.[11]

While no Chinese emperor ever travelled to the West, some imperial scholars were fascinated by the benefits of Western technology. The political theorist and reformer Kang Youwei (K'ang Yu-Wei, 1858–1927) understood that while China possessed 'principles, institutions, and culture' which were the 'most elevated in the world', due to unenlightened customs and 'a dearth of men of ability, she is passively taking aggression and insult.'[12] Some traditional scholars demonstrated surprising flexibility. Zhang Zhidong (Chang Chih-Tung, 1837–1900), a scholar famed for his phenomenal memory and knowledge of the Confucian classics, was criticised for paying too much attention to current affairs rather than classical learning. In fact, when he became governor of the important southern province of Guangdong he not only promoted the distribution of printed books for the dissemination of knowledge but created an arsenal for manufacturing shells, established a school for training naval officers and purchased new warships. He also brought German instructors to train a modern military force. Later, as Governor of Wuchang, he sponsored a project for a railway from Peking to Hankow[13], and from his action in founding an iron-and-steel works evidently understood very well the importance of industrial development.[14] In his book *Exhortation to Study* (1898) he coined the still-cited slogan 'Chinese learning for the fundamental principles (*ti*), Western learning for practical applications (*yong*).' This meant that scholars should 'glance over the philosophical works and belles-lettres and exquisite writings. And then they can select and make use of that Western knowledge which can make up our shortcoming.'[15] Zhang's book was an immense success, and the emperor himself ordered its distribution to all officials and students.[16]

There were other armaments factories built in Shanghai and Suzhou, new arsenals in Shanghai and Nanjing, new dockyards, the creation of an office to deal with foreign affairs, schools of foreign languages and translation, and, parallel to the example of the 'House of Sciences' in Tehran, the beginning of programmes to send Chinese students to study abroad – 120 boys were sent to the United States between 1872 and 1881, and soon afterwards naval students were sent to study shipbuilding in Britain, France and Germany.

But technology generated concern even then. The court official Liu Xi Hun (Liu Hsi Hun), who in 1876 travelled with the first Chinese embassy to London, wrote in his *Journal* that if railways were introduced to China 'the people who bare their thighs and forearms, who hold to the whip and the cord, who row the boats, who pull the carriages, to carry people or cargo, would all lose their jobs.'[17]

In China and Iran, the same western authors were studied, as we will now see in the parallel cases of a Chinese naval student who became a significant reformer and translator of authors such as Adam Smith and John Stuart Mill, and a Persian aristocrat who became Prime Minister and in his retirement dedicated himself to translating Shakespeare. These men arrived in England by different routes and for different reasons in exactly the same year, 1877, and the profound impact of Western culture conditioned the future life of each man – and thus of his country.

Yan Fu (or Yen Fu; 1853–1921) was one of the first Chinese students to be sent abroad, and learned English well enough to become an eminent translator.[18] The son of a doctor in a scholar-gentry family of Fujian province, he was destined for the official exams which could lead to government office. But on the death of his father when he was thirteen, this costly and arduous process – which required private tutors and years of study – became impossible for him, and a family friend helped him to enter the Fuzhou Arsenal Academy. There, the curriculum was quite different. Technical subjects like astronomy, navigation and the various branches of mathematics were taught together with English, a far cry from the rote learning of the Confucian classics and their commentaries which constituted the traditional scholarly career. He graduated from the academy in 1871 and then spent six years at sea before being selected to study naval science in England.[19]

This opportunity transformed the young midshipman, who gradually reverted to his scholarly background. He travelled as part of a group of twelve, initially to Portsmouth, and then to the Royal Naval College in Greenwich, where he studied from 1877 to 1879. Given this background, he could have become an excellent naval commander, but events in China led him to exploit his linguistic talents to translate works he believed would be useful for his country and its growing self-awareness. As David Wright observes, 'his heart was indeed not in technical translation, but in the transmission of the political ideas which he had discovered in the West, and which he felt to be of urgent relevance to the future of China.'[20] Above all, he wanted to understand what it was about this small country, England, which had enabled it to become such a great military and economic power. In the process, he became one of Westernisation's strongest advocates, first as a professor in Fuzhou, then at the Tianjin Naval Academy for nearly twenty years, at a school of Western studies in Beijing known as the 'School of all the Arts', and as Head of the College of Letters at the National Peking University, now Peking University. He also founded newspapers and journals, but became most famous initially for a series of modernising essays in which he developed his ideas, and then for translations of works which were to have a significant impact on Chinese intellectual life.

An example of the essays was *Strength*, published in 1895 after the disastrous Sino-Japanese War of 1894–5 and the ensuing loss of face which China had suffered. Yan's idea of strength was based on the concept of moral, physical and intellectual education developed by Dr Thomas Arnold, Headmaster of Rugby School, who had emphasised the value of physical exercise and sport. The new China he envisaged would be possible only if the people were physically stronger: he noted how dominant nations in the past – such as Greece and Rome – had been 'strong and beautiful, able to withstand suffering and capable in war, ruling over their era.'[21] This adapted version of social Darwinism had significant influence on the rise of competitive sport in China, after centuries in which the queue (pigtail) had rendered many sports physically difficult.

The books Yan Fu translated were among the major texts of evolution, economics and political philosophy of recent British history, and appeared in rapid succession: *Evolution and Ethics* by T.H. Huxley in 1898 (which the author Lu Xun tells us he devoured at a single sitting while he was studying at the School of Railways and Mines[22]), *The Study of Sociology* by Herbert Spencer in 1902, *The Wealth of Nations* by Adam Smith in 1902, *On Liberty* by John Stuart Mill in 1903, and *Logic*, again by John Stuart Mill in 1905. In just a few years, he opened up a new world of ideas for the Chinese intellectual élite which read them voraciously: concepts like the 'struggle for survival' and 'natural selection' had a profound effect on Chinese readers accustomed to their classics.

Many years later, the authors of a controversial Chinese television documentary series shown in 1988, *River Elegy* (discussed below), made an unfavourable comparison with Hirobumu Ito, Prime Minister of Japan (1892–96), arguing that he had been a fellow student of Yan's at Greenwich but had made better use of his knowledge since as a result of it he 'quickly led his nation into the community of powerful nations'.[23] That they were fellow students is unlikely however, since Hirobumi was twelve years older and already in government service at the time his Chinese counterpart went to study at the Naval College. But the comparison does point up a significant difference between China and Japan. For Hirobumi, who was a strong advocate of adopting Western technology and ideas, wrote the new Japanese constitution in 1889, and also supported the war with China which spurred Yan Fu's interest in translating Western works. Indeed, Hirobumi also participated in negotiations for the infamous (from the Chinese point of view)

Treaty of Shimonoseki which at the end of the Sino-Japanese War ceded Taiwan to Japan. The authors of *River Elegy* claim that while Yan studied enlightenment thought and sponsored social reform in China, as well as translating fundamental texts, he 'eventually retreated back into the embrace of Confucius and Mencius'. In other words, although he advocated modernisation and Westernisation fervently, he could not totally escape the shackles of his early classical education. Indeed at least one reader, the reformer and author Liang Qichao, complained that 'those who have not read many ancient books found his translations most difficult to comprehend.'[24]

Following a different and more privileged route, the Persian aristocrat Abul Ghassem Khan Gharagozlou arrived in England in the same year as Yan Fu, 1877, aged twenty-one.[25] His father also had died relatively young, but he was lucky enough to be brought up by a wealthy and influential relative, his grandfather Mahmoud Khan, known by the title Nasser ul-Molk, who was the Persian Minister for Foreign Affairs. Thus it was arranged that when Nasir ed-Din Shah left Persia for his first European journey, the young man would travel with the court and then stay in England to study at Oxford. Abul Ghassem lacked the basic qualifications, and to pass the entrance exam was required to master not only the English language but also Greek, Latin and mathematics. He must have been an astonishing student, first because with a determination which is almost unimaginable today he managed this in just nine months, and second because he was accepted as a student by Benjamin Jowett (1817–93), one of the greatest of Oxford dons, Regius Professor of Greek, translator of Plato and Thucydides, and Master of Balliol when the young Persian arrived. Jowett is credited with having made Balliol the preeminent college of the university during his mastership, linked to Rugby – and thus to the sporting ethos which enthused Yan Fu – through a college tutor who succeeded Dr Arnold. In Jowett's words, the objective of following the Oxford curriculum was 'not primarily to obtain a first class, but to elevate and strengthen the character for life.' During a tutorial he would dictate a passage from English literature and expect his pupils 'to extemporise viva voce into Latin or Greek.'[26] The effect was such that forty years later, Abul Ghassem Khan could still translate Plato or Thucydides with the same ease that he read Shakespeare.[27] A fellow student, Cecil Spring-Rice, called him 'one of Jowett's pets, a good historian, immensely hard-working, and an eloquent opponent of Curzon's in our debating society.'[28] But beyond the academic excellence there were social, literary and political associations, so that the young Persian met men of letters like Swinburne, Tennyson and Oscar Wilde, or future political figures like Edward Grey and George Curzon – the last of whom wrote some of the best books about Persia and Central Asia before becoming Viceroy of India, and remained a life-long friend. He gained the nickname 'Abul Cursim Can', a tribute to his intellectual qualities.[29]

Balliol left an indelible mark on Abul Ghassem Khan. He himself became Nasser ul-Molk, serving as Minister of Finance and Prime Minister of Persia.

Indeed his Balliol years and British connections saved his life in 1907, when during the constitutional crisis of that year the Shah decided to have him killed. He was only saved by the timely personal intervention of the Oriental Secretary at the British Legation, George Churchill, who rushed to the royal palace and demanded the release of a man who held one of the highest orders of British Chivalry.[30] For in 1889, whilst accompanying Nasir ed-Din Shah on his third visit to Europe, Queen Victoria had made him a Knight Commander of the Order of St Michael and St George, and eight years later on another official visit to London awarded him the higher grade of Grand Cross of the Order of St Michael and St George.[31] Later in life, in retirement, after a long and distinguished political career, he returned to the life of the scholar and translated both *Othello* and *The Merchant of Venice* into Persian.

In the summer of 1969, I had the good fortune to meet and talk several times with Abul Ghassem Khan Gharagozlou's son Hossein Ali Gharagozlou, who himself went up to Balliol in 1923. Given his background and education, it was natural that he should have become aide-de-camp to Shah Mohammad Reza Pahlavi at the beginning of his reign, but they later fell out and he returned to Europe in voluntary exile. He was as much an English gentleman in language and manner as a Persian could be, with immaculate three-piece suits and a white handkerchief tucked into his left jacket sleeve. He then lived in Paris, and we met both at the home of his ex-wife Iran Teymourtache on Boulevard Murat and at the Téhéran Restaurant, a centre of Persian expatriate and exile communities in a street just off Avenue Wagram near the Arc de Triomphe. The restaurant itself was a piece of the émigré Persian world, with antique carpets on the walls, authentic food, and a clientele of mostly elderly refugees from various periods of difficulty, where these men and women could eat their *chelo-kabab* and drink their *dough*, and conspire to their hearts' content. Not by chance did Ayatollah Khomeini plot his return to Tehran from Paris – where his first President, Abdol-Hassan Bani-Sadr, was also living in the late 1960s and frequented the Téhéran. But what I recall most of all in a series of animated conversations with Hossein Ali Gharagozlou was his passion for the works of John Stuart Mill, and his desire to translate *On Liberty* with the same elegance that his own father had translated Shakespeare, just as Yan Fu had been inspired to do sixty years earlier. For the same books and ideas resonated throughout the then imperial world.

Perhaps these two 'Balliol men', father and son, are the source of Christopher Sykes' portrait of Bahram Kirmani in his book *Four Studies in Loyalty* (1946). Sykes recounts how he had been able for the first time ever to arrange for foreign visitors to enter the mosques in Isfahan. Bahram claimed to be a graduate of Balliol in the late 1880s, and in fact possessed the broad knowledge of Oxford and England befitting someone who had studied there – even though he claimed to have been sent down and never took a degree. Dressed in a coat, trousers, waistcoat, collar and tie, he certainly looked like a Balliol man to Sykes, and sounded like one as he spoke in 'over-faultless' English: 'Here, my dear fellow, we are in the Maidan-i-Shah, the Place Royale, so to speak ... Vanished days! I had the privilege of teaching Miss Marie Corelli how to smoke opium in the North British Hotel in Edinburgh.'[32] He was a Sufi, but appeared to love England and Englishness above all else, and constantly referred to Balliol and men he had met in London such as Balfour, although he had gone on to make a fortune in Russia. He claimed to have known Tolstoy, Chekov and Rasputin. Reduced to penury during the Bolshevik Revolution, he had returned to Persia as a beggar until through the discovery of Sufi texts he had become a dervish and finally returned to his native Isfahan.

The problem was that none of his stories was true, and that no such person had ever studied in Oxford – although Sykes eventually discovered that he *might* have visited the city and indeed Balliol itself briefly as a schoolboy on holiday from an academy in St Petersburg at which he really seems to have studied. In Sykes' words: 'Nothing is known except one tremendous fact: that the soul of a Persian boy was smitten with a love whose fire blazed on to the end of his days.'[33]

The story has a twist which makes it worth recounting here, for Bahram's apotheosis was quite extraordinary. In 1940, German propaganda had instilled in many Persians an enthusiasm for Hitler, encouraged by a press attaché who was a devoted follower of Goebbels. Wishing to bolster the German position in order to convince the British-educated Persians who rejected his message, this attaché learned of an impoverished gentleman in Isfahan, 'without principles' and in desperate need of money, surviving on vodka and arak, who might be able to perform the service. Bahram was summoned to the German Legation, where the attaché made an offer he assumed the old man would be unable to refuse: that he should accept a job as leader-writer on a newspaper, which the attaché could arrange, and live a comfortable life by writing articles based on his knowledge of England extolling the virtues of having the Germans as allies to his country. At the 'supreme moment of his life', as Sykes relates, Bahram rose to the occasion with true style: 'I am surprised,' he said, 'that you are so foolish as to make such a suggestion to a Balliol man.'[34] Suddenly, in this new light, Bahram becomes an exemplar of the positive influence of Western values.

Certainly Sykes knew Hossein Ali Gharagozlou (and his ex-wife), who remembered him well from Tehran in the 1930s and recommended me to contact him in their name. He visited the Gharagozlou mansion on at least one recorded occasion, when together with his travelling companion, Robert Byron, he attended a reception in January 1934.[35] Moreover, his college biographer relates how on a final trip to Balliol, in 1924, Abul Ghassem Khan Gharagozlou 'walked across the Quad and said he would like nothing better than to be given one of the rooms in College, so that he could continue to live there quietly and continue his studies.'[36] This is very much in the character of Bahram Kirmani, and of those like Yan Fu who adopted these positive Western attributes.

The Twin Crisis of 1911

But the foreign influence also had its negative aspects. In December 1911, both China and Persia were on the verge of disappearing as nations. In China, there were 'widespread rumours' that the country was about to be sliced into pieces like a pie and distributed to the foreign imperial powers which already occupied parts of her territory.[37] In Persia, it seemed that the country would lose its fragile independence, and that, after the period in which it had been divided into British and Russian 'spheres of influence', attacking Russian forces would now occupy the entire country, thus achieving Russia's perennial dream (more recently manifest again in Afghanistan) of creating a corridor southwards to the Indian Ocean.[38]

The two countries had experienced their first attempts at political reform around the turn of the twentieth century: in Persia, with the Constitutional Revolution of 1905–11; similarly, in China, with a reform movement which gathered pace from the moment in 1905 when the Dowager Empress Cixi ordered the creation of a study group to research into the working methods of foreign governments (Japan, America and Britain among others) and culminated with the demise of her dynasty at the end of 1911. Thus, eventually, the introduction of new 'foreign' ideas brought down both the Qajar and the Qing, astonishingly, in the same month.

In China, the first provincial assemblies met in the autumn of 1908, and by 1910 their success was such that there was considerable pressure on the Qing court to speed up the process of reform and convene a national assembly in Peking. Sun Yat-sen returned from abroad to be elected as 'provisional president' of a new republic on 29 December.[39] In Persia, after an initial attempt to establish a constitutional government in 1905 with an elected parliament, or *Majlis*, there were attempts at restoring traditional power by Muhammad Ali Shah after his accession to the throne in 1907 – including a coup against the *Majlis* at the end of that year. In July 1909, two nationalist armies, one departing from Rasht on the Caspian and one from Isfahan, marched towards Tehran in order to restore the constitutional government; with fewer than five hundred casualties in five days of street fighting, Muhammad Ali Shah was deposed.[40] The Shah, on a regal pension granted by Russia and Britain, travelled around Europe visiting sympathetic exiles much like his successor in the 1980s, plotting to regain the throne.

The year 1911 began with two assassinations: that of a cousin of the Governor of Isfahan during an attempt on the Governer himself, whose putative assassin took refuge in the Russian Consulate, and that of the Minister of Finance, Saniu'd-Daulah, in Tehran. In this case, too, the assassin was protected by Russia. Abul Ghassem Khan Gharagozlou, now using the hereditary title Nasser ul-Molk, was appointed regent for the fourteen-year-old heir Ahmad in the Shah's absence. He, unsurprisingly for a Balliol man, attempted to introduce a party system based on the British Parliament, while factions led by the *mujahiddin*, or guerrilla fighters, and the Bakhtiari tribe agitated for control of Tehran. At the same time, an American expert, W. Morgan Shuster, attempted to put the country's finances in order. Outside the capital, rebellious warlords and rival tribes vied for position: in the important southern city of Shiraz, for example, the Governor-General was a virtual prisoner besieged by the Qashqai tribe and rebellious Arab groups, while even brief trips were unusually hazardous.[41] Then, in July, Muhammad Ali Shah returned to Persia with a load of boxes of weapons falsely labelled 'Mineral Water',[42] intending to attack Tehran. A four-pronged assault failed in what Peter Avery described in a chapter title as the 'Eclipse of Hope', and by September the ex-Shah had once again escaped via the Caspian Sea on a Russian ship.

Persia still risked dismemberment, or, worse still, becoming part of Russia, as an article in the *St Petersburg Bourse Gazette* in October 1911 explicitly stated:

> Russian diplomacy ... has put an end once and for all to the idle talk about dividing Persia into a northern sphere of influence belonging to Russia and a southern sphere belonging to England. There can be no division of spheres of influence in Persia, which, together with the waters which bathe its shores, must remain the object of Russian material and moral protection.[43]

In November, the Russian government delivered an ultimatum, together with a request for an indemnity for military expenses, every bit as humiliating as the Twenty-One Demands made by Japan to China just over three years later. For in China there had been similar fears for a long time of dismemberment by foreign military intervention, at least since an explicitly titled nationalistic essay 'On the Preservation or Dismemberment of China', published by Sun Yat-sen in a radical newspaper in 1903. But in the event, both countries survived the end of the dynasties which ruled them, thanks mainly to nationalistic fervour and the skills of the political figures who guided the new phase in their history.

Death Throes of two Dynasties: the End of the Qing and the Qajar

The expansion of imperial power highlighted weaknesses in the ruling dynasties of both China and Persia, with modernisation and new political ideas threatening their hold on power. As we have seen, the defeat of Fath Ali Shah by the Russians, when Persia lost Georgia, Armenia and Azerbaijan, mirrors in scope that of Emperor Daoguang (1821–1850) during the Opium Wars, when defeat led to the opening of the Treaty Ports, the concession system, and the ceding of Hong Kong to Britain. Later, Mozaffar-e-din Shah (1896–1907) in Persia was just as weak and ineffectual as Guangxu (1875–1908) in China.

Formally, the Qing dynasty ended with the abdication of the last Manchu emperor on 12 February 1912, with Sun Yat-sen having been provisional president of the new republic since the beginning of the year (he resigned the next day). But imperial ambitions and nostalgia were not yet extinguished. In fact the new president, Yuan Shikai, attempted to make himself emperor in 1915. At the same time, confusingly, the nine-year-old ex-emperor Puyi, the 'Last Emperor', was allowed to keep his imperial title and was even restored to full powers for twelve days in 1917. Thus the death throes of the Qing Empire were prolonged through years of plot and counterplot. For many, life continued pretty much as before. In the words of a contemporary observer:

> The Tutuhs, or Military Governors, acting precisely as they saw fit, derided the authority of Peking and sought to strengthen their old position by adding to their armed forces. In the capital the old Manchu court, safely entrenched in the vast Winter Palace from which it has not even to-day [ie. 1917] been ejected published daily the Imperial Gazette, bestowing honours and decorations on courtiers and clansmen and preserving all the old etiquette.[44]

Puyi himself writes of that year that 'the Forbidden City was as active as it had been in the old days', and in fact he still maintained a personal staff of 700.[45] So it might be argued that the death throes of the empire were only finally exhausted on 5 November 1924 when Puyi was driven out of the Forbidden City forever. By this time, of course, the Chinese Communist Party had already been founded, and since 1922 the Republic of China had maintained diplomatic relations with the new Republic of Iran, one of the first foreign countries to do so.

For in a similar moment of plots and political convulsions, and what one scholar called the 'disunifying pressures',[46] the last Shah of the Qajar dynasty, Sultan Ahmad (1909–1925), was overthrown by a military coup in 1921 led by the British protégé and fervent nationalist Sayyid Zia (Sayyid Ziau'd-Din Tabataba'i; 1888–1969) and the future Reza Shah (1878–1944) then a colonel in the Persian Cossack Brigade known as Reza Khan.[47] But, as in China, the old system was not easily overthrown and replaced, and it was only after rebellions and insurrections throughout the country and attempts to establish a soviet socialist republic in the northern province of Gilan, that Reza Khan took effective control of the country and in 1923 exiled Sultan Ahmad to Europe. At that time, it was generally thought in Persia that a republican form of government would be established the following year, but the abolition of the Caliphate in Turkey in March 1924 had such a negative impact on the clergy that their Persian colleagues were terrified. Such a move in Persia became impossible as the result of their fierce opposition. [48] In fact, Sultan Ahmad was only formally deposed on 31 October 1925, almost exactly one year after the expulsion from the Forbidden City of Puyi. Unlike China, however, where Yuan Shikai's imperial ambition and Puyi's restoration were thwarted, Reza Khan became the first Shah of a new dynasty called Pahlavi before the end of the year.

Nation, Nationalism and Identity: China, 1919; Persia, 1921

It has been said of the Persian mind in the past that it was always torn between local patriotism and universalism, and that the Persian was 'too civilized to indulge in the narrowness of nationalism' as a result of his 'superior self-assertion and self-esteem'.[49] The same might have been said about the Chinese mind.

In both cases, these qualities survived unimpaired well into the first half of the nineteenth century. But the realities of colonial expansion, and modern firepower, revolutionised this placid and confident state of affairs. For the arousal of nationalist sentiments which led to constitutional movements and revolution were the result of aggression by Russia and Britain: in the Persian case, in a more or less balanced way; in the Chinese case, predominantly by the British.

The reference points of intellectuals in each country were often the same: nineteenth century thinkers like John Stuart Mill, Huxley and Darwin whom Yan Fu translated. Literary fiction also played an important role. In 1921, two writers published short works of fiction that are considered the first to be written in the modern vernacular of languages that had until that time been heavily influenced by classical forms and content: Lu Xun's *Ah Q: The Real Story* and Mohammad-Ali Jamalzadeh's collection of six stories entitled *Once Upon a Time*. Both are replete with colloquialisms, social criticism and implicit political comment.

Lu Xun's story begins with reference to the difficulties of Chinese names, and the problem of how to write the name of an illiterate peasant whose family name and given names were both unknown to the narrator, and who did not have a courtesy name, but who was known as Ah Quei. The problem was whether the 'Quei' character used should be the one that means 'laurel' or another that means 'high rank'. After an amusing two-page discursus on the problems of naming, the narrator settles on the 'foreign word' Q. Yet in spite of his illiteracy and minimal employment on odd jobs, Ah Q considered himself to be above all the other villagers, even the two young *literati*. He builds for himself a psychological defence mechanism which enables him to transmute what others see as a defeat into a victory in his own mind. In other words, he adopts an extravagant way of keeping face, which Lu Xun implicitly ridicules.[50] He also chastises blind reverence for authority, or snobbishness. For the defence mechanism is taken to absurd extremes when after being beaten by the headman of the village, Mr Zhao, Ah Q finds solace in the fact that he had been – albeit temporarily – associated with such an important man and had therefore become famous. Thus Lu Xun shows Ah Q's ignorance and follies to be symptomatic of the Chinese national character of his time, which was unable to face up to the reality of the political situation or shrug off traditional social rules and structures.[51] Most importantly, it is done in extremely colloquial, or non-literary, language.

Similarly, in *Once Upon a Time*, Jamalzadeh blended comment on social conditions in his country with criticism of religious fanaticism and Western influence, which in his case is ironic since he lived abroad and the book was first published in Berlin. The story 'Persian Sugar', written in a colloquial style, plays off 'one of those typical Europeanised young men who would remain Iran's symbol of insipidness, foolishness, and lack of education for generations to come' against 'something shiny and white that resembled a cat curled over a bag of coals' and making hissing sounds. This turns out to be a mullah – whose turban was the 'cat' on the 'bag' which was his cloak, and the hissing the sound of his prayers in Arabic. After enduring a 'bubbling' and 'abstruse' rant in Arabic from the mullah, and recitals in French of verses from Victor Hugo by 'Monsieur Europe', the narrator wonders why people can't speak Persian – echoing Lu Xun's criticism of the abolition of Chinese characters in *Ah Q*. In the Persian context, moreover, Jamalzadeh's ferocious portrayal of the mullah was hardly likely to endear him to clerics.[52] The 'Fake Foreign Devil' in Lu Xun's story and the caricatured 'Monsieur Europe' in Jamalzadeh's represent the deep resentment of foreign influence.

Taken as a whole, this intellectual ferment led to the creation of new political parties at the same time and with the same original aims of Westernisation and modernisation through a process of democracy: the Communist Party in China and the Nationalist Party in Persia, both founded in 1921. The lives of two more surprisingly similar figures will best illustrate this phase.

Sun Yat-sen (known today as Sun Zhongshan; 1866–1925) is considered the 'father of modern China'. A key figure in the demise of the Qing Dynasty, he became the first President of the new Republic of China in January 1912. Although born into a poor family in Guangdong in southern China, he went to live with his emigrant brother in Hawaii at the age of thirteen and thus acquired excellent English at high school there. He later studied medicine in Hong Kong and worked as a doctor for a few months in 1893, although interestingly he once dreamed of entering a naval academy in Jiangnan or Fuzhou and becoming an officer like Yan Fu.[53] Then, fired by enthusiam for the new ideas of scholarly reformers like Kang Youwei and Liang Qichao, both of whom were also from Guangdong, but never accepted him because of his low birth and lack of classical education, and the need for China to obtain technological know-how from the West, he devoted himself to politics. Initially in favour of a new monarchy, he gradually shifted to a position based on the abolition of the monarchy and the establishment of a republic. Above all, Sun saw himself as a mover, and is reported to have said to Yan Fu during a meeting in London in 1915: 'How long can a man wait for the river to clear? You, sir, are a thinker, I am a man of action.'[54]

In fact his first overt political action was an attempted but failed insurrection in Guangzhou, and his career was in some ways a catalogue of failed uprisings

– thirteen in all. Ironically, at the time of the revolutionary episode that eventually brought him to real political power, the Wuchang Uprising of 1911, he was in Denver, Colorado, and gleaned the information from a newspaper headline seen on his way to breakfast.[55] For Sun led a peripatetic life. He spent long periods of residence abroad, especially in Hawaii and Japan, and during his life visited or resided in cities throughout Asia, Europe and North America – wherever there was a Chinese community. In 1896, he was kidnapped and briefly held prisoner by the Chinese Legation in London, a mysterious episode which however enhanced his reputation as a revolutionary. During this period, Sun feared being poisoned and refused all food offered to him by Legation staff; he survived on bread and milk.[56] It was only with the help of Dr James Cantlie, his long-term friend and mentor, and director of the College of Medicine for Chinese where he studied in Hong Kong (and who wrote approvingly of Sun's medical ability), that he was released after twelve days as he awaited a ship for transportation and probable hanging in China. [57] He managed to turn what might have been a disaster into what one author has called 'one of the greatest triumphs of his career',[58] and write a book entitled *Kidnapped in London* (1897). This was widely read in China and Japan as well as in Europe and the United States and made Sun a celebrity both at home and abroad. The man of action became a man recognised as a potential future leader, and matured into a political thinker who influenced each of the rival parties which struggled for dominance until 1949, the Kuomintang of Chiang Kai-Shek and the Communist Party led by Mao Zedong.

Sun's final political formulation was that of the 'Three Principles of the People' (*sanmin zhuyi*): nationalism (*minzu*), democracy (*minquan*), and the people's livelihood (*minsheng*), in a volume of that title published in 1924. For Sun, these were 'by the simplest definition, the principles for our nation's salvation'.[59] The principle of *minzu* entailed a nationalism which would unite the five main ethnic groups in a single nation strong enough to withstand imperialistic aggression. Sun defined *minquan* as 'the people's sovereignty', by which he meant both the power of the people to vote and the power of a government to administer them, in a lengthy argument in which he cited Rousseau, the Civil War in England and the American War of Independence, and asked whether such methods could be imported into China. He concluded that it would in fact be possible to realise 'an all-powerful government seeking the welfare of the people.'[60] The first occurrence of the phrase 'people's livelihood' was as early as 1905, with the *principle* of the people's livelihood being used as a synonym for socialism.[61] In his later lectures he defined it as 'the welfare of the nation', by which he meant four main practices: first, using government to guarantee education, and provide health services and safe working conditions; second, the nationalisation of transport and communications to improve them; third, taxing capitalism to provide financial resources for the state (on the model of Germany and Great Britain); and, fourth, socialised distribution, by which he meant a system which reduced the costs of commodities and improved distribution by taking them out of the hands of traditional merchants.[62]

On a more practical level, he wrote an ambitious little book, *The International Development of China* (1922), which was essentially a list of infrastructure projects that prefigured those of Mao three decades later and even the current Politburo. The focus of the book was on railways, roads and ports, with shorter sections on food, housing and mining. There were specific recommendations for factories, for example to build large-scale cement works in Shanxi and along the Yangtze River, since 'steel and cement are the basis of modern construction', and for factories building railway engines and cars, and also shipbuilding yards.[63] Sun saw the 'colonisation' of Mongolia and Xinjiang as a complement to his vast railway scheme, based on similar successes that he had observed in the American West, Canada, Australia and Argentina. He explained his idea as 'simply a matter of applying waste Chinese labour and foreign machinery to a fertile land for production.' This 'waste labour' included over a million soldiers 'about to be disbanded', who needed work and whose employment in these regions would save the enormous expenditure of providing welfare for them. No religious or ethnic considerations at all. But he did add that self-government and local administration with 'perfect democratic spirit' should follow economic success.[64] He concluded his book with a sentence which anticipates the 'socialism with Chinese characteristics' and 'get rich is glorious' formulations of Deng Xiao Ping half a century later: 'In a nutshell, it is my idea to make capitalism create socialism in China, so that these two economic forces of human evolution will work side by side in future civilization.'[65]

In the end, the impossibility of quickly unifying China into a single nation defeated Sun's grandiose projects. He died of cancer before the warlords ruling large areas of the country could be brought under control. But his vision underlies modern China. For his 'Three Principles of the People' survive in Communist doctrine, and subtend the 'development trend of China's advanced productive forces', the 'orientation of China's advanced culture' and the 'fundamental interests of the overwheming majority of the Chinese people' which are presented as the essence of 'socialism with Chinese characteristics' as outlined in the first paragraph of the general programme of the Chinese Constitution.[66] During the ongoing arguments about whether the Chinese should adapt Western forms of dress or adhere to traditional costumes, it was Sun who devised the compromise wrongly known today as the 'Mao suit'. Items of dress were vital accoutrements of modernisation in both China and Iran, as we shall see. Above all, Sun Yat-sen was a man of genuine nationalistic fervour, a vision for his country, and possessed of incredible perseverance. As his friend James Cantlie remarked in 1912, 'that he has succeeded so far as to bring China within sight of deliverance stamps him as one of the most remarkable men of our time.'[67] In spite of later setbacks and errors, it is fitting that the words *Sanmin zhuyi* (Three Principles of the People) are still today the opening words of the Chinese national anthem.

The 'father of modern Iran' was Sun's near-contemporary Prince Abdul Hosein Khan Teymourtache (1883–1933), who served as the Minister of Court to Reza Shah from 1925 until his death, a man of similar nationalistic fervour and perseverance. It was he who placed the crown on the head of the new Shah in 1926 during a ceremony in the Gulistan Palace.[68] Indeed many people believed that the more sophisticated Teymourtache together with the journalist and political visionary Sayyid Zia-ul-Din were puppeteers who placed the simple soldier on the throne and planned to direct policy from behind the scenes.[69] For they knew – as Sun knew but could not achieve – that future success depended upon a strong military leader who could bring sufficient unity to the country to initiate the process of modernisation. Thus they preferred to work behind the scenes, once again reminiscent of Sun as he stepped aside from the presidency after just forty-five days to make way for Yuan Shikai – whom he recognised as possessing the authority necessary to run the country, even though his decision proved to be a mistake.

Teymourtache was a dynamic and brilliant man who pushed through important reforms and worked for the emancipation of women; his daughter, Iran, was the first woman to appear in public without a veil. His palace in Tehran was 'the centre to which all the intellectuals of Persia repaired to enjoy the discussion of momentous problems with him.'[70] He spoke excellent French and German, knew English, and translated Lermontov and Turgenev from Russian to Farsi before beginning his political career as a deputy in the *Majlis* or 'consultative assembly'. The German Ambassador to Persia, Wipert von Blücher, who knew the Minister well, provides a vivid portrait in his memoirs. He describes him in his European-style house in front of a giant portrait (*Kolossalgemälde*) of Reza Shah as a man of medium height with a muscular figure and well-cut features. But, more important, he had a charming personality and a 'spiritual fire which flashed from his eyes', and was a sophisticated man who was relaxed in conversation but retained the elegance of the Russian cavalry.[71]

Born to greater privilege than Sun, as the son of an aristocrat with a princely title and huge estates in Khorassan, Teymourtache too was sent abroad to study as a boy, but in this case to the exclusive Nikolaev Military Academy in St Petersburg. On returning to Persia he joined the Young Persian Party, and was always a fervent nationalist – naming his daughter Iran, for example, and his son Manuchehr after the legendary shah who ruled Iran in Ferdowsi's *Shahnameh*, or *Epic of the Kings*, the Persian national epic (Ferdowsi, like Teymourtache, was himself a native of Khorassan, always a hotbed of nationalism). He represented Khorassan in four sessions of the *Majlis* from 1909-1924,[72] became Governor of Gilan in 1919 and Minister of Justice in 1922. A year later he decided to throw his weight behind the rising Reza Khan, who was then Prime Minister, and became his Minister of Commerce. In 1925, he became Minister of Court to the new Shah, and the second most powerful man in the country. He was an excellent and energetic administrator: in the words of *The Times* he was the 'chief lieutenant' who provided 'the energy and driving force to give effect to his Majesty's commands.'[73] Thus his efficiency was one of the main factors behind modernisation: 'It was largely due to Timurtash that bottlenecks were cleared away and momentum maintained in the complicated and confused efforts to transform and build up the economic life of Iran.'[74] He also played the key role in the Abolition of Capitulations in 1928, that is to say the abolition of the treaties which conferred extraterritorial privileges to foreign governments. Apart from Britain and Russia, beneficiaries had included Austria, Belgium, Czechoslovakia, France, the Netherlands and Sweden.[75] But the real problem for the new Persia concerned oil.

The wealth of Iran – which in this case was more fortunate than China – the power of Reza Shah, and the downfall of Teymourtache were all connected to the discovery of oil in Persia. For on 26 May 1908, a British geologist in south-western Persia had announced the discovery of the largest known oilfield in the world, after a long search that began with an exclusive oil concession granted seven years earlier to the entrepreneur William K. D'Arcy.[76] The next year, a company called the Anglo-Persian Oil Company was formed to exploit this field, later becoming the Anglo-Iranian Oil Company, in 1935, and then British Petroleum or BP, in 1954. The D'Arcy Concession, as it was known, became the greatest thorn in Anglo-Persian relations for decades after a further agreement in 1914 granted fifty-one per cent of the company to the British Government. It was also a key factor in Britain's success in the First World War, since this contract guaranteed supplies of oil to the Royal Navy for thirty years at a fixed price, lower than market price, just as it converted its warships from coal to oil.

From the point of view of a government avid for modernisation, and therefore for cash, the terms of the D'Arcy Concession seemed both unjust and a humiliating survival of colonial 'occupation'. It was also no longer adequate to the much larger scale of the Anglo-Persian Oil Company's operations: by the end of the 1920s, the company had 30,000 employees and was producing nearly six million tons of oil annually.[77] The conflict came down to a triangular confrontation based upon the negotiating parties, Teymourtache and Sir John Cadman, Chairman of the APOC, with the dark shadow of Reza Shah forming the third point. The main bone of contention was the royalties paid to the Persian government, which had been fixed at sixteen per cent of net profits. Persia demanded twenty-five per cent of the shares of the company, and a greater share of profits. Negotiations dragged on in Tehran, London and Lausanne, with Teymourtache and Cadman travelling to and fro, and with the situation exacerbated by the economic crisis that engulfed Western markets in 1929. Revenues slumped by eighty per cent by 1931,[78] and Cadman refused to negotiate further. A furious Shah with a limited understanding of world economics and frustration at his inability to control the situation cancelled the concession. In doing so, he contradicted a strong statement by his Minister of Court made three years earlier that the concession 'is a Law which cannot be altered amended or repealed without the full consent of both parties. I will go even further and say that as far as the present Government is concerned it is a sacred document.'[79] With hindsight, it was a rash declaration.

Both the company and the British Government demanded that the Shah withdraw the cancellation, and on being rebuffed took the issue to the Permanent Court of International Justice. Naturally, Reza Shah refused to accept the jurisdiction of this court, so Britain went to the League of Nations in December 1932. Within two weeks, Teymourtache was in prison, where he remained when a new concession was signed the following April.

Like Icarus, perhaps Teymourtache over-reached in his desire to protect the pro-British and imperialistic D'Arcy Concession. Not only was he against its cancellation, he was, in the words of a contemporary newspaper, 'the only man who would have dared to tell the Shah that he had made a mistake.' For it was evident 'that the Government did not govern, and that Timurtash [sic] was the real brain and power of the Persian Government. He it was who did everything and carried out the Shah's ideas, as interpreted by himself.'[80]

But there may have been another reason for his downfall: simple jealousy on the part of the Shah, who lacked the intellectual brilliance, charm and international knowledge and experience of his minister. There was also fear that someone would prevent his son Mohammad from succeeding him and perpetuating the dynasty. From about this time there were rumours in Tehran that Reza Shah was suffering from stomach cancer and that his son the crown prince would be murdered when he came back from school in Switzerland.[81] Since Teymourtache himself had suggested the Swiss school, and even sent his own son Mehrpour there together with the crown prince,[82] similar rumours could only have added to the Shah's suspicions. His daughter Iran related the following conversation, which took place on the evening of 23 December 1932:

> TT: When I asked you two years ago why you finished with Firuz, you said you no longer needed him. Now me?
> RS: I want my son to be Shah.
> TT: Of course, so does everyone else. I don't have the temperament to be Shah.
> RS: I am obliged to finish you.
> TT: Here is my revolver. I was educated as an officer and know how to use it. If I wanted to kill you, I could do so now. I could leave and annouce myself as the new Shah and no one would dare to argue. But I will place it on the table. I do not wish to be Shah. [83]

The following day Iran was preparing to go to the country when a valet announced that her father was no longer Minister of Court, that the trip was postponed, but that he believed he would be able to retire and live at home or on his country estates in Khorassan. There were even rumours that he might be nominated ambassador to Washington. On Christmas Day, Iran noticed during a reception at the British Embassy that Sir Reginald Hoare still kept a photograph of Teymourtache on the piano; then, the next day, his home was surrounded by police and family members were refused entry. Iran Teymourtache's account is confirmed by a detailed narrative of events by Wipert von Blücher. Moreover, the ambassador relates a more sinister cause of the sudden fall. One of Teymourtache's closest friends and associates Diba was an inveterate gambler in spite of his position as Controller of the Royal Chest, and well known as a slightly suspicious figure who had made money by selling entry permits to White Russians. One evening, he bankrupted the Shah's father-in-law by winning a large sum of money from him, after which the old man died of a heart attack. Following this tragedy, Diba was sacked and Teymourtache avoided gambling parties. But Von Blücher suggests nevertheless this was the origin of the sudden change of attitude to the Minister of Court.[84] If so, the Shah appears to have regretted his actions: he never trusted anyone again, developed extreme paranoia and xenophobia, and lived in 'a sort of sealed isolation and developed the mind of a tyrant, demanding submission pure and simple.'[85]

Teymourtache suffered a classical slow Persian prison death: at first in a well-furnished cell with carpets and thirty servants, and his cook being allowed to go shopping outside; then, furniture and privileges were gradually reduced over the months until he had only one servant. Like Sun Yat-sen in the embassy during his London 'kidnapping', he refused to eat prison food because he was convinced it would be poisoned, a tradition as strong in Persia as in China. In the end, Von Blücher tells us, 'the spoiled, sick man lay on the bare cold stone floor of his damp cell.'[86] It is likely that he did indeed die of poison, on 3 October 1933, after eventually accepting prison food. But nobody will ever know.

Perhaps the obituary of this extraordinary man in *The Times* was closest to the truth: 'the fact that he was tried *in camera* makes it the more difficult to judge whether he was condemned for what he had done or for what he might do.'[87] In this, his fate in not being allowed to complete his modernisation is similar to that of Sun Yat-sen.

What is certain about these men, Sun and Teymourtache, is that their native intelligence, experience of the world and immense political skill rendered their situations potentially perilous in the presence of figures such as Reza Shah and Chiang Kai-Shek (not to mention Mao). Writing of events a thousand years earlier, Edward G. Browne observed that 'royal jealousy excited by envious rivals … has caused, and will probably continue to cause, the fall of every great Minister whom Persia has produced.'[88] Three exceptionally gifted men – and friends – provided the knowledge and skills to modernise Persia: Firuz Mirza (Minister of Justice and Finance in successive cabinets), Teymourtache, and Ali Akbar Davar (Minister of Agriculture, Commerce, Justice and Finance). The first two were accused of bribery and murdered, 'if not by Reza Shah personally, undoubtedly with his approval'.[89] Davar committed suicide in 1936, apparently fearing a similar fate.

Sun and Teymourtache had much in common, as do the cultures from which they emerged. Here is a description of one of them by a modern biographer: 'His extreme geographic mobility nurtured his equally great versatility of mind and temperament. He could cross cultural boundaries as easily as geographical ones, adapt to all societies, all types of men.'[90] These words are used of Sun, but could equally well be used of his Persian counterpart. One was a product of maritime and mercantile China, the other of the tribal aristocracy of the Persian desert; each was fired by early travel, a foreign education and a desire to bring the benefits of Western modernisation and political thought to his country. In the end, both died without having accomplished what they might have done, the former at fifty-nine, having for a brief moment achieved the highest post in his land, the latter at fifty, having been in the second highest post of his land for eight years. In the end, however, both preferred to work behind the scenes as 'king-makers' rather than kings. Perhaps what they wished to do first required the sweeping away of multilayered pasts, which is what the 'kings' they made, in one case directly and in the other indirectly (since there was also the rivalry of Chiang Kai-shek), tried to do. For both indulged in an operation of what we might describe as 'cultural cleansing'.

Destruction of the 'old' by Reza Shah and Mao Zedong

These sophisticated and constructive founders of the new nations were followed by disruptive leaders who sought to destroy the religious and cultural foundations of the 'old' society into which they had both been born in relatively humble situations, first Reza Shah Pahlavi and later Mao Zedong.

Reza Shah's policy for modernisation was based on three pillars not dissimilar to those of Sun Yat-sen: national unity; material westernisation; and secularisation.[91] Whereas earlier Persian authors and politicians had derived *ideas* from the West, there had been little attempt at the practical implementation of Western models. The difference with Reza Shah lay in his natural indifference to 'intellectual fineries' and a tendency to look to the West in terms of Persia's need for 'material improvements and desire for action.'[92] His thoughts constituted a Persian variant of Kang Youwei's distinction between 'Chinese learning for the fundamental principles' and 'Western learning for practical applications'.

Descriptions of the new Shah vary widely. Sir Percy Loraine, the British Minister in Tehran during his rise to power, described him as quietly spoken and having 'no awkwardness of manner' and 'considerable natural dignity',[93] which is quite a compliment from the scion of an ancient Northumberland family and baronetcy renowned for his elegance and manners. Loraine's direct counterpart, the Persian Minister in Britain, Mirza Hussein Khan Ala, suggested in a speech in London that the Shah 'has great charm of manner and affability'.[94] But a later American observer wrote that 'there was little humour in that face, no trace of human kindness'; worse still, it was 'an immobile face that very rarely smiled but could express the savage temper he often loosed.'[95]

Certainly Reza Shah was possessed of notable energy, and devoted himself to the task of freeing his country from foreign influence and to make it strong by introducing Western-style reforms and technology - a strategy similar to that pursued by his son in the 1970s. His role model was his almost exact contemporary Mustafar Kemal Ataturk, who from similar beginnings in the army had succeeded in westernising and secularising Turkey. But first he had to break the traditional stranglehold on regional power of the tribes, the great landowners (like Teymourtache), and the clergy.

As in the case of Sun Yat-sen in China, one of Reza Shah's best strategies was the construction of the Trans-Iranian Railway – the objectives of which were strategic and anti-traditional as well as economic. In fact, reflecting imperialist schemes in the past, several short sections of railway already existed, such as an Indian Northwestern Railway extension into Zahedan, a Russian line south from Azerbaijan to Tabriz, and a British section in the oilfields. Reza Shah's grand addition was the Trans-Iranian line, some 850 miles of track constructed through harsh mountains and desert with hundreds of bridges and tunnels. Started in 1926 and completed in 1938, it linked the new port of Bandar Chapour on the Persian Gulf (built on the east side of the top of the Gulf, as far away from British Iraq as possible) with Bandar Shah on the southeastern corner of the Caspian Sea (in this case, as far away from Russian influence as possible), passing through Qom and Tehran. Further plans to extend the system with lines west to Tabriz, east to Mashad and southeast to Yazd, thus linking most of the major cities of Iran, were truncated by Reza Shah's departure and the Second World War.[96]

The new railway played an important role in gaining control of areas distant from the capital. For when Reza Khan assumed power in 1922, three economically important provinces like Gilan, Azerbaijan and Khorassan in the north were in separatist mood, while Khuzistan – where the oilfields are located – was an autonomous and British-sponsored sheikdom ruled by the hereditary, and Arab, Sheikh of Mohammarah. In fact there were Arab calls for Khuzistan to be incorporated into Iraq as late as 1946.[97] The first step towards breaking such provincial autonomy was to make Tehran the only clearing house for both economic and commercial purposes, assuming central government control over foreign trade and creating monopolies for products such as sugar and tobacco. Traditional commercial centres like Tabriz and Isfahan were brought to their knees: 'When the trans-Iranian railroad was built, Tehran alone of Iran's major cities was given rail access to both the Caspian and the Persian Gulf. As a result there was a mass exodus of merchants and other middle-class elements from the provinces to

Tehran.'[98] Thus the railway project finally brough the huge areas once dominated by independent tribes into a unified nation. But even in 1940, with a population of 14 million, less than twenty per cent of Iran's GDP was derived from industry and only twenty-two per cent of the inhabitants lived in urban areas.[99] There were still only 7,000 employees in industrial factories compared to 31,000 in the oil industry, 60,000 in the carpet industry and 25,000 in textiles and hosiery.[100]

Reza Khan's greatest ire was reserved for the clergy, although after initial resistance from them he made symbolic pilgrimages to Najaf and Karbala.[101] Certainly he was a man of little education, the self-confessed illiterate son of a humble father before Pahlavi hagiography upgraded the latter *a posteriori* to military officer status,[102] uninterested both by educational limitations and by inclination in the sophistry of the intellectuals and the clergy. He served from the age of fourteen in the Cossack Guards, where 'the whip was freely used both within the organisation and in its relations with the Persian public,'[103] and was known to have a ferocious temper. This was observed at least once in public, when Reza Shah suspected a Turkoman jockey of committing a foul during a race and struck him a violent blow with his riding crop. Wipert von Blücher was present together with the rest of the diplomatic corps and recounts that the blow was struck with the technical skill of a boxer; in the privacy of his memoirs, he speculated undiplomatically on the violence which the Shah might have committed in private.[104] Similar wrath could also be directed at the clergy: once, in 1928, Reza Shah's consort had allowed her veil to slip during a religious ceremony at Qom and was publicly denounced by the cleric who was preaching at the time. The next day the Shah arrived with troops and two armoured cars; he entered the mosque without troubling to take his boots off, and thrashed the offending mullah.[105] Interestingly, the subtle and very Persian Bahram Kirmani had enabled Christopher Sykes' visits to Isfahan mosques by convincing the governor that such visits would be in line with Reza Shah's anti-clerical policies.

In his anticlericalism Reza Shah was in tune with the times; at that moment there was an increasing number of Persian Muslims who in view of the technological superiority of the West were no longer certain about the superiority of Islam.[106] Thus one of the key elements of the new nationalism was secularisation, so much so that initially there was talk of establishing a secular republic with Reza Khan as president – an enterprise the Chinese had previously attempted and in which Ataturk had recently been successful. One reason why the clergy preferred a new imperial dynasty was fear that Reza Khan might institute something akin to the new Turkish Republic (founded in 1923) with the separation of church and state; similar fears of the new had facilitated Yuan Shikai's brief elevation to the role of emperor from late 1915 to his death in the summer of 1916. Had the Persian clergy known what would soon hit them, one contemporary author surmised, they would 'probably have preferred to take their chances with a more democratic form of government.'[107]

In light of the popular view of Iran today, it is interesting to note the emphasis on women's education and voting rights in early-twentieth-century Tehran. Reza Shah, an early biographer wrote, 'was bent upon emancipating Persian womanhood. But he did not know how to go about it. Court Minister Teymourtache, at a Minister's council, suggested that some high-born lady should visit a Persian café.'[108] The lady, according to Teymourtache's family, was the minister's own wife, whom he affectionately called Nightingale. There were also significant legislative changes in this regard. In August 1931, for example, a law was passed giving women the right to seek divorce and raising the minimum age for marriage for girls from sixteen to eighteen.[109]

Another directly anti-clerical move was to confiscate clerical *vaqf*, or mortmain – land held in perpetuity by the church – which led to a notable loss of wealth and power for the religious. Some clerics were retained to administer the *vaqf* for the government, but they did so as civil servants. Key religious ceremonies such as those to celebrate Moharram were 'so curtailed that the majority lost interest in their enactment', rites such as self-flagellation were banned, with new national holidays taking their place, and the solar calendar was introduced in place of the lunar calendar used by Islam.[110] Other significant new legislation included the 1926 Penal Code, which abolished the Law of Retaliation and was derived from French law; this was followed by a new Civil Code in 1928, which although it was based upon the traditional Islamic law or *shari'a* also included important adaptations from French law. These moves were more important than they might seem, since attacking the clergy in this way 'deprived them of their chief social function and principal source of legitimate revenue.'[111]

One symbolic gesture was the abolition of the veil in 1935, by which Persian women were encouraged to wear European dress. The following year the Shah and his Queen went to a public meeting with their two elder daughters unveiled and all three women wearing European dress. Thenceforward, veiled women could not be served in shops, nor were they allowed to use public transport. In their shame, some women never left their homes again until 1941, when Reza Shah was forced into exile. Men had also been compelled since 1928 to wear European-style clothes, and in particular a new form of headgear known as the Pahlavi cap, whose peak was an affront to Muslims: when wearing it, they were unable to touch the ground with their foreheads in prayer without removing the cap. It also had the advantage of reducing the visibility of tribesmen in the cities by removing the picturesque fur busbies of the Turkomen, the high white felt hat of the Bakhtiari, and the silk-fringed turbans of the Kurds. In 1935, European headgear was prescribed, and apparently hatters in provincial bazaars not only borrowed trilby hats from travelling Englishmen to make copies but even made cheap versions in painted recycled tin.[112]

Reza Shah attempted to cleanse Farsi of its Arabic influences, but was not prepared to go as far as Ataturk and introduce a new alphabet – yet another

Chinese problem in the same period, with various failed attempts made at imposing a romanised script on a pictographic language. But there was always notable resistance from the clergy. One example was in the field of modern medicine, and the introduction of medical training. When the clergy realised that vaccines for smallpox, which together with diphtheria was a major epidemic problem, used serums deriving from human beings, they waged a propaganda war against vaccination and hampered new legislation that provided a free service for all Persians.[113] The real problem was that while many of the 'old' values were removed, nothing had taken their place – a difficulty which Mao Zedong and his successors were later to encounter. Later, Reza Shah's son was to face similar problems with the clergy, and ultimately it would be the clergy – in the person of Mohammad Shah's old adversary Khomeini – which would bring down the house of Pahlavi. Rarely has seething long-term resentment had such dramatic and unforeseen consequences.

Something similar happened in China, and led to the weakening of Mao Zedong's immediate authority and long-term prestige. For during the notorious Cultural Revolution, Mao launched a ferocious campaign against the 'four olds' of Chinese civilisation: old customs, old habits, old culture and old thinking.

In some ways, traditional Chinese ideas had long been a barrier to 'progress'. At the turn of the century, for example, there had been resistance first against the introduction of telegraph wires and then against the development of railways on the grounds that they would disturb the ancient rules of *feng shui*. But the new campaign went much further. It was started in late May of 1966, by students at the Tsinghua University's high school in Beijing, with the specific purpose of protecting Mao. He accepted their ideas with enthusiasm after seeing posters they had written, welcoming their initiative with 'warm support', causing the Red Guards (*hong weibing*) to bloom into thousands of units in a matter of weeks. The underlying motive was to allow Mao to alienate the Party, so that he could assume all power in his own person and use the teenage Red Guards as his shock troops.

On 8 August, the Communist Party Central Committee passed a 'Decision Concerning the Great Proletarian Cultural Revolution', sometimes called the 'Sixteen Points'.[114] The first point stressed that while the 'bourgeoisie has been overthrown, it is still trying to use the old ideas, culture, customs and habits of the exploiting classes to corrupt the masses, capture their minds and endeavour to stage a comeback', while the 'proletariat must do the exact opposite' and use new ideas, culture, customs and habits 'to change the mental outlook of the whole of society.' Ominously, the second point made reference to the Red Guards when it stated that 'large numbers of revolutionary young people, previously unknown, have become courageous and daring pathbreakers.' Ten days later, on 18 August, over a million of these 'courageous pathbreakers' gathered at a mass rally in Tiananmen Square; Mao himself was there for six hours that day. The American sympathiser and long-term Beijing resident Sidney Rittenberg writes that, approaching Tiananmen from the west the crowds were such that it was impossible to move beyond the entrance to the leadership compound at Zhongnanhai, half a mile before the square.[115] In the midst of this enthusiasm, Lin Biao, then Mao's designated successor, launched into an inflammatory speech urging the audience to go out from their schools, rebel, and literally 'smash up' the 'olds'. He argued that 'we will vigorously destroy all the old ideas, old culture, old customs, and old habits of the exploiting classes ... we will sweep away all vermin and remove all obstacles!'[116] In effect, this gave the Red Guards licence to destroy or remove anything that reeked of ancient or bourgeois culture, and to launch *ad hominem* attacks. These could be against someone who had merely had a Western education or had dealt with foreign businessmen or missionaries, as well as against any intellectual who might be accused of feudal or reactionary thinking.[117] Thus, on the morning of 19 August, thousands of young Red Guards fanned out through the capital with the intention of obliterating the rather vaguely defined 'olds' with fanatical zeal and in an often random manner. Slogans like 'Smash the Old World; Establish a New World', which appeared on giant posters, did not attempt to explain what the 'new' would be.

The Red Guards stopped girls in the street to cut off long hair, confiscated jeans and coloured shirts, and destroyed shop signs and street names they deemed offensive: the sign for a famous Peking Duck restaurant, Quanjude, for example, was destroyed because they held that the old name of the restaurant had Confucian connotations. Street names were changed, so that the 'old' Chang'an Avenue (or 'Eternal Peace Avenue'), the highly symbolic thoroughfare which intersects Beijing east to west and passes between Tiananmen Square and the Forbidden City, was changed to East-Is-Red Avenue. The popular shopping – and hence in their minds decadent – street Wanfujing (or 'Prince's Palace Well') became the unwieldy Preventing-Revisionism Street. Rittenberg, shocked even though he was a long-time communist and admirer of Mao, who he had known personally since the 1940s, watched guards there pulling down and destroying painted wooden and neon signs from the shops and knocking apart 'anything old and fancy that suggested bourgeois consumerism.'[118] There were even plans to change the 'old' name of the capital itself to East-Is-Red City.[119] In the coming weeks the students entered private homes in search of 'olds', ransacking rooms and rooting out books, pictures and anything they considered to be worthy of their fury. Many still recall the fear of those weeks, and eloquent artistic testimony may be found in such beautiful examples as the film *The Red Violin* (1998) where its owner in Shanghai carefully hides the violin under the floorboards in terror that this nasty 'old' – purportedly a Stradivarius – would be discovered and destroyed.

Beijing was never such an intensely religious city as Tehran, not to mention the doctrine-driven fastness of Qom, but here too there was a focus on religious activities and clerics which would make Reza Shah seem a lamb by comparison. For the Shah rarely if ever *destroyed* places of worship. In Beijing alone, of 7,000 cultural relics selected for preservation in 1958, 5,000 were damaged by Red Guards in a matter of weeks.[120] The objects of ire included churches, mosques, temples, stelae, inscriptions, statues of Buddha, missionary graveyards, idols and books. Important temples which now seem oases of peace amidst the bustling city such as Biyunsi and Yonghegong were ravaged, and the tomb in which the Jesuit missionary Matteo Ricci had reposed well away from the centre of the city since 1610 was destroyed.

Mao himself was little better in his public expression, although in private he seems to have been completely different. Already three years earlier he had attacked all art forms as 'feudal or capitalist' and sent thousands of writers, poets, singers and dramatists into the countryside to be 'seriously reformed'.[121] Now he complained about books, especially novels. This literary and obsessive reader argued that 'the more books you read, the more stupid you become', while he himself had enjoyed a classical education, wrote poetry in traditional style and professed his love both of the 'old' novels like Cao Xueqin's *Dream of Red Mansions* (1791), and the stories of a modern writer like Lu Xun. The same was true of traditional opera. Mao always enjoyed opera, especially the more salacious kind; he owned hundreds of tapes, and one of his favourites was the fairly explicit *The Emperor Seduces the Barmaid*, which he enjoyed in private even as the 'four olds' campaign was in full flush.[122] For the campaign transcended his personal pleasure. In 1964 there had been a festival of 'revolutionary Peking opera', a rather oxymoronic event by the sound of it, and an attempt to create proletarian versions of this traditional art form since operas based on the stories of emperors and traditional scholars cannot 'foster proletarian ideology.'[123] On one infamous occasion, after a bonfire of theatrical props and costumes from the traditional Peking Opera in a courtyard of the Temple of Confucius, the author and playwright Lao She, author of popular and translated works such as the novel *Rickshaw Boy* (1936; also translated as *Camel Xiangzi*) and the play *The Tea House* (1957), was brutally beaten by Red Guards. Ordered to wear a humiliating placard, the sixty-seven-year-old author instead chose suicide in Taiping Lake.

In both China and Iran, the campaign to eradicate old culture was ultimately a failure because nothing new was created to take its place; 'old' place names and customs quickly reassumed their role in the everyday life of the inhabitants. Both Reza Shah and Mao Zedong appeared frustrated by this failure, and each slipped into old age as a rather sad and solitary figure unable to trust others – becoming increasingly both misanthropic and xenophobic. The genuinely new, the modern version of their respective countries, was yet to emerge as these rough and ready attempts were truncated: in the first case by invasion and exile, in the second by rapid physical decline and death.

Notes

1. '...*i Cinesi sono diversi dagli indigeni per la razza, la religione, la civiltà ed i costumi quanto gli Inglesi in India, e vivono appartati dalla popolazione maomettana, senza curarsi di impararne neppure superficialmente la lingua, in città separate, recinte da alte mura, dove sono rinchiusi i funzionari, le guarnigioni armate e una piccola popolazione di bottegai cinesi che provvede ai loro bisogni.*' de Filippi, Filippo, *Storia della Spedizione Scientifica Italiana nel Himàlaia Caracorlim e Turchestàn Cinese (1913–1914)*, p. 484.
2. See my detailed refutation of this view in Burman, *Stealth Empire*, Chapter 1.
3. Ellis, Henry, *Journal of the Proceedings of the Late Embassy to China; Comprising a Correct Narrative of the Public Transactions of the Embassy, of the Voyage to and from China, and of The Journey from the Mouth of the Pei-ho to the Return to Canton*, London: John Murray, 1817, 2 vols.
4. Wright, *The English Amongst the Persians*, p. 150; Spence, *The Search for Modern China*, pp. 159–166.
5. Pottinger, *Travels in Beloochistan and Sinde; Accompanied by a Geographical and Historical Account of Those Countries*, p. 69; see Chapter IV on the Baluchis.
6. Compare Plan I and Plan II in the Appendix to Pakravan, *Vieux Teheran*, unnumbered pages inside the back cover.
7. Redhouse, *The Diary of H.M. the Shah of Persia, during his tour through Europe in A.D. 1873*, p. 250.
8. Ibid. p. 224.
9. Avery, *Modern Iran*, p. 82-4.
10. Cresson, *Persia: The Awakening East*, p. 61; Curzon made the same point when he wrote that the 'era of the Thousand and One Nights, with its strange mixture of savagery and splendour, of coma and excitement, is fast fading away, and will soon have yielded up all its secrets to science.' *Russia in Central Asia in 1889 and the Anglo-Russian Question, p. xii.*
11. Cresson, *Persia*, p. 93
12. Quoted in Teng & Fairbank, *China's Response to the West*, p. 153.
13. Wuchang and Hankow, on opposite banks of the Chang Jiang and linked by a bridge for the first time in 1957, were combined together with Hanyang in 1927 to form the present industrial city of Wuhan.
14. See his biography in Hummel, *Eminent Chinese*, Vol. I, pp. 27-31.
15. Teng & Fairbank, *China's Response to the West: a documentary survey 1839–1923*, p. 169.
16. Hummel, *Eminent Chinese*, p. 30.
17. Translated in Frodsham (Ed.), *First Chinese Embassy to the West: The Journals of Kuo Sung-t'ao, Liu Hsi-hung, and Chang Te-y*, pp. 110, 114.
18. The two main sources of biographical information on Yan Fu are Boorman and Howard's *Biographical Dictionary of Republican China* and Benjamin Schwartz's *In Search of Wealth and Power: Yen Fu and the West.*
19. Most details in this paragraph are taken from Schwartz, *In Search*, pp. 22–7. China at that time was focused on building a modern navy and modern weapons, and had founded two arsenals for that purpose, first the Jiangnan Arsenal in Shanghai (1865), where a 'School

for the Diffusion of Languages' was created in order to translate technical materials from English, and then the Fuzhou Arsenal (1866), to which was attached a 'School for Naval Administration', with 'divisions' specialising in English and French. For a detailed account of these arsenals and the activity of translation, see Benjamin A. Elman, 'Naval Warfare and the Refraction of China's Self-Strengthening Reforms into Scientific and Technological Failure, 1865–1895', *Modern Asian Studies* (2004), Vol. 38, pp. 283–326. An earlier version of this article, presented at a conference in Chicago in 2002, is available at http://uts.cc.utexas.edu/~rhart/conferences/chinesescience/papers/elman.pdf.

20. Wright, 'Yan Fu and the Tasks of the Translator', p. 237.

21. Ibid., p. 15.

22. Wang Shiqing, *Lu Xun: A Biography*, Beijing: Foreign Languages Press, 1984, p. 41.

23. Su and Wang, *Deathsong of the River: A Reader's Guide to the Chinese TV Series Heshang*, p. 209–11.

24. Quoted in Schwartz, *In Search of Wealth and Power*, p. 93.

25. The biographical information below has been provided in the English translation of the Persian *Introduction* to Nasser ul-Molk's own translation of *The Merchant of Venice* by his grandson Fereydoun Ala. It is quoted with Mr Ala's permission. The same material was used in Anthony Wynn's brief article, 'Abul Ghassem Khan Gharagozlou, Nasser ul-Molk: The First Persian at Balliol', *Balliol College Record*, 2006.

26. Quoted from the chapter on Jowett in Noel Annan's *The Dons: Mentors, Eccentric and Geniuses*, London: HarperCollins, 1999, pp. 61-78.

27. Wynn, 'Abul Ghassem Khan Gharagozlou, Nasser ul-Molk, The first Persian at Balliol', p. 19.

28. Quoted in Wright, *The English Amongst the Persians*, p. 81, n; Sykes, *Four Studies in Loyalty*, p. 47.

29. Ibid.

30. Browne, *The Persian Revolution of 1905–1909*, p. 163.

31. Wynn, 'Abul Ghassem Khan Gharagozlou', p. 19.

32. Sykes, *Four Studies in Loyalty*, p. 47.

33. Ibid., p. 57.

34. Ibid., p. 79.

35. Byron notes the reception on 18 January 1934. He observes: 'Indeed Madame Nasr-al-Mulk [ie. Hosein Ali's mother] is said to be the one person living who occasionally speaks her mind to Marjoribanks [Byron and Sykes' nickname for Reza Shah]. I can believe it. She spoke her mind to me when she thought I was going to spill some lemonade over a brocade chair.' Byron, *The Road to Oxiana*, p. 129. Christopher Sykes was a cousin of Sir Reginald Hoare, the British Minister in Tehran, who was himself a personal friend of Iran's father, as we shall see below, and according to her kept a signed personal photograph of her father on the grand piano in the Legation drawing room.

36. Wynn, 'Abul Ghassem Khan Gharagozlou', p. 20.

37. Fung, *The Military Dimension of the Chinese Revolution*, p. 195.

38. Browne, *The Persian Crisis of December, 1911*, p. 3.

39. For a good general account of this period in China, see Spence, *The Search for Modern China*, pp. 243–63.
40. Browne, *The Persian Crisis*, p. 3.
41. Wilson, *S. W. Persia*, p. 188; on the dangers of travel there are several examples in this acutely observed book, including Wilson's own capture by brigands and near-death (pp. 135–99 *passim*).
42. Avery, *Modern Iran*, p. 155–6.
43. Browne, *The Persian Crisis*, p. 16.
44. Weale, B.L. Putnam, *The Fight for the Republic in China*, ch. 3. This was the literary pseudonym of Bertram Lennox Simpson (1877-1930).
45. Aisin-Gioro Pu Yi, *From Emperor to Citizen*, p. 87 and p. 144.
46. The title of Chapter II of Joseph Upton's *The History of Modern Iran* is 'Sources of Disunifying Pressures in Modern Iran', referring to the period 1906–1921.
47. In my opinion the best accounts of this difficult period remain those by Joseph Upton in *History of Modern Iran,* Peter Avery in *Modern Iran*, and by Laurence Elwell-Sutton in *Modern Iran.* Both Avery and Elwell-Sutton knew Sayyid Zia personally.
Personal Note: in 1969/70, apart from meeting Iran Teymourtache and Hossein Ali Gharagozlou in Paris, I enjoyed long conversations on this period with Mr Avery in King's College, Cambridge and with Professor Elwell-Sutton in Edinburgh. I was also privileged to have several lunches and conversations with Sir Roger Stevens, the Vice-Chancellor of Leeds University, where I was then an undergraduate; Sir Roger had been British Ambassador to Iran from 1954–58 and was the author of *The Land of the Great Sophy* (1962). In 1971, I applied to do a D.Phil/PhD in Modern Persian History at St Anthony's College, Oxford and at Edinburgh University, and was interviewed by Albert Hourani at the former and Professor Elwell-Sutton at the latter. I was accepted at Edinburgh on condition that I did an intensive Farsi course during the first year, but since my degree was in Philosophy, and at that time I had only been to Iran on a short visit, it was impossible to obtain funding. I went to live in Rome instead, moving from there to Tehran in 1974. Later, however, I did use Elwell-Sutton's *Elementary Persian Grammar* (Cambridge: CUP, 1963).
48. See the detailed account of this episode in Upton, *History*, pp. 48–52.
49. Haas, Iran, pp. 149–50
50. This is not so unusual. A similar case is that of a Section Chief interviewed in 1986: 'I've gone out with several girls, but each time it came to nothing. The girls always called it off. No. I didn't feel it a loss of face. Do you mean that I lose face when I can't get a girl? I don't feel ashamed if she ditches me. It's her fault not mine.' In Zhang and Sang, *Chinese Profiles*, p. 30.
51. The story has been translated several times. My preference is for the version, with excellent notes, by William A. Lyell, in *Lu Xun: Diary of a Madman and Other Stories*, Honolulu: University of Hawaii Press, 1990.
52. English versions of these stories were published in Jamalzadeh, Mohammad Ali, *Once Upon A Time*, Trs. H. Moayyad and P. Sprachman, Delmar, NY: Caravan Press and Bibliotheca Persica, 1985.

53. Bergère, *Sun Yat-sen*, p. 27.
54. Quoted in Schwartz, *In Search of Wealth and Power*, pp. 146–7.
55. Bergère, *Sun Yat-sen*, p. 207.
56. Ibid., p. 63. Sun's friends expressed the same fears to the *New York Times*, reported in an article entitled 'A Chinese Doctor Kidnapped in London', 22 October 1897.
57. See Cantlie's own account of the episode interspersed with writings by Sun himself in Cantlie and Sheridan Jones, *Sun Yat Sen and the Awakening of China*, pp. 42–6. In stereotypically British fashion, Dr Cantlie's first instinct was to contact Scotland Yard.
58. Schiffrin, *Sun Yat-sen and the Origins of the Chinese Revolution*, p. 114.
59. Sun, *San Min Chu I: The Three Principles of the People*, p. 1.
60. Ibid., p. 150.
61. Bergère, *Sun Yat-sen*, p. 167.
62. Sun, *San Min Chu I*, pp. 151–60.
63. Sun, *The International Development of China*, p. 61, p. 138 and p. 97.
64. Ibid., pp. 23-4.
65. Ibid., p. 161.
66. Quoted from the amended version adopted at the 17th Party Congress in October 2007, in *Documents of the 17th National Congress of the Communist Party of China*, Beijing: Foreign Languages Press, 2007, p. 83.
67. Cantlie and Sheridan Jones, *Sun Yat Sen and the Awakening of China*, p. 12.
68. See the account of the ceremony in Mohammad Ahsan Farooqi's hagiographic life *The Silver Lion: Biography of Reza Shah*, Calcutta: Upper India Publishing House, 1939 pp. 82–4; there is a descriptive chapter on the coronation in Vita Sackville-West's *Passenger to Tehran*, London: Hogarth Press, 1926, pp. 123–42.
69. See, for example, Farooqi, *The Silver Lion*, pp. 124-5.
70. Ibid., p. 126.
71. Von Blücher, *Zeitenwende in Iran*, p. 198.
72. The second Majlis was in session from 1909–1911, the third from 1914–15, the fourth from 1921–23, and the fifth in 1924.
73. *The Times*, 11 September 1928.
74. Upton, *The History of Modern Iran: An Interpretation*, p. 59.
75. Ramazami, *The Foreign Policy of Iran: 1500–1941*, p. 243.
76. The message was sent by the geologist, G. B. Reynolds, to the British Resident at Bushire, Major Percy Cox (later Sir Percy [1864–1937], Minister in Tehran, High Commissioner in Baghdad, who in 1922 established the frontiers between Iraq, Kuwait and Saudi Arabia), in the cryptic form of verses from the Psalms: 'See Psalm 104 verse 15 third sentence…' : 'That he may bring out of the earth oil to make him a cheerful countenance.' Quoted in Longhurst, *Adventure in Oil*, pp. 32–33.
77. See the summary of operations in Longrigg, *Oil in the Middle East*, pp. 54–8.
78. From £1,436,000 in 1929 to £1,288,000 in 1930 and then to £307,000 in 1931; Longrigg, *Oil in the Middle East*, p. 58.
79. Quoted in Longhurst, *Adventure in Oil*, p. 76.

80. *The Near East and India*, 12 January 1933, p. 27.
81. Reported by Robert Byron, in *Road to Oxiana*, p. 125.
82. Mohammad Reza Shah Pahlavi, *Mission for my Country*, p. 60.
83. Personal conversation in Paris with Iran Teymourtache in 1969 at her home at 92 Boulevard Murat, Paris 16e. She remembered the day well because it was the first anniversary of her wedding to Hossein Ali Gharagouzlou.
84. The sum was 25,000 tomans. See the account in Von Blücher, *Zeitenwende in Iran*, pp. 255–9.
85. Haas, *Iran*, p. 147.
86. This information comes from Von Blücher, who had a paid informant on Teymourtache's staff in order to have regular news and continued to visit the Minister in his cell until the end (*Zeitenwende in Iran*, pp. 258–9). Robert Byron wrote on 5 October: 'News arrived this evening that Teimur Tash died in prison at ten o'clock the night before last, after he had been deprived of all comforts, including his bed.' (*The Road to Oxiana*, p. 54).
87. *The Times*, 9 October 1933. The family was swiftly rounded up. Iran divorced her husband so that she would not be spared prison because of the influence of her husband's family, and on the same day joined her brother, grandmother and Teymourtache's sisters, who remained in prison until 1941. As she told the story to me, she had married Hossein Ali just before her father fell into disgrace, and he – ever the gentleman – had offered to protect her from imprisonment. In her late sixties, Iran Teymourtache was still a striking woman, especially when she was enthusiastic about something, so it is easy to believe the story that the last Shah was infatuated with her as a teenager. Her flat was a shrine to Persian culture, with some of the most beautiful carpets and furniture I have ever seen. Both she and her ex-husband were friends with many French intellectuals, including André Malraux (then still alive), whose novel *The Human Condition* was set in Shanghai, although I remember that Hossein Ali's favourite French novelist was Anatole France.
88. Edward G. Browne, *A Literary History of Persia, Volume II: From Firdawsi to Sa'di*, 1906, p. 185.
89. Upton, *The History of Modern Iran*, p. 58.
90. Bergère, *Sun Yat-sen*, p. 6.
91. The Third Session of the Majlis in 1914 had already proposed such revolutionary changes as the creation of a teachers' training college for women, and the transformation of religious schools into secular elementary schools (Banani, *The Modernization of Iran*, p. 34).
92. Banani, *Modernization*, p. 30–1.
93. Quoted in Waterfied, *Professional Diplomat: Sir Percy Loraine*, pp. 73–4.
94. Reported in *The Near East and India*, 16th May 1935, p. 600.
95. Melvin Hall, *Journey to the End of an Era*, New York: Scribners, 1947, p. 198.
96. Avery, *Modern Iran*, pp. 300–3; Banani, *Modernization*, pp. 132–5; see also the map of transportation in Iran in the 1930s in Upton, *History*, pp. 18-9.
97. Cottam, *Nationalism in Iran*, p. 115.
98. Ibid., pp. 98–9.

99. Floor, 'Industrialization in Iran 1900–1941', p. 6.
100. Ibid., p. 27.
101. Cottam, *Nationalism*, p. 147.
102. A reliable contemporary observer, F.A.C. Forbes-Leith, describes him thus and says he worked with his father before entering the Cossack Guards at fourteen (*Checkmate: Fighting Tradition in Central Asia*, London: George G. Harrap, 1927, p. 235); Mohammad Shah claimed that Reza Shah's father and grandfather had both been 'officers in the old Persian army' (Mohammad Reza Shah Pahlavi, *Mission for my Country*, p. 35). But even he agreed that his father was 'completely illiterate' at the age of fourteen (ibid., p. 36), which seems to be a contradiction in a family of military officers.
103. Upton, *History*, p. 49.
104. Von Blücher, *Zeitenwende in Iran*, p. 211; Byron also mentions the episode in *Road to Oxiana*, p. 126.
105. Avery, *Modern Iran*, p. 288.
106. Banani, *Modernization*, pp. 150–1.
107. Young, 'The Problem of Westernization in Modern Iran', pp. 53–4.
108. Farooq, *The Silver Lion*, p. 115.
109. *Annual Review*, p. 263.
110. Young, 'The Problem of Westernization', p. 54.
111. Avery, Modern Iran, p. 284.
112. Ibid., p. 291
113. Banani, *Modernization*, pp. 62–3.
114. Taken from Róbinson Rojas, *La guardia roja conquista China*, Santiago de Chile: Causa ML/Editorial Prensa Latinoamericana, 1968, pp. 430–40, available at http://www.rrojasdatabank.org/16points.htm .
115. Sidney Rittenberg, *The Man Who Stayed Behind*, p. 318.
116. From New China News Agency's English service reporting Li Biao's speech, in *Asia Research Centre, The Great Cultural Revolution*, pp. 376–8.
117. Spence, *Search for Modern China*, p. 575.
118. Rittenberg, *Man Who Stayed Behind*, p. 321.
119. These examples are taken from Li, Dray-Novey and Kong, *Beijing: From Imperial Capital to Olympic City*, p. 199.
120. According to statistics of the Municipal Bureau of Cultural Relics, quoted in Li, Dray-Novey and Kong, *Beijing: From Imperial Capital to Olympic City*, p. 200.
121. Jung Chang and Jon Halliday, *Mao: The Unknown Story*, London: Jonathan Cape, 2005, p. 508.
122. According to his personal doctor, Li Zhisui, in *The Private Life of Chairman Mao*, London: Arrow Books, 1996, p. 479.
123. From an editorial in Hung-ch'i, No 12, 1964, 'A Great Revolution on the Cultural Front', reprinted in Asia Research Centre, *The Great Cultural Revolution*, pp. 26–8.

Chapter 3

Routes to Modernisation

After the initial failures at modernisation, sponsored by the 'fathers' of the respective nations and imperfectly executed by the men who assumed the trappings of power as Shah and Mao, their successors made a second attempt. In both cases, the old enemy became temporarily a friend as President Richard Nixon, accompanied by Secretary of State Henry Kissinger, not only made the first visit by an American president to Beijing in 1972, but he also – a fact generally overlooked – made an important stopover in Tehran en route to China to meet the Shah. Thus that trip marked the return to respectability for both China and Iran: China as a country emerging from unique travails to regain prestige on the international scene; Iran emerging as a major balancing power in the Middle East on behalf of the Western powers, and gaining formal approval for the acquisition of American weapons.

Mohammad Reza Shah in the 1970s

Mohammad Shah Pahlavi succeeded his father as Shah in 1941, when Reza Shah was forced into exile in South Africa. After years in which Reza Shah had played Russia against Britain for his own benefit, the coming together of these two powers in alliance brought him down as they invaded his country together to forestall German designs on the oilfields. Britain launched the attack symbolically at Abadan in refinery country, while Russia attacked from the north by sea and by land. Throughout the Second World War, supplies were sent from British and American sources through Persia to the Soviet Union: the main route was by rail or road northwards from the Persian Gulf; a secondary route led from Chabahar on the Gulf of Oman, whence lorries drove due north on a newly-paved military road through Birjand to Mashad (a few white Roman-style stone milestones with distances marked in English could still be seen along this road in the 1970s).

The Shah sat hapless in Tehran, biding his time. He was seen by many of his own people, in Peter Avery's phrase, as 'still a rather shadowy figure.'[1] He struggled to establish his legitimacy amidst the growing power of the Soviet-inspired *Tudeh* party and demands for the nationalisation of the oil industry, and in 1949 survived an assassination attempt. Then, in 1951, he made the major error of appointing the popular nationalist politician Dr Mohammad Mossadegh as Prime Minister after the previous holder of the position had been assassinated. This was something of a step backwards, since Mossadegh was a descendant of the Qajar dynasty and his wife a granddaughter of the modernising Nasir ed-Din Shah Qajar. But Mossadegh was also a fervent supporter of nationalisation, and in fact nationalised the Anglo-Iranian Oil Company within days of his appointment. Bolstered by this success, Mossadegh sought greater powers and over the next two years antagonised most sectors of public life; he was fired and reinstated as Prime Minister, and political life was gradually absorbed by arguments over the future of the monarchy. In a convoluted preview of 1979, there were riots and street battles, hundreds of deaths, and parades of tanks through the streets of Tehran. To preserve his chances of survival, Mohammad Shah fled into exile in Rome in August 1953. It was the year of *Roman Holiday*, and they were in time to participate briefly in the *dolce vita*, like the Shah's one-time brother-in-law, King Farouk of Egypt. The Shah's sojourn – and that of his beautiful second wife, Soraya – was still remembered in the 1970s in Via Veneto, where they stayed near the American embassy at the Excelsior, and by the Roman paparazzi. Filmstar-style photographs of the glamorous couple could still be seen on the walls of favourite restaurants like Doney's.

But soon the Shah returned to Tehran, sustained by the CIA and American financial support. Thus he began his second life, at first sight in ominous conditions. Oil revenues had shrunk virtually to zero, so the first thing he did was to negotiate an agreement with a consortium of eight foreign oil companies – with the AIOC being known from the following year as British Petroleum. Oil output rose steadily, from a low-point of 1 million tons to 45 million tons by the end of the decade.[2] Together with a credit of $150 million from the United States, and one of £10 million from Britain, oil revenues enabled the Shah to recommence the process of modernisation. As in China, one of the first essentials was the redistribution of land to peasant farmers, beginning with some of the Shah's own extensive holdings and continuing with government land; until that time, large landowners had possessed lock, stock and barrel hundreds of villages each, including the lives of the inhabitants. Towards the end of the decade, oil concessions were signed with AGIP of Italy and Pan-American, a subsidiary of Standard Oil, for new exploration and production in southern Iran, with much more favourable terms which assigned to Iran seventy-five per cent of profits (as opposed to the sixteen per cent of the D'Arcy Concession and fifty per cent of the post-Mossadegh agreements).

On the basis of this excellent start, the economy quintupled in size over the next ten years, with steady growth in domestic demand, low inflation and political stability. These stable and financially solid conditions allowed the Shah to introduce his 'White Revolution' in 1963, with the purpose of building a new and modern Iran. The provisions and policies of this 'revolution' read well: further distribution of land to peasant farmers, the creation of collectives, and the introduction of profit-sharing for factory workers. Together with new electoral laws which gave the votes to women and measures for eliminating illiteracy and improving health services, the reforms pointed in the right direction.[3] In 1961, the literacy rate was as low as fifteen per cent in rural areas, and elementary education was available to only about a fifth of village children.[4]

The White Revolution also spurred significant improvements to national infrastructure, with an improved transport system in terms of sea, road, rail and air transport: a National Shipping Company was set up, initially operating two oil tankers and two cargo vessels; plans were announced to link remote villages to the existing highway system; rail links to Tabriz and Mashad proposed thirty years earlier were finally completed and diesel engines introduced; the Shah began to dream of direct links from Tehran to London in the west and to Calcutta in the east 'in a few years'.[5] Air services were strengthened by an agreement in 1962 which merged two existing airlines, Iranian Airways and Pars Airways, to create the new flag-carrier, Iranair, which was based at the new international airport in Tehran. These investments and improvements were part of a well-planned effort to drive Iran into the modern world, upgrading from an agricultural economy with exports based on hand-woven carpets, tobacco and dried fruit to a genuinely industrial economy. To this end, emphasis was placed on the development of a domestic steel industry and new petrochemical industries, which would 'provide a broader base for the next phase of industrialisation.'

In a short period of rapid growth, Iran had become the leading regional economic power, and began to invest heavily in military equipment in line with its new ambitions. While China was in the grip of the Cultural Revolution, Iran was enjoying phenomenal growth. But at the same time these rapid reforms caused friction amongst conservative and religious opponents.

In fact the White Revolution was more fateful than anyone could have realised, for it provoked the ire of a certain Rouhollah Mousavi Khomeini, then sixty-one, who had been accepted by the Shi'a in Qom as their spiritual leader after the death of the more moderate Ayatollah Boroujerdi two years earlier. Khomeini and other clerics now signed a manifesto which listed ways in which they considered the Shah had violated the Persian Constitution and Islamic Law, strongly condemning what they perceived as the spread of moral corruption – even though the Shah had made a public show of religiosity by going on pilgrimage to Mecca in 1957. On 3 June 1963, Khomeini attacked the Shah in a speech demanding his departure from Iran if he was not prepared to change his policies. The Ayatollah was arrested the next day and taken to prison in Tehran, but was released with equal rapidity after pressure from the clergy and violent protests in cities throughout the country: troops opened fire on demonstrators near the bazaar in Tehran in a preview of what would happen in Tiananmen Square twenty-six years later to the day, for the arrests and killing took place on 4 June. Thousands of demonstrators bore placards with the words 'Down with the Shah!'; in 1978, this was upgraded to 'Death to the Shah!' Just as to Persians this event is known simply by its date as the 'Uprising' of 15 Khordad (which was actually the following day), so the events in Tiananmen are known to Chinese as the 'Fourth of June'. Again, as in China later, there were widely varying estimates of the carnage: while the Shah's Prime Minister Amir Asadollah Alam claimed that the resulting deaths were eighty-six, other estimates ranged up to 10,000.[6]

Undeterred by his brief imprisonment, indeed galvanised by the deaths of the faithful, Khomeini did not desist from strong criticism. In October, after he had urged the boycotting of elections and protested the Shah's decision to provide immunity from prosecution for American military personnel in Iran, reminiscent of privileges accorded to foreigners in China in the nineteenth century, he was again arrested. This time he was held prisoner by the Shah's notorious secret police, SAVAK. Released on 4 May 1964, he again protested vociferously throughout the summer, and was finally and formally exiled in November, when SAVAK re-arrested him in Qom and flew him to Turkey. A year later, he moved to a long-term residence in the Shi'a holy city of Najaf in Iraq, where he was to reside for thirteen years. Intriguingly, it was said to have been Hossein Ali Gharagozlou, something of an expert in the subject, and brother-in-law of Prime Minister Alam, who persuaded the Shah to send Khomeini into exile while others wished to execute him.[7] The Shah's hope that at such a distance the disruptive cleric would be forgotten proved to be over-optimistic.

But for the moment Shah Mohammad Pahlavi was firmly in control. Steel production began after the White Revolution, with a contract signed in 1965 with the Soviet Union to build a factory in Isfahan for the National Iranian Steel Company (NISC). Earlier plans had been complicated by the fact that at a moment of Allied invasion the construction of blast furnaces, rolling mill and steel factory and other infrastructure had just been assigned to a German consortium involving Demag and Krupps.[8] The new Isfahan plant began operation six years later, and in the same period a privately-owned company, the Iran National Steel Industries Group (now a subsidiary of NISC), established steel rolling plants in Ahwaz.[9] Today, Iran is the twentieth biggest steel producer in the world, with ten million metric tons in 2006 placing it a little above South Africa and Australia, and a little below Poland, Belgium and the United Kingdom (China is in a class by itself, at 422 million, over three times more than second-placed Japan).[10]

At about the same time, in 1967, the first car-assembly plant was built by the Iran Khodro Industrial Group, which began by assembling imported kits of a car known in Iran as the Paykan. This was in fact a Hillman Hunter, which was at first assembled from kits supplied by Rootes in Britain and later produced with locally-made parts and an imported engine, supplied by Peugeot after it had acquired Rootes. The Paykan was the Fiat 500 of Iran (a locally produced Renault 5 was later also very popular), with over two million of them over the decades offering mobility to less wealthy families at a reasonable price when import duty on cars was around 300 per cent. It was also the vehicle of choice for taxi drivers, and could be seen in rural areas in a pick-up version.[11] It remained in production until 2005, and now, in a fine twist of fate, the same company assembles the 'new Paykan', known as the Samand, in Belarus.[12]

Modernisation saw another acceleration in the 1970s with financial muscle augmented by the windfall following the 1973–4 oil crisis. Iran had been a founder member of OPEC, and was an enthusiastic supporter of the decision not to supply countries which supported Israel and to increase oil prices after the failure to agree on a price mechanism with the western oil majors. When the consequent embargo ended in March 1974, prices had quadrupled and the following year Iran's income from oil rocketed to $19 billion as petrol prices in the USA and Europe reached unimagined levels.

This led naturally to rapid growth in the petrochemicals industry. The National Petrochemical Company (NPC, originally NIPC) had already been founded in 1963 with overall responsibility for the development and operation of Iran's petrochemical sector, beginning in line with the Shah's agricultural reforms with a fertiliser plant in Shiraz. Over the next two decades, until development was brought to a halt by the Iran-Iraq War, the NPC opened seven major petrochemical complexes for the production of fertilisers, and petrochemical and chemical bases for domestic consumption. Foreign expertise was brought in to provide technical know-how, one of the most successful joint-ventures being the Abadan Petrochemical Company between the NPC and the American company B.F. Goodrich, which had a minority stake of twenty-six per cent. A plant was established in 1966 to produce PVC (for plastics), DDB (for detergents) and NaOH (caustic soda). Then, as a result of the new-found wealth, in 1973 a new and larger plant was begun in order to double the production. It became operational in 1975 but four years later, of course, NPC 'acquired' the stake of its American partner.[13] Joint-venture plants between the NIPC and foreign partners included petrochemical plants in Khuzistan at Bandar Chapour (now Bandar-e Imam Khomeini) and Farabi, both with Japanese firms.[14]

Something similar happened with plans for nuclear energy, with which in the beginning the United States was deeply involved. The country's nuclear programme also received a boost in the 1970s, but the story began when a small nuclear reactor was given to Iran as the result of President Eisenhower's 'Atoms for Peace' programme in 1953. Cooperation between the United States and Iran began in 1957, when the pro-US Shah was perceived as a vital regional military ally. Ten years later, it became operational with the establishment of the Tehran Nuclear Research Center, which had an American-supplied five megawatt research reactor. In the following year, 1968, Iran signed the Nuclear Non-Proliferation Treaty and the Shah announced a plan to build twenty-three nuclear power stations by the end of the century, beginning with a plant in Bushehr to supply electricity to the city of Shiraz. The United States, as the Shah's main ally, favoured Iran's nuclear policy, but with some reservations. However, many other Western powers provided assistance with supplies, training and in other ways, including France, West Germany, Britain, Italy, Belgium and Canada.[15]

In 1975, the German company Thyssen Krupp began work on this ambitious plan for power stations. The next year, when the White House Chief of Staff was a certain Dick Cheney and the Secretary of Defense one Donald Rumsfeld, the American government agreed to sell to Iran reprocessing facilities for extracting plutonium from nuclear reactor fuel. According to Dr Akbar Etemad, considered the father of Iran's nuclear programme, nuclear adviser to the Shah and president of the Atomic Energy Organisation of Iran from 1974 to 1978,

> our negotiations with the Americans started in 1974. From the beginning, they had the precondition that they should have complete control over our nuclear fuel cycle. Both the Ford and Carter administrations told us privately that they didn't have any issues with the Iranian government. The problem was that Yugoslavia and Egypt were waiting to see what Iran and the US agreed.[16]

But in any case this cooperation, and concerns about Yugoslavia and Egypt, came to an abrupt halt in 1979 with the Revolution, when suppliers and contractors in France, Germany and the United States reneged on earlier deals. When, as we shall see, the nuclear programme made a fresh start in the 1990s, the new partners were China and Russia.

Oil wealth also facilitated the acquisition of weapons and the build-up of a strong military presence, for defence was the third prong of what one of the Shah's biographers described as the 'Pahlavi trident' – together with oil and SAVAK (which ironically, from today's perspective, received assistance and training from both Mossad and the CIA).[17] From 1971 to 1978, arms spending in the United States alone totalled $19 billion, while in the latter year government spending on defence, steel, atomic power and the petrochemical industry accounted for sixty-five per cent of the national budget.[18] In the fiscal year 1976–1977, as much as twenty per cent of the entire national budget, or $9.3 billion,[19] was spent on defence purchases such as Chieftain tanks from Britain, and F-14 fighters and *Spruance*-class destroyers from the USA, with the most sophisticated weapons systems then available. At that time, when the author was living in Tehran, most people assumed that by the mid-1980s Iran would become the world's fourth power in military terms after the USA, the Soviet Union and China. The Shah himself often boasted in his speeches that Iran would soon have one of the world's five biggest economies.

Just as for the Shah, the wresting of control of the oil industry in 1973 meant revenge for humiliations imposed by foreign oil companies after the Mossadegh coup, thus representing restoration of Persia's past greatness, so from the Chinese perspective it was also seen in an extremely favourable light. China, intuitively understanding from its own experience, praised Iran's success in the struggle against 'western petroleum monopoly groups' and the people's 'protracted struggle to protect their oil rights and interests'. It produced evidence of the way in which 'imperialists and superpowers' had amassed their wealth at the expense of Third World countries.[20] China also saw the broader international oil crisis positively, as an important victory against American hegemony in the form of the 'Seven Sisters', all but two of which, Shell and BP, were US-owned.[21] At the same time, ironically with hindsight, the United States perceived Iran as a crucial model of development and stability in the Middle East. The mainly American multinationals were rapidly increasing their presence there, in particular military-oriented companies like McDonnell Douglas, Westinghouse, Grumman, Lockheed and Bell Helicopter, those working with the nuclear programme, and companies engaged in large-scale computer projects such as IBM, Honeywell and EDS. A non-American company like Mercedes Benz, which since 1959 had a joint-venture called Khavar-Benz manufacturing lorries under license, was building a factory for passenger cars in the late 1970s. The new middle-class dressed in Western style, enjoyed local wine from vineyards laid down during Reza Shah's time using South African vines, and drove expensive imported cars – especially Mercedes models, which together with the Peugeot 504 were considered the most rugged cars on local roads. By then, few middle-class women under thirty wore the *chador*.

Thus, as Tehran began 1978 there was a semblance of a rapidly modernising city, and much of the country was engaged in a process of industrialisation. There were signs of the Western-inspired boom everywhere, with a new ski resort under construction in the mountains behind Tehran, and residents proudly showing off the glass-fronted Coca Cola bottling plant to new visitors as they drove into town from the airport on what was still called Eisenhower Avenue. The new middle class went on shopping trips to London and Paris, often to visit their children in universities there, and each year more foreign products became available in bright new supermarkets, especially in Tehran. Covered in winter snow, many streets in the tree-lined northern suburbs of Tehran might easily have been in Switzerland, with high whitewashed walls protecting elaborate villas with marble floors and furniture imported from Italy. There were nightclubs as lavish as those of Europe, and a millionaire's paradise on Kish Island in the Persian Gulf which served as an forerunner to modern Dubai – especially the Madinat Jumeirah quarter with its faux traditional restaurants (including a Persian one) and bazaar, and the extravagant Burj Al Arab Hotel.[22] In fact, the only other places where entrepreneurs dream of seven-star hotels are Shanghai and Beijing, and the Atlantis Hotel which opened on the artificial Palm Jumeirah Island in Dubai in late 2008 bears striking similarities in its architectural detail to expensive apartment buildings in Shanghai.

Tehran was once a rival to such developments: never-implemented plans for a new 554-hectare city centre to be called Shahestan Pahlavi, with spectacular office buildings, housing for 36,000 people, cultural centres and fountains built as a 'spine' above a new metro system leading to an equally new international airport, and at the centre a square destined to be one of the biggest in the world, sound and look like a half-way-house between Dubai and Shanghai. The objective was to transform Tehran into 'one of the major capitals of the world'.[23] One of the architects made ambitious comparisons with Shah Abbas' early-seventeenth-century plan for Isfahan, Pope Sixtus V's slightly earlier plan for Rome, and Baron Haussmann's plan of Paris.[24] In the midst of this extravagance, the Shah himself frequently exhorted his subjects with the slogan 'Get Rich!' in an uncanny pre-echo of Deng Xiao Ping's 'to get rich is glorious!'

Then, towards the end of 1978, it all began to unravel. An apparently minor protest against the removal of Khomeini from Iraq mushroomed into genuine revolution. The wealthy suddenly began to spirit their money out of the country. There were bazaar rumours of hundreds of millions of dollars a day being transferred, and a printed list of guilty names circulated in photocopies. Then the rich began to flee in person, blocking all outward-bound flights; an acquaintance of the author's flew to London via Singapore in desperation. Western-educated female colleagues and friends who had laughed and smiled in fashionable imported outfits and high-heeled shoes quite suddenly and simultaneously appeared without make-up in *chadors* as if by some invisible sign. Nationalistic sentiment and religious fervour could be felt in the air. Foreigners began to leave too, following the abrupt cancellation of a large number of contracts and projects involving multinational companies.

For an Englishman then living in the capital, the date on which the possibility of revolution became tangible is indelibly fixed. For from the north of Tehran, a city which stretches up along what was originally built as Pahlavi Avenue,[25] from the old city on the plain to the district of Shemiran at around 1,700 metres above sea level, it was in the late afternoon of 5 November that the first gunshots could be heard. Columns of black smoke rose from bonfires of old tyres in the streets far below. Ash-heaps in downtown streets the next morning resembled the smouldering remains of Guy Fawkes pyres the day after.

Deng Xiao Ping in the 1980s

In Beijing, at precisely the moment Mohammad Reza Shah's doomed modernisation burst into flames, and strikes and protests against him gained momentum, Deng Xiao Ping was preparing for the Third Plenum of the 11th Central Committee of the Communist Party, which opened on 18 December as Iran descended into chaos.

In a historically important keynote speech Deng initiated the process of substitution of Mao's negative 'four olds' with the positive 'four modernisations' of agriculture, industry, science and technology, and the military. In fact, the idea of the modernisations dated back to Zhou Enlai in 1965, and had been reiterated in 1976; this accorded them a certain respectability. The main issue, Deng now argued, was how to 'emancipate our minds, use our heads, seek truth from facts and unite as one in looking to the future.'[26] In order to begin this process, he needed to overcome the ideological taboos of the Gang of Four, explain the merits of Mao in creating a 'New China' which would not have existed without his past leadership, pardon Mao's fallibility, and seek a long-term evaluation of the 'shortcomings' of the Cultural Revolution. In essence it was a ritual cleansing and healing of the past two decades, after which he and the Party would be ready to 'study the new situation' and focus on the economic issues necessary to realise the four modernisations. One consequence of a tentative new opening was the celebrated stretch of 'Democracy Wall' just to the west of the Forbidden City and Tiananmen Square and reaching the external wall of the leadership enclave known as Zhongnanhai, which began to host posters and slogans in November and December 1978 that even dared criticise Mao and Deng. On one famous poster displayed on 5 December, the ex-Red Guard Wei Jingsheng went so far as to speak of the 'Fifth Modernisation', which would be democracy. Although Deng may have permitted and encouraged some of the earlier criticisms, this and harsher criticism of the Party itself led to a crackdown the following month which brought fifteen years in prison for Wei.[27]

Deng had begun his own less radical mission a few years earlier, when he opened a speech at a Party internal meeting in the spring of 1975 – a year before Mao's death – by asserting the importance of what he called a 'two-stage development' of China:

> the first stage is to build an independent and relatively comprehensive industrial and economic system by 1980. The second will be to turn China into a powerful socialist country with modern agriculture, industry, national defence and science and technology by the end of this century…

In extremely explicit language he complains that some comrades 'only dare to make revolution but not to promote production.' These comrades paradoxically assert that the former is safe, while the latter is dangerous. 'This is utterly wrong,' Deng asserts.[28] His speech marked the birth of the 'four modernisations', and of a leader determined enough to be able to push them through.

Deng began slowly by introducing agricultural reforms which ended the era of collective farming with a mild form of privatisation. Under the 'household responsibility system', individual farmers only had small plots of land and were obliged to sell some of their produce to the government at low prices. Once these quotas were completed, however, they were free to sell extra produce at market prices. With such an incentive, there was a rapid increase in production, so much so that agricultural production grew by around ten per cent per year from 1979 to 1984.

The first major economic reform was the creation of the Special Economic Zones. Beginning in 1979 with Shantou, Shenzhen, Xiamen and Zhuhai, fourteen other cities were thus designated in 1984, together with the island province of Hainan. Given the first group's status as ports and the importance of Shantou and Xiamen – previously known in the West as Swatow and Amoy – as providers of emigrants, it was natural for these zones to focus on manufacturing for export through their own overseas networks. The Teochiu speakers who come from seven villages near Shantou represent the most successful of all overseas Chinese communities, constituting the majority Chinese population in Thailand and the second largest group in Canada, Hong Kong, Malaysia, Singapore, the United States and Vietnam.[29] The second wealthiest group is that of the Hokkien speakers from Xiamen, who are in the majority in Indonesia, Malaysia, Singapore, Taiwan and the Philippines. In fact, investment into the province of Fujian (including Xiamen and Shatou) in the period from 1979 to 1993 was mainly from these communities - with as much as 65.7 per cent from Hong Kong and 16.5 per cent from Taiwan against 3.1 per cent from the USA and Canada together. [30] These supposedly foreign investors put their money where they speak the local dialect: Hokkien speakers from Hong Kong and Taiwan, for example, represented ninety-eight per cent of 'foreign' investment in Xiamen.[31] In other words Deng, himself of Hakka origins, was tapping into the vast wealth of the overseas Chinese and understood from the inside the strong loyalty of these tightly-knit groups to their hometowns. A network of existing banks, factories and markets at home and abroad stood ready to assist China's economic growth.

This facilitated the 'four modernisations' which became a pillar of reform during the 12th Party Congress in 1982 and set the stage for economic and political reform in the next few years as Deng evolved the concept of 'socialism with Chinese characteristics'. Two years later, his vision was spelled out even more precisely, speaking at a ceremony to mark the thirty-fifth anniversary of the foundation of the PRC:

> Our primary job at present is to reform systematically everything in the existing economic structure that is impeding our progress … We shall redouble our efforts in scientific and technological research, in education at all levels and in the training of workers, administrative staff and cadres.'[32]

The next few years were to see a remarkable resurgence in the economy of China and an all-round improvement in the lives of its people.

Much the same could be said of Beijing a decade later, with the first entrepreneurs, a new restaurant culture, and the sending of bright students to study abroad on government scholarships. Already in 1988, there were 261 foreign joint-venture companies in Beijing, including one set up by American Motors to build the 'Beijing Jeep',[33] and new luxury hotels managed by entrepreneurs from Hong Kong. At the same time, medium-sized state-owned enterprises had been put up for auction to private entrepreneurs as well as to the more politically-correct collectives. Following Deng's exhortation about wealth, civil servants left the government to set up new private businesses. At the same time, there were massive new projects in the areas of coal-mining, dam-building and oil production which necessarily entailed central government planning and investment, and were vital for future growth of the country. They all generated the desired prosperity.

In the same year, 1988, newspapers listed the ten best construction projects of the decade, based on readers' votes. They included emblematic buildings of the new modernity and its accoutrements such as the Central Color Television Center, the second terminal at Beijing Capital Airport, the China Theatre, and one of the new subway stations.[34] The list reads as a striking harbinger of present nationalistic fervour and its dramatic expression in architecture, in parallel or 'successor' buildings like the spectacular leaning CCTV Tower by Rem Koolhaas, the huge third terminal at Capital Airport by Norman Foster, the flying-saucer-like National Theatre by Paul Andreu, and five totally new subway lines currently under construction.

By that time, the city had a new ring road which followed the line of the city walls Mao had demolished (the present Second Ring; now as the Sixth nears completion there are plans for a Seventh Ring), two subway lines which transported 800,000 passengers every day, over 200 taxi companies with 20,000 cars, while the ancestors of those who today upgrade from bicycle to car were purchasing motorcycles. Moreover, there were plenty of places to go for leisure activities, which were previously unknown. There were historic buildings open to the public for the first time, such as the Lamaist temple at Yonghe Gong which had once been the home of the emperor Qianlong, and the Palace Museum in the Forbidden City. Restaurants, teashops and roadside food-stands began to reappear after decades, together with bicycle repair shops and bourgeois businesses such as hairdressing salons which would have been unthinkable during the lifetime of Mao or in the Cultural Revolution. There were by that time around 150 restaurants offering a much wider choice of fare than the pork and cabbage traditional to the inhabitants of the capital. On one count, the number of small businesses such as convenience stores, barbers and restaurants increased from 15,000 in 1978 to 100,000 ten years later – of which three-quarters were privately owned.[35] Shops sold goods such as televisions, tape recorders and refrigerators that had been unavailable a decade before; there were cafes in which to meet, and newly-opened churches offering divine service.

There were families like that of the wheeler-dealer 'Ten-Thousand Yuan Household', two childless ex-peasants who in 1986 gorge in an expensive Tianjin restaurant on six dishes including fish and king prawns, the most expensive dishes, beer, and even a chicken bought in the street and taken inside. They toast with beer, and boast of having 'wads of tenners' when a schoolteacher's monthly salary was less than 100 yuan and a bus conductor earned 70. The wife is obsessed with cash, calling the martens she raises as a sideline her 'three hundred yuans'; she boasts of the Hong Kong clothes she buys through Shenzhen, frequent trips to Beijing, their colour television, tape-recorder, refrigerator and the house they own. 'After three years as a ten-thousand yuan household,' she concludes her interview, 'never mind Shenzhen, even a trip to the US wouldn't be such a big deal for us.'[36] Another example was an twenty-nine-year-old itinerant tailor who earned as much as 1,200 yuan a month and was seeking to save 20,000 so that he could live on the interest and take a wife. When he first returned home to Qingpu, near Shanghai, from the north, he had so much cash with him that his family were convinced he had robbed a bank.[37] Equally typical is the case of the ex-member of the 'Peasants' Rebel Regiment' and participant in Mao's rallies for the Red Guards, now a buyer and salesman for a privately-owned factory in Zhuoxian, south of Beijing. He boasts of spending 239 yuan on a meal at the Dasanyuan Restaurant in the capital, and observes that there's only one thing his company is good at compared to a State-Owned Enterprise, which is supplying drink and cigarettes: 'Raise your glasses and forget about policy; once the chopsticks start moving everything's possible.'[38] These examples illustrate the new environment of 'getting rich is glorious', and remind the author of the frenzied solo dancing of traders in Tehran in popular nightclubs near the bazaar like the Golden Horizon (*Ofoktalaiyi*), with wads of cash bulging in their pockets and bottles of Chivas balanced on their heads; everything was possible there too when the chopsticks started moving.

In fact popular music re-emerged in China after years of official propaganda songs, and drove a craze for dancing. This took place in public squares with tape-recorders, as it still does on summer evenings today, but also in discotheques such as those organised in the Friendship Hotel in western Beijing and the Peace Hotel in the central shopping district. Hotel restaurants turned into cabarets after dinner, with a five-yuan entry fee which young entrepreneurs could afford and official permission to perform one foreign song for every three Chinese songs; in one case, the five band members themselves earned ten yuan each evening.[39] The first popstars gained widespread notoriety, most of them coming from Hong Kong and Taiwan singing what was known as *gangtai* music, from the Mandarin name for Hong Kong, Xiang*gang* plus *Tai*wan. Several Chinese acquaintances have recounted to the author how as teenagers they listened furtively to the love ballads of Teresa Teng, known in Chinese as Deng Lijun, whose soft and beautiful voice they heard on tapes under sheets to ensure no one else would overhear such reactionary behaviour. The instruments were mainly Western, but some of the most attractive songs also used traditional Chinese instruments, and her songs are still today a stalwart of parties and karaoke. Sadly, she died from an asthma attack at the age of forty-two. It is difficult for us to imagine how exciting these rather corny and mellifluous songs must have sounded for people whose only music for over a decade had been songs in praise of the *patria* or Mao himself. Moreover, the rapid diffusion of tape recorders in the same period facilitated the use of 'private' music, to be enjoyed at home rather than in mass gatherings and politically-inspired occasions.

In 1986, a young singer called Cui Jian created a sensation in Beijing with a rock-style song called *Having Nothing*, sung at a huge public concert with over a hundred singers. It struck a chord with youth and especially with university students, who identified strongly with the message of this so-called love song whose roots went much deeper. From a world in which they had literally had nothing, no food, no studies, no personal identity, no self-belief, no cultural history, this song presented 'a whole new ethos that combined individualism, nonconformism, personal freedom, authenticity, direct and bold expression, and protest and rebellion, in short, the essence of Western rock culture.'[40] A song about personal feelings and experience was a revelation, and offended the old propagandistic notion that the Chinese had everything they needed. It was the same hint of protest and rebellion which Western youth had sensed two decades earlier in the music of the Rolling Stones and Bob Dylan, which could now be heard thanks to growing numbers of foreign students and cassette recorders. Many years later, in 2006, the two came together when Cui Jian sang the Stones' song *Wild Horses* together with Mick Jagger at the Shanghai concert of the Rolling Stones' world tour.

Life was restored to 'normal' in many other ways. Universities re-opened after forced closure during the Cultural Revolution, and from 1978 Chinese students began to travel abroad for postgraduate studies – sometimes with state funding but often with money provided by their families as they reached decent income levels.

New ideas from the west spurred entrepreneurship. One businessman who had been sent down to the countryside during the Cultural Revolution recounted learning from Alvin Toffler's *Third Wave* (1980) and John Naisbitt's *Megatrends: Ten New Directions Transforming Our Lives* (1982), and was then inspired by Arthur Haley's novel *Hotel* (1970) to enter the hotel business.[41] But access to Western experience and ideas also stimulated questions about China, its past and its future. Intellectuals began to discuss democracy openly just as they had in Tehran. In December 1986 there were large-scale protests demanding freedom and democracy in Beijing, Nanjing, Tianjin, Kunming, Chongqing and Shenzhen, with as many as 30,000 students and 40,000 townspeople joining demonstrations in Shanghai. Such protests were soon banned, with sympathetic politicians being purged and new rules on censorship and control established.[42] But the momentum did not diminish, and in 1989 new calls for a form of democracy were made. Demands were made by prominent intellectual for the release from prison of Wei Jingsheng. The same intellectuals and students, enjoying new-found freedoms, pushed once again to see how far they could go when they saw the opportunity provided by the death in mid-April of former Secretary-General Hu Yaobang, who had been purged for his responsibility in allowing the student protests of 1986 to grow. In Jonathan Spence's words:

> By launching a pro-Hu Yaobang demonstration, and demanding a reversal of the verdict against him too, the students would ensure that all the issues of 1986–1987 pro-democracy protests, and perhaps also those of Democracy Wall in 1978–1979, would once more be at the forefront of the nation's attention.[43]

Few imagined the immediate dramatic consequences, or the long-term effects, of these student protests in Tiananmen Square.

Backlash: Khomeini and Tiananmen

Few saw the revolution coming in Tehran either, or imagined its consequences. Yet with hindsight, as in Beijing, the deep causes and immediate trigger were easy to understand. The fateful year of 1978 began with religious protests against the regime in January, when several protesters were shot dead by the army, and in February shouts of 'Death to the Shah' were heard for the first time in a commemoration of the same episode in the northwestern city of Tabriz.[44] Similar protests continued through the summer, with deaths which had little resonance in the local press and everyday life in Tehran. The Shah himself seemed unperturbed. 'And then', he said to his ambassador to the United Nations in April, 'who can oppose me? Khomeini? He doesn't count for much!'[45] On 26 June 1978 he declared to *US News and World Report* that 'Nobody can overthrow me. I have the support of 700,000 troops, all the workers and most of the people.'[46] And, he might have added, 5,000 élite members of SAVAK, the ferocious secret police who most Persians the author spoke to at the time believed would be able to repress any rebellion.

In the summer the bazaars in Tehran, Tabriz, Mashad and Qom (the latter being the major centres of Shi-ism in Iran) went on regular strike together with other shops. Still the Shah maintained a studied calm, claiming that protests were the price to be paid for democratisation, and insisting that Iran would reach the standard of living and freedom of Europe within ten years: in August he confidently announced that the following June there would be 'one hundred per cent free elections'.[47] Two weeks later, following other protests, nearly 400 people died when a cinema, seen by clerics as a negative symbol of modernity, was set on fire in Abadan, followed by other protests in early September and continuous agitation from distant Najaf. Feelings against the Shah ran high, but it still seemed that he would be able to suppress any real attempt to depose him even if protests increased. He began to exercise pressure on Iraq to exile Khomeini, and changed ministers and prime ministers in his own government.

Then, on 8 September, martial law was imposed throughout Iran. The Shah, in an interview in a palace surrounded by tanks, informed *Time* that without martial law his opponents 'could have taken over the country – and I don't mean slowly'.[48] There was a growing number of strikes by small businesses and shops, including a general strike on 1 October, but these were mainly aimed at the problem of galloping inflation. On 26 October, the Shah's birthday, students demonstrated again him in Tehran University even though he used the occasion to release 1,000 prisoners.[49] But in spite of these protests, strikes, oppression and rumours, at the end of October most people in Tehran went about their daily business in the normal way. All knew about feelings against the Shah, and heard of threats emanating from Khomeini, but believed that the military might of the Shah together with the American backing that he had enjoyed before would carry the day. So did he.

Clearly, he had failed to recognise increasingly deep resentment as he assumed, literally, more imperial powers by crowning himself Shahanshah, King of Kings, in 1967, as he began to perceive himself as the heir to Persia's imperial legacy. In 1971 he held extravagant celebrations to mark the 2,500th anniversary of the creation of the ancient Persian Empire by Cyrus the Great – whose tomb is thought to be in Persepolis. Thus by association he assumed ancient titles such as the as 'king of the universe' and 'king of the four quarters', and styled himself *Aryamehr*, 'Light of the Aryans'. A temporary city of gold-spangled tents was set up in a star shape amongst the ruins of Cyrus' capital, Persepolis, with catering by Maxims – with thirty cooks and 150 maitres – and gold-embroidered uniforms by Lanvin; convoys of lorries brought furniture, bedding, crockery and much else from France. A new motorway was built from Shiraz for the occasion, and a telephone exchange using satellite telephony for the 500 VIP guests, including sixty from amongst foreign royalty and heads of state. Flowers had been planted with precise planning so that they would bloom during the celebrations, including a specially-bred variety of rose called Persepolis. Flying in the face of Islamic decorum, there were casinos and beauty parlours to keep the guests entertained.[50]

For a while, things went in the Shah's favour, in spite of this extravagance, as when government revenues multiplied after the oil crisis. This was to be the birth of a new country, on the model of the birth of Cyrus' empire – a sign of the depth of historical feeling equivalent to Sun Yat-sen's inaugural speech as President of China, when he pledged to free China of 'foreign' Manchu power as the Ming had freed the country from the Mongols 700 years earlier.[51] The Shah spoke again of Iran becoming the fifth largest economy in the world, the leading power in the Middle East, the only regional power with a nuclear programme. Such self-aggrandisement culminated in 1976 when the Shah imposed the use of a new calendar dating back to the foundation of the Persian Empire by Cyrus, antagonising the clerics since the traditional calendar was dated from the *hegira* of Mohammad rather than a fairly arbitrary historical date in the pre-Islamic past. Persians now had to deal with three separate calendars: the Gregorian Calendar, the Persian or *Jalāli* Calendar (devised, amongst others, by Omar Khayyam), and the new Pahlavi Imperial Calendar; thus a single year was 1976, 1355 and 2595 respectively, with the latter used by newspapers and official documents.

Against the hubris, pressure had been building for some time. In June 1975, there were demonstrations on the anniversary of 15 Khordad which continued for three days. Khomeini participated at a distance, with a message in which he said that the demonstrations were a sign of hope that 'freedom from the bonds of imperialism' was close at hand. Three years later, it must have seemed even closer, at least to him.

At last Iraq agreed to deport Khomeini, and on 24 September his house in Najaf was surrounded by troops. He was informed that continued residence in Iraq was contingent on his abandoning political activity, a condition he rejected. Refused by Kuwait, and after considering the alternatives of Algeria, Lebanon and Syria, he embarked for the traditional exile's refuge of Paris just over a week later. Journalists from around the world travelled on pilgrimage to the house which other exiles had rented for him in the suburb of Neauphle-le-Chateau, and the severe image and words of Ayatollah Khomeini became a daily feature in the media.

In Iran, the presence of Islam had remained important in spite of Reza Shah's attempts to secularise his country. The elderly recited their prayers daily, and bazaaris shifted beads on the rosary as they talked with customers, although in the author's experience of visiting mosques throughout the country there were very few young men visible on the prayer rugs. The Persians are a fun-loving people, for whom weddings and parties were a great event, and music and drinking an essential part of these festivities (many Persians claim that their country invented vodka, and in remote villages it was then common to welcome visitors with the even stronger *arak* – which on one occasion in Baluchistan I remember *diluting* with Smirnoff vodka). But at the same time there were signs of fundamentalist pressures against modernity. In the holy city of Qom, a city of nearly sixty Islamic seminaries and seat of the leading *ayatollahs*, women who ventured outside the home without a *chador* were quickly accosted by zealots. During a visit there in December 1978, local residents seemed keener to show me a burnt-out cinema than the religious monuments. Whereas on earlier visits it had been possible to walk round the beautiful golden-domed Shrine of Hadrat Ma'sumah, if not enter it, that time we were turned away at some distance by youths armed with clubs.

Thus on 5 November, the pyres began and resentment at a century of humiliation by colonial powers was focused into a slogan that the author heard for the first time that night: *Morg bar faranghi*, 'Death to foreigners!' accompanied by the more familiar *Allah-o Akbar*, 'God is great'. It became a frequently heard chant, in my own case accompanied by the banging of shovels on the metal garage door under my bedroom and stones thrown against the windows in the night. Protests and demonstrations continued into the next month, with troops again shooting into the crowds.

On 11 December, a day of great religious and emotional significance for the Shi'a as the tenth day of the month of Muharram and the anniversary of the martyrdom of Mohammad's grandson Hossein at the Battle of Karbala in 680, there was a peaceful procession in Tehran with hundreds of thousands of participants. For this day, known as *Ashura* (literally 'the tenth day'), marks the birth of Shi'ism. There were violent demonstrations in Isfahan and strikes in the oilfields of the south-west, but officially and internationally the situation was still calm. Armenian vendors set up rows of Christmas trees against mud walls as in previous years, and the mood in northern Tehran was positive. So much so that, unhindered by the advantages of hindsight, I drove towards the south-east with a friend on a planned Christmas trip to visit ancient cities near Zabol, near the Afghan border, where we did not hear about the killing of an American oil-worker in Ahvaz, or about advice to American citizens in Iran to travel home. There were petrol shortages as a result of the strikes, but no sense of real danger even in Qom.

Elsewhere, there was more tension in the air. 200 kilometres south of Qom, in the town of Ardistan, we took an old caravan route about twenty kilometres east to a village called Zavareh to visit a twelfth-century mosque and an even older minaret. We parked on a small enclosed square at the beginning of the village, and were approached by a group of armed young men who in a very matter-of-fact manner explained to us that we were welcome to visit but that if we tried to take photographs they would kill us. In Zabol, where we were the first and only visitors in a huge newly-opened government guesthouse, the manager was so concerned for our safety (and his job!) that he personally escorted us in the area for two days with an armed employee. Driving north from Zabol to Birjand, along the Second World War military road, we were stopped at a roadblock by thirty or so men who first tried to force the doors of the car open with shovels and picks and then tried to overturn it. I accelerated through them, and we were followed through open desert for many miles as three men standing in the back of a white Toyota pick-up shot at us with rifles. There was no doubt that they wanted to kill, but fortunately their petrol seemed to run low and they pulled back. Back in Tehran two days later, most shops were closed and it was necessary to queue for days – people slept in their cars – for a few litres of petrol, or else pay black-market prices. Every night the shouts of *Morg bar faranghi* resonated from nearby rooftops and gunshots cracked through the mountain air.

The 'changeover' began a week later, on 16 January, when the Shah was sent into exile, first to Egypt. Two weeks later, Ayatollah Khomeini left Paris for Tehran. They were violent times, with a nightly curfew and proliferating road-blocks manned by the Shah's army. Finally, on 10 February, Khomeini ordered that the curfew should be defied. The next day the Supreme Military Council withdrew its support from the Shah's last Prime Minister, Shahpour Bakhtiyar, and on 12 February 1979, following a night of sporadic street gunfights, all organs of the Pahlavi regime, political, administrative, and military, finally collapsed. The revolution had triumphed.[52]

In many ways, the situation in Beijing in the spring of 1989 was similar to that in Tehran in the autumn of 1978. In both cases there had been calls for more open government, social tensions which threatened the process of industrial development, problems of corruption amongst officials, and growing unrest in the universities. Intellectuals – assuming the role of the Persian clergy – urged Deng Xiao Ping to exploit what was the 200th anniversary of the French Revolution, the 70th of the Fourth May Movement and the 40th of the foundation of the PRC to introduce more flexibility and democracy.[53] But most families were less concerned about democracy than with acquiring the 'Eight Bigs' which had substituted the 'Four Olds': colour television, refrigerator, stereo system, camera, motorbike, suite of furniture, washing machine and electric fan; and younger men with the 'Three Highs': salary, education and five feet six inches, necessary to find a wife, just as most wealthy Persians were concerned about getting enough cash to the USA or Switzerland to guarantee the future of their children.[54] As in Tehran, years of strong central government and the presence of a well-trained army led people to believe that everything was under control. No one imagined the drama which would ensue.

The catalyst in this case was the death on 15 April of the purged but popular leader Hu Yaobang, the Chairman and General Secretary of the Communist Party who had spoken up for freedom of speech and of the Press until his purge in 1986. Jonathan Spence has suggested that 'students in Peking saw a means of pressuring the government to move more vigorously with economic and democratic reforms and also keep alive memories of the Democracy Wall and other pro-democracy protests.'[55] There was a large student rally in Tiananmen Square on 17 April, a sit-in in front of the Great Hall of the People (on the western side of the square) the next day, and more demonstrations when the funeral took place on 22 April. The Prime Minister, Li Peng, refused to meet the students on that day when they requested politely to talk to him, and on 24th they began a boycott of classes in the many universities in the capital. Up to that moment, as Spence observes in his summary of the events, there was still every possibility of reaching a compromise. Zhao Ziyang, General Secretary of the Communist Party, may even have considered exploiting the protests to his own advantage and to remove conservative figures such as Li Peng and Deng Xiao Ping. On 4 May, a highly emotional day in modern Chinese history, as many as a hundred thousand students joined a rally in Tiananmen Square, with many similar rallies and marches in other Chinese cities.

Fatefully, a few days later, on 15 May, President Gorbachev was expected in Beijing for a summit meeting with Deng Xiao Ping which was intended to restore relations between the two communist parties after an estrangement of thirty years. Gorbachev himself was on the crest of a wave after two years of successful political and economic reforms, expounded in a book entitled *Perestroika: New Thinking for Our Country and the World* (1987) and the freedom of speech guaranteed by his concept of *glasnost*. He was flying to China after the first ever democratic elections to the Congress of People's Deputies had taken place in Moscow. For this reason, the hotels near Tiananmen were bursting with over 1,000 foreign journalists and television camera crews. The upper floors of the western end of the Beijing Hotel where many stayed offered an excellent vantage point for watching and filming the ensuing drama. It was too good an opportunity for the students to miss, for, as the *New York Times* expressed it, 'many of the students see in Mr. Gorbachev a vigorous symbol of political liberalization and regard his visit as an implicit rebuke to the ageing leadership of China.'[56] Thus began what the newspaper described as a 'vigil for democracy', with thousands of students demonstrating and beginning a hunger strike on the square. Two days after Gorbachev arrived, as many as 10,000 students slept in the square, bearing his portrait and refusing to leave in order to facilitate official ceremonies at the Great Hall of the People. In the daytime there were as many as a million demonstrators.

On 20 May, Martial Law was declared, as in Tehran on 8 September 1978, but as in the earlier case its effects were minimal. Even the PLA could not clear the square of the mass of demonstrators. Worse still, once more as in Iran, ordinary Beijing families and workers began to express solidarity with the students, erecting barricades and deflating tyres to hamper the army, and telling the troops that they should not open fire on Chinese citizens. Their own protests were motivated rather by increasing inflation and the scarcity of produce in the shops than by a desire for Western-style democracy, and they certainly did not envisage the consequences of their actions. When they heard shots later in the night, many believed they were being fired into the air; even when they were told that troops were firing into the crowd, they believed the PLA was using plastic bullets. No one imagined there would be a massacre (in Tehran, too, it was believed until the last that the changeover would occur 'not with rifles, but with faith and persuasion'[57]). At eleven o'clock on the evening of 3 May, a Chinese-speaking foreign journalist and good friend of the author left the scene in Tiananmen Square, convinced as were all the people he met in the streets, journalists, students and ordinary Beijingers alike, that nothing more would happen that night. He filed a report to his news agency in the diplomatic quarter, and then went home to sleep.[58]

The events of the following day are too well-known to need repeating here. But, as so often in this parallel story, it is an uncanny fact that the time from the peaceful demonstrations on 11 December to the arrival of Khomeini on 31 January (fifty-one days) coincides with that from demonstrations on Hu's death on 17 April to the events of 4 June (forty-eight days). No one could anticipate such speed, and such violence, although in fact both were implicit in the deep and parallel resentments in the respective countries. One regime fell by the sword, while the other, more ruthless, survived by virtue of its determination.

In both cases, however, the processes of modernisation and democratisation were violently truncated as deep-rooted conflicts emerged once again. Ironically, on the very same day as the Tiananmen massacre, the process *began* for the countries whose Soviet-inspired regimes collapsed in the coming months, with the surprise victory of *Solidarność* in Polish elections.

Notes

1. Avery, *Modern Iran*, p. 404.
2. Mohammad Reza Shah Pahlavi, *Mission for my Country*, p. 277.
3. Summaries of the key documents are given as appendices to Sanghvi, Aryamehr, *The Shah of Iran, A Political Biography*, pp. 345–74.
4. Avery, *Modern Iran*, p. 496.
5. Mohammad Reza Shah Pahlavi, *Mission for my Country*, p. 150.
6. Zonis, *The Political Elite of Iran*, pp. 72–3; Laing, *The Shah*, pp. 168–9.
7. Wynn, 'Abul Ghassem Khan Gharagozlou', p. 21.
8. Floor, Willem, 'Industrialization in Iran 1900–1941', pp. 33–5.
9. http://www.niscoir.com .
10. *World Steel in Figures 2007*, Brussels: International Iron and Steel Institute, 2007 p. 4; available at http://www.worldsteel.org .
11. This made the price of imported cars astronomical, but did not deter wealthy Tehranis from importing monsters like the Mercedes 450 SEL 6.9, which with its hydropneumatic suspension system could be lifted two inches by pulling a knob under the speedometer and therefore cruise safely over the stones commonly found on country roads outside the capital. The Rolls was beyond ordinary mortals, since it could only be imported by members of the Shah's family.
12. The car may be seen on the company website, http://www.ikco.com/default.aspx ; an expatriate named Roger Tagg produced a slim paperback of suggested short trips in and around Tehran, and called it *Travels with a Peykan* (Tehran: Rayka, 1975).
13. http://www.abadan-petro.com/en/index.aspx?page=about-history.
14. http://www.nipc.net/about/historyen.htm.
15. See the account of the Shah's programmes in Quillen, 'Iranian Nuclear Weapons Policy', pp. 7–20.

16. See the interview with Dr Etemad by Maziar Bahari, 'The shah's plan was to build bombs', *New Statesman*, 11 September 2008; http://www.newstatesman.com/asia/2008/09/iran-nuclear-shah-west.
17. Laing, *The Shah*, p. 197.
18. Hoveyda, *The Fall of the Shah*, p. 69.
19. *Financial Times* 21 June and 11 August 1976, quoted in Laing, *The Shah*, p. 203.
20. Quoted from the *People's Daily* and Xinhua) of the period by Garver, *China and Iran: Ancient Partners in a Post-Imperial World*, p. 37.
21. China's view was in fact prophetic, since in 2007, according to the *FT*, seven new state-owned sisters (of those outside the OECD) controlled a third of the world's oil and gas, all of them having escaped from or avoided American control: Aramco (Saudi Arabia), Gazprom (Russia), CNPC (China), NIOC (Iran), PDVSA (Venezuela), Petrobras (Brasil) and Petronas (Malaysia). *Financial Times*, 11 March 2007.
22. But Tehran never lost its essential Persian nature, while the cosmopolitan Dubai sometimes seems very un-Arabic. I recall an angry elderly Dubai native, with a ticket problem concerning a flight to Oman, railing against foreign employees of Emirates at the airport and furious that he could find no one who could speak the language of his own country.
23. Robertson, 'Shahestan Pahlavi: Steps Toward a New Iranian Centre', p. 47.
24. Ibid., p. 44.
25. Briefly known as Mossadegh Avenue in 1979, and now called Valiasr Avenue, after the 12th or Hidden Imam Vali Asr.
26. See the speech 'Emancipate the Mind, Seek Truth from Facts and Unite as One in Looking to the Future', delivered on 13 December to the closing session of the Central Working Conference which prepared for the Plenary Session, and which served as the basis for his keynote address, in *Selected Works of Deng Xiaoping*, Vol. II (1975–82), Beijing: Foreign Languages Press, 1995, pp. 150–63; also in *Deng Xiaoping, Speeches and Writings: Second Expanded Edition*, Oxford: Pergamon Press, 1987, pp. 62–74.
27. See the account in Spence, *Search*, pp. 624–30.
28. From the speech 'The Whole Party Should Take the Overall Interest into Account and Push the Economy Forward', 5 March 1975, in *Selected Works of Deng Xiaoping*, Vol. II (1975-82), Beijing: Foreign Languages Press, 1995, pp. 16-19.
29. Seagrave, *Lords of the Rim*, pp. 116–7; Lynn Pan, *Sons of the Yellow Emperor*, pp. 13–17.
30. Lever-Tracy, *The Chinese Diaspora*, p. 76, quoting the Fujian Statistical Yearbook
31. Ibid., p. 171.
32. Deng Xiao Ping, *Fundamental Issues in Present-Day China*, Beijing: Foreign Languages Press, 1987, p. 62.
33. Quoted from Chinese sources in Li, Dray-Novey and Kong, *Beijing: From Imperial Capital to Olympic City*, p. 213.
34. Ibid., p. 217.
35. Ibid., p. 218.
36. 'The Head of a Ten-Thousand Yuan Household', in Zhang and Sang, *Chinese Profiles*, pp. 51–61.

37. 'An Urbanised Peasant', in in Zhang and Sang, *Chinese Profiles*, pp. 100–112.
38. 'Drinks and Smokes', in Zhang and Sang, *Chinese Profiles*, pp. 237–44.
39. From an interview with a singer in Zhang and Sang, *Chinese Profiles*, pp. 268–71.
40. Baranovitch, *China's New Voices: Popular Music, Ethnicity, Gender, and Politics*, p. 32.
41. 'The Third Wave', in Zhang and Sang, *Chinese Profiles*, pp. 352–64.
42. Spence, Search, pp. 683–4.
43. Ibid, p. 697.
44. Reported in Hoveyda, *The Fall of the Shah*, p. 13.
45. Ibid., p. 17.
46. Ibid., p. 23.
47. Ibid., p. 24.
48. Ibid., p. 34; a summary of the interview, from which the quotation is taken, is available at http://www.time.com/time/magazine/article/0,9171,916375-2,00.html .
49. Ibid., p. 40.
50. These details are taken from an article entitled 'A Feast Fit for 60 Kings', in *The Sunday Times*, 22 August 1971.
51. Bergière, *Sun Yat-sen*, p. 214.
52. The downturn in US-Iranian relations which persists to this day began with the capture of the hostages in the American embassy in Tehran on the eve of 5 November in 1979. But this was not the first anti-American violence aimed at diplomatic representatives in that country. In the summer of 1924, the American Consul in Tehran, Robert W. Imbrie, who was a personal friend of Allen W. Dulles (then also a diplomat, later the first civilian director of the CIA), was murdered by an angry mob consisting of clergy and soldiers after visiting a Bahai shrine in Tehran. The real cause of this violence was probably the fact that he wanted to take pictures for *National Geographic Magazine* (see the account in Michael P. Zirinsky, 'Blood, Power, and Hypocrisy: The Murder of Robert Imbrie and American Relations with Pahlavi Iran, 1924', *International Journal of Middle East Studies*, Vol. 18, No. 3, August 1986, pp. 275–292, especially pp. 275–6). We should also recall the vehemence of Khomeini's attack against the Shah's decision to grant old-fashioned colonial-style immunity to American citizens in Iran in 1963.
53. Spence, *The Search for Modern China*, p. 696.
54. Ibid., p. 693.
55. Ibid., p. 697.
56. *New York Times*, 15 May 1989; available at http://query.nytimes.com/gst/fullpage.html?res=950DE2DE1F3BF936A25756C0A96F948260.
57. Words of the supporters of Abol-Hassan Bani-Sadr, elected as the first President of the Islamic Republic in January 1980; quoted in Dreyfuss, *Hostage to Khomeini*, p. 196.
58. Personal communication from the author's friend Francesco Sisci, now the correspondent in South-East Asia for La Stampa, who read Chinese at the University of Venice and at SOAS in London; in 1989 he was studying at the Academy of Social Sciences in Beijing and writing for the Italian news agency Ansa. He published, in Italian, an excellent book on the period from a student's perspective, *La differenza tra la Cina e il mondo: La rivoluzione degli anni Ottanta*, Milano: Feltrinelli, 1994.

Chapter 4

History in Popular Art

Two popular television programmes defined the mood and summarised the underlying tensions during these two backward-looking moments better than any subsequent work: in Iran, *My Uncle Napoleon* ('*Daee Jan Napoleon*') a drama series which was broadcast in 1976; and, in China, *River Elegy* ('*Hesheng*') a six-part documentary broadcast in 1988 which became as popular as *My Uncle Napoleon* even though it enjoyed a shorter shelf life.

My Uncle Napoleon was the television adaptation of a comic novel by Iraj Pezeshkzad (b.1928) published three years earlier and set in Tehran in 1940–1. 'Uncle Dear', as the Persians say, using the suffix *jan* affectionately after the names of close friends and family to mean 'dear' (as in Edward-*jan*, Mary-*jan*, hence *Daee-jan*), is a hilariously paranoiac head of a family with noble pretensions which lives in three separate houses within a single large garden compound. Daee Jan, whose grandiose delusions of being Napoleon Bonaparte have won him the mocking title 'Uncle Napoleon', is the patriarch of the clan. Superficially it is a love story about Dear Uncle's daugher Layli and the narrator, who is never named but is the son of Dear Uncle's brother-in-law, with all the ramifications of conflict within a large extended family. It often reminds the reader of the intrigues, love stories, feuds, political setting and ancestor worship of another large family in its compound, the Yao family in Lin Yutang's *Moment in Peking,* published in 1940. This novel is thus contemporary with the setting of *My Uncle Napoleon,* and has references back to the Boxer rebellion of 1901 parallel to Dear Uncle's references to the Constitutional Revolution of 1906. Once again the uncanny similarities of time-scale in the two countries' painful process of sloughing off the imperial past are evident. The novel is full of wonderful characters, like Dear Uncle's devoted servant Mash Qasem, and the massive, murderous butcher Shir Ali, who for an English reader is reminiscent of the blacksmith in the village cricket match in A. G. Macdonell's *England, Their England.* We feel that the English blacksmith who makes the earth shake as he 'thunders over the crest' to bowl and knocks up a cloud of dust when he falls, could easily be interchanged with the Persian butcher who causes nuts to fall to the ground when he crashes into a walnut tree.

But for our purposes it is the sub-plot about Dear Uncle's obsession with the English, who are responsible in his mind for all evils and events, which is most interesting. This is the cause of his love for Napoleon, because in his view there was no greater enemy of the English. As he himself puts it:

> That hypocritical wolf called England hates everyone who loves the soil and water of his own country. What sin had Napoleon committed that they harried him like that? That they separated him from his wife and children like that? That they broke his spirit like that so that he died of grief? Just that he loved his country. And this for them is a great sin.[1]

In public fantasies about the military exploits of his youth, aided by Mash Qasem, who is so engaged in his master's delusions that he begins to believe he was always present too, Dear Uncle recounted such exaggerated episodes of valour in battle against the English that his brother took to reminding him that the English would never forget about his deeds and that he should always be careful. Thus he begins to fear their revenge and 'became suspicious of everyone and everything' – to the extent of sleeping with a revolver under his pillow and muttering Milligan-like 'I know they'll get me in the end.'[2] When his brother wants to appease Dear Uncle after a prolonged row, he flatters him with invented stories from the past which feed his paranoia, of how a 'well-known person' he refuses to name because it is too dangerous informed him that in all the East there was no one who had harmed the plans of the English as much as Dear Uncle (whose formal family name was 'Master'). This person had heard that 'there were two people who'd really given the English a hard time, one the Master in World War I, and the other Hitler in this war…'[3]

Later, when he learns that one of his tenants who has rented a house opposite the garden is Indian, a certain Brigadier Maharat Khan, Dear Uncle is enraged and becomes convinced that the English have sent the Brigadier to spy on him. Even worse, the Brigadier has an attractive blonde English wife. When Dear Uncle learns that she has been looking at a photograph of him as a young man in the uniform of the Cossack Guards (Reza Shah's old regiment), he faints with his hand on his heart: but, hilariously, he quickly raises his head and screams when he overhears the narrator's father say he would call Dr Naser al-Hokama. The doctor, he exclaims, suddenly recovered, is a 'lackey of the English' since his cousin works for the Anglo-Iranian Oil Company.[4] This is pure paranoia, since in a city of only 900,000 inhabitants and a country of around 15 million,[5] living in large extended families, it was highly likely that each person in the capital has a cousin who happened to work in a company employing at that time around 50,000 Persians throughout the country.[6] Thus when Dear Uncle learns of the (real) British invasion from Iraq in August 1941, he is convinced that the first thing the invading forces will do on reaching Tehran is to come to get him. In the television series, funnier than the book even with my imperfect Farsi at that time because so much of the humour was visual, every noise or movement in the night was instantly attributed to the presence of the English, and any comment made by others was interpreted with suspicion. To give one final example, when an innocent itinerant photographer who has often taken pictures of the family arrives one day, Dear Uncle threatens to shoot him because he believes the photographer is working for 'them' and wishes to take a picture for 'their' dossier on him.[7] Everything is, in one way or another, an English plot; towards the hysterical finale, Dear Uncle has to take tranquilisers, but as soon as the effect of the drugs wears off, he again sees the 'lackeys of the English' everywhere.[8]

In fact, Pezeshkzad tapped into a deep reservoir of anxiety, for such paranoia has deep roots and at one time or another the British have been held responsible for everything. The journalist Sayyid Zia, who as we saw played a key role in the coup d'état which brought Reza Shah to power, was openly supported by the British Minister in Tehran, Herman C. Norman, and by the head of the military mission, Major-General W.E.R. Dickson.[9] One astute observer of the political scene in Tehran at that time wrote in his memoirs how at the beginning of 1919, after the negotiation of an Anglo-Persian treaty, the British seemed to be behind every activity:

> A financial mission under the direction of Mr Armitage-Smith was already in Teheran preparing a plan of reorganisation for the financial system. A military mission with General Dickson, who had been in command of the East Persia Cordon … and Lieutenant-Colonel William Fraser, were discussing with the Iranian officers Sardar Moktader and Lieutenant-Colonel Fazlollah Khan the organisation of a new Iranian army. British engineers were surveying the Teheran-Khanegin route for the building of a railway line to Baghdad. Prince Firuz Nosrat-ed-Dovleh, the Finance Minister, was in London negotiating the loan which would be advanced under the treaty.[10]

They were beating a well-trodden trail: in 1912, an American mission headed by W. Morgan Shuster was sent to organise the Persian government's revenues and expenditure, and a Treasury Gendarmerie set up to ensure the collection of taxes was headed by Captain C.B. Stokes, who had just retired as Military Attaché to the British Legation. Thus everybody was assumed to be in British pay.[11] Teymourtache, for example, was thought by some to be in the pay of the British simply because he was a personal friend of both the resident director of the Anglo-Persian Oil Company, Tommy Jacks, and its Chairman, Sir John Cadman.[12] In this case, the paranoia was double, for the Russian secret service agent Georges

Agabekov states that members of Teymourtache's family were GPU agents, which implicitly suggests personal involvement since he was a cadet in St Petersburg.[13] It is more likely, as in traditional Chinese foreign policy, that Teymourtache, Reza Shah and others were simply playing off the two powers against each other.

Perhaps the paranoia was calculated. Robert Byron comments on how the Persians believed that petulance on their part struck terror in London, and provides a hilarious example of counter-attack when *The Times* reported the jockey-whipping incident cited above: the Persian press retorted that 'in England the King dare not leave his palace without a guard of 3,000 men, while the Prince of Wales keeps 100 dogs that climb on to his bed by a special ladder and sleep there.'[14] Yet relationships had been formally excellent, with the grudging admiration of the English which we read in Nasir ed-Din Shah's account of his visit to England in 1878: 'In justice [we can but say that] the demeanour of the English, and everything of theirs, is extremely well regulated and governed, and admirable. In respect to populousness, the wealth of the people, the commerce, the arts, business, and dolce far niente, they are the chief of all nations.'[15] Neither did the old prejudices die easily: as late as 1971 Mohammad Reza Shah suggested during an interview that Khomeini was a salaried British agent.[16] Pezeshkzad was spot on!

The contrast between secular pleasure and Muslim seriousness is also given play in *My Uncle Napoleon*, for example when the narrator's father decides to give a party for his wedding anniversary, which happens to coincide with the commemoration of an important martyrdom. His wife comments: 'How can you possibly give a party tonight? On that side of the garden people beating their chest in mourning … and on this side music and dancing and getting drunk … who'd dare to sit at the party … those toughs who come to mourning ceremonies from the bazar would tear you all to pieces.'[17] The martydom in question was that of Muslim ibn-Aqeel (in the novel transliterated as 'Moslem ibn Aghil'), who was murdered at Kufa – a holy city now in Iraq, near Najaf – while on a diplomatic mission for his cousin. Since this cousin was the third Shi'a imam, Ali's younger son, Hossein ibn-Ali (d. 680), and therefore a direct descendent of Mohammad, the narrator's father commits sacrilege when he replies: 'But I know this business of the martydom of Moslem ibn Aghil is just a fabrication!' This captures perfectly the near-schizophrenia of Persians regarding Islam and pleasure, of revolutionary guards who patrolled the streets a few years later while drinking parties went on behind high walls: I am reminded of a restaurant where vodka was served instead of wine so that guards looking in would think we were drinking water (or pretend to think so, in exchange for payment), and of a wealthy Azerbaijani friend who in late 1978 hired a mechanical digger to excavate a vast cellar beneath his walled garden, and then filled it up with what he calculated would be enough whisky and vodka for his lifetime. Later in the novel, in an episode prophetic of the Islamic revolution, when the narrator's father advises the tenant of a chemist's shop he owns in the bazaar to close down for the day, he tells him to write a notice and stick it on the door. But what should he write? 'Due to a pilgrimage to the sacred shrine in Qom...'[18] That way, no one would dare to complain, or to desecrate his property.

The first episode of *River Elegy* opens with an example of similar paranoia, with the description of a tragedy directly caused by nationalist fears of inferiority, when in the summer of 1987 two teams of Chinese rafters died in an attempt to raft down the Yellow River, the 'mother river of our nation'. This attempt was inspired by a similar rafting expedition the previous year, when a well-known American white-water rafter, Ken Warren, paid $325,000 for the privilege of being the first person to raft down the Yangtze River on what was called the Sino-U.S. Upper Yangtze River Expedition, an adventure described in the book *Riding the Dragon's Back*.[19] That a foreigner should have done this wounded national pride, for, as the narrator explains, the youth of China cannot forget the British gunboats which sailed up the same river over a hundred years earlier 'in disregard of China's rights'.[20] Warren saw the descent, like many others he made on the great rivers of Asia, as a sporting challenge; the Chinese, in *their* paranoia, saw it as an affront to their national dignity. So, too, in their pride the Chinese often refused knowledge which might have been useful: 'Matteo Ricci', the narrator relates

> brought from the West a fifteen-chapter edition of Euclid's *Elements*, of which he and Xu Guangqi (1562–1633) translated the first six chapters. After the fall of the Ming dynasty, the work of translation was interrupted for exactly two hundred years. Yet during those two hundred years, Xu Guangqi's translation was brought to Japan where it stimulated scientific development there.[21]

This national paranoia, the continuous resort to memories of past humiliations and victimhood, are taken to task as the narrator asks: 'Has our current state of mind been created by our past century of history, in which we were always the helpless victim? Or has it been created by the poverty and backwardness of the past few decades?'[22] *River Elegy* is a deeply serious, at times philosophical study in the conflict between past and present, and hence on the future. Why, it asks, 'did the large oriental country that made Marco Polo sigh with surprise, the great people that frightened European rulers into fabricating the theory of the "yellow peril", the sleeping lion that made the peerless Napoleon warn the West not to wake it up, in recent times fall into such a helpless state that others carved up its land?'[23] Why instead did Chinese civilisation turn inwards, avoid the open sea and seek to enclose itself within a wall – which in Chinese is the same word as city (*cheng*)? For the need for walls, a defining characteristic of Chineseness,[24] may also be read as a sign of paranoia, as in the walled garden of Dear Uncle in which he seeks to defend himself against the invading British as uselessly as China sought to defend itself by a wall against steam-powered iron gunboats.

The fifth episode of *River Elegy*, 'Sorrow and Worry', returns to the Yellow River, noting that while it is usually renowned for nourishing the so-called 'cradle' of Chinese civilisation, is also known as 'China's Sorrow'. The only way out, the last episode shows, is to renounce the sorrows of a yellow infertile land in favour of the blueness of the sea: it opens with footage which shifts from the Yellow River to the deep blue ocean and includes images of the azure Adriatic in Venice.[25] The time had come to shake off 'the accumulated sentiment of feudalism'[26] by opening to trade and reinvigorating culture and country through maritime engagement with the world. The series concludes with an aerial view of the meeting of the yellow waters and the blue sea of the open ocean.

River Elegy treats with philosophical seriousness the same problems of identity and becoming modern that *My Uncle Napoleon* deals with in satire. Both are currently banned in the countries in which they were written and filmed, because they cut too close to the truth about pasts that need to be exorcised: the psychological power of the Yellow River on the one hand, and the negative forces of Islam on the other. For both were part of the complex forces which spurred the backlash against modernisation. The words of *River Elegy* might serve for both: 'Our thousand-year old dream of empire already came to an end long ago … Now the most important thing is not to cheat ourselves again.'[27] Sadly, the two countries did so. In the first case by the unexpected and sudden reversion to the values of Islam, in which the Persian people 'cheated' themselves by believing they were ready for something better than the Shah; and, in the second case, by the government reaction to the events of the Fourth of June.

As the authors of *River Elegy* observe, 'frightening social turmoil is neither remote nor unfamiliar' for the Chinese people. The Cultural Revolution had passed, like other historical turmoils, but such turmoil and floods can never be predicted; the problem is that if another major flood were to occur along the course of the Yellow River, it will 'greatly threaten China's modernization'. Thus, they argue prophetically, 'A Sword of Damocles is hanging high above our heads, yet we do not know when it will fall!'[28] Alas, too soon after the broadcasting of *River Elegy*, the Chinese 'cheated' themselves again, and are only now recovering.

But, as the proverb has it, 'once bitten, twice shy': these two great countries are unlikely to make the same mistake again, especially if a future decision is to be made in common interest.

Notes

1. Pezeshkzad, *My Uncle Napoleon*, p. 68.
2. Ibid., p. 218.
3. Ibid., p. 191.
4. Ibid., p. 236.

5. There was no official census until 1956, but these approximate numbers are found in several sources, for example in Julian Bharier, 'A Note on the Population of Iran, 1900–1966', *Population Studies*, Vol. 22, No. 2 (July 1968), pp. 273–279, p. 273.

6. See Longrigg, *Oil in the Middle East*, p. 129.

7. Pezeshkzad, *My Uncle Napoleon*, pp. 257–9.

8. Ibid., p. 419.

9. Dickson knew Persia very well, since his father, William Dickson, had been interpreter and translator to the British Legation for over thirty years, from 1852, and he had lived in Tehran as a child (Wright, *The English Amongst the Persians*, p. 124n.).

10. Arfa, *Under Five Shahs*, pp. 87–8.

11. Just as in 1979 all Anglo-Saxons were presumed to be Americans, Shuster was probably seen as an Englishman by most Persians.

12. T.L. (Tommy) Jacks was Resident Director in Persia from 1926 to 1933. Sir John Cadman, previously Professor of Mining at Birmingham University, was a Director from 1921 and Chairman from 1927; he became Baron Cadman of Silverdale in King George VI's Coronation Honours in 1937 (Longrigg, *Oil in The Middle East*, p. 52; Rowland, *Ambassador for Oil*, p. 159). Cadman's biography has a picture of Lady Cadman with 'Madam Teymourtache' standing in fashionable clothes both with long fur stoles in front of one of the gates of Tehran, and one of Sir John himself in the garden of the Teymourtache family (Rowland, *Ambassador for Oil*, opposite p. 97 and p. 129 respectively). Teymourtache's close friend the author and translator Ali Dashti (1894–1982), known in the West as the author of *In Search for Omar Khayyam* (London: George Allen & Unwin, 1971) – a wonderfully civilised man I had the good fortune to meet and who had the unique experience of having being imprisoned by both Reza Shah and Khomeini – translated Edmond Demolins's *A quoi tient la supériorité des Anglo-Saxons?* (1897) into Farsi.

13. Quoted in Lenczowski, *Russia and the West in Iran*, p. 114.

14. Byron, *The Road to Oxiana*, p. 126.

15. Redhouse, J.W. (Trs), *The diary of H.M. the Shah of Persia, during his tour through Europe in A.D. 1873*, London: John Murray, 1874, p. 214.

16. During an interview with the Tehran correspondent of *Le Monde*, quoted in Hoveyda, *Fall of the Shah*, p. 11; this is a thesis sustained at length in Robert Dreyfuss's *Hostage to Khomeini*, p. 196.

17. Pezeshkzad, *My Uncle Napoleon*, p. 76.

18. Pezeshkzad, *My Uncle Napoleon*, p. 108.

19. Richard Bangs, *Riding the Dragon's Back: The Race to Raft the Upper Yangtze*, New York: Atheneum, 1989.

20. Su and Wang, *Deathsong*, p. 102.

21. Ibid., p. 188.

22. Ibid., p. 103.

23. Ibid., p. 113.

24. For wall-building was not an isolated or unusual occurrence in ancient China, but what Owen Lattimore described as 'the characteristic of an age' (Lattimore, *Inner Asian Frontiers of China*, p. 429).

25. I remember, two years later, working in Rome with some Chinese telecommunications experts who had come from Shanghai. After two days of lectures about telecoms strategies and technical visits, they were given an afternoon free and asked whether they would like to visit St Peter's or the Forum. But their only interest was to see the 'blue sea', so we took them to Anzio – where they spent an hour photographing the sea. The significance was lost on me at the time!

26. Su and Wang, *Deathsong*, p. 216.

27. Ibid., p. 115.

28. Ibid., p. 189.

Part II

The Convergence of the Twain

IX

Alien they seemed to be:
No mortal eye could see
The intimate welding of their later history.

X

Or sign that they were bent
By paths coincident
On being anon twin halves of one august event,

XI

Till the Spinner of the Years
Said 'Now!' And each one hears,
And consummation comes, and jars two hemispheres.

from Thomas Hardy, 'The Convergence of the Twain', in Satires and Circumstances, 1914

Chapter 5

Parallel Needs

One of the primary features of the foreign policy of each of these remarkably similar countries is the will to create a space which is free from American hegemony. Military bases in Japan and Turkestan constitute a thorn in the side of China, while the American presence in Iraq and close relations with Israel are the equivalent for Iran. Both echo the older, British presence.

Chinese foreign policy has in recent years been focused in three main directions: first, maintaining carefully balanced relationships with the major world powers, especially at present in economic terms the USA and the EU and its most important member countries; secondly, developing close relationships with energy-producing countries (such as Venezuela and Russia) and with countries black-listed by First World powers (Iran, Sudan, and smaller states in Africa); and, thirdly, building tighter and mutually rewarding relationships with neighbouring states. From 1996 this was achieved as a 'dialogue partner' with ASEAN (Brunei, Cambodia, China, Indonesia, Laos, Malaysia, Myanmar, Philippines, Singapore, Thailand and Vietnam), which was originally created as a bulwark against Communism. Then, to the West, as a founding member of the Shanghai Five, again in 1996 (with Russia, Kazakhstan, Kyrgystan and Tajikistan), which became the Shanghai Cooperation Organization (SCO) with the addition of Uzbekistan in June 2001. This web of alliances may also be seen as what one expert calls a 'stealthy strategy toward global dominance,' integrating military, economic, and diplomatic instruments and aiming to displace the United States as the world's pre-eminent power.[1] More specifically, behind the rhetoric and smiling faces of group photographs, the SCO, whose secretariat is in Beijing, was designed to limit American power in Turkestan – although the United States is not the only potential hegemon since all the member countries, and Iran, have in Russia a much larger neighbour and previous overlord to counter.

This logic also lies behind the extensive sale of Chinese weapons to Iran, in particular from 1980 when China became one of Iran's closest international partners in the latter's ferociously anti-US period and during its war with Iraq. Not only did this trade become 'more quantitatively and qualitatively comprehensive and sustained than that with any other country' in this period,[2] but, as we shall see below, it involved both the direct sale of conventional weapons and assistance with much more lethal nuclear, chemical, and biological weapons.

In the second week of May 1989, just before Gorbachev's dramatic visit to Beijing, a new phase in Sino-Persian relations began when the President of Iran, Ayatollah Ali Khamenei (b.1939), made the first ever visit to China by such a high official, together with the Foreign Minister and a large delegation representing the principal ministries. His first objective was achieved when he returned to Tehran with an agreement for China to double its purchases of oil. But shortly after this propitious visit there was a notable acceleration in China's strategy concerning Iran as a consequence of three apparently unrelated events, which were however closely linked in time: the first meeting of the Congress of People's Deputies in Moscow on 25 May, the death of Ayatollah Khomeini on 3 June, and the events in Tiananmen Square on 4 June.

The First Sino-Persian Anti-hegemony Partnership 1989–1996

The newly elected Congress represented the first step in the reforms of President Gorbachev which led to the demise of the Soviet Union just over two years later. The old Soviet Union, for all its faults in Chinese eyes, had represented a consistent and reliable bulwark against global domination by the United States, especially in the Middle East. That bulwark was now fading, and a replacement was needed by China. At the same time, the Middle East was an area in which a sole superpower could easily become embroiled to the extent of weakening its ability to intervene in other parts of the world, notably in what China perceived as its own sphere of interest in East Asia. This, indeed, is exactly what happened with American involvement in Iraq from 1991 and in Afghanistan from October 2001; with the superpower's attention deflected elsewhere, China was able to plough its own furrow undisturbed. The policy of cautiously developing relationships with Iran was also amply rewarded when the United States failed to discover anything more than slight circumstantial evidence of that country's complicity in the 9/11 attacks, but further antagonised Iran by its threats and sanctions and drove her into China's waiting arms.

The second key event was the election of President Ali Khamenei (b.1939) as Supreme Leader of the Islamic Republic to succeed Khomeini, and the elevation of Akbar Hashemi Rafsanjani (b.1934) to the role of President. This occurred on 4 June 1989, a date which keeps cropping up!

The pure fanaticism and genuine faith of Ayatollah Khomeini, who argued in favour of nurturing diplomatic relationships exclusively with other Islamic nations, was tempered by the extreme pragmatism of Rafsanjani. Unlike Khomeini, who came from a prestigious family of clerics, he was born into the ranks of small provincial business-owners and farmers. Rafsanjani, who virtually ruled Iran from 1989 to 2005, was not only responsible for re-establishing relationships with China but followed Deng in a staunch belief in the advantages of a free market economy. In an article entitled 'Millionaire Mullahs' in *Forbes*, his and his family's business deals were compared with the crony capitalism of post-Soviet Russia. As the 'father' of Iran's privatisation programme he revived the stock market, sold off state-owned companies to insiders, liberalised foreign trade - especially with countries not connected to the United States - and re-opened the oil industry to private enterprise. Much of the best of these privatised companies, such as hotel groups, car companies, and the manufacturers of drugs and consumer goods, finished up in the hands of 'mullahs, their associates and, not least, Rafsanjani's own family'.[3] The family is extensive: two of his brothers controlled Iran's largest copper mine and the state television network, a cousin has a virtual monopoly on the important pistachio export business, while his sons have important roles in the Ministry of Oil and the project for the Tehran Metro system. At that time, things were similar in China. To take Deng Xiaoping's own brood as an example of the ramification of the power of the so-called 'princelings', we find his sons Deng Pufang as Chairman of the China Disabled Persons Federation and Deng Zhifang as President of the Sifang Group, his daughters Deng Lin as Vice-Director, China Council for International Friendship, Deng Nan as Vice Chairman and First Secretary of the China Association for Science and Technology and Deng Rong as Chairman of Shenzhen Huayue Industry Corporation, and his sons-in-law Wu Jianchang as General Manager of the China Non-Ferrous Metals Company, Zhang Hong as Director of the Science and Technology Bureau of the Chinese Academy of Science, and He Ping as Director of the Armaments Department of the PLA General Staff Headquarters. Here then, in Rafsanjani, was a man who the equally pragmatic members of the Poliburo in Beijing could understand.

In the aftermath of June 1989, the Chinese government sought diplomatic support in Third World countries to counter-balance the extreme hostility of Western governments led in spirit by the United States. Diplomatic relations had been interrupted, sanctions announced, foreign-invested projects cancelled, while the World Bank taps ran dry. In this case too, which country better than Iran, one of the world's leading oil suppliers, with a vigorously anti-American diplomatic stance to boot, could begin to fill the void? For in Chinese eyes, their explicit support of Iran 'penalised' the United States for its anti-China policies 'and demonstrated to Washington the U.S. need for China's cooperation in the

Middle East'.[4] Moreover, the newly wealthy country was a good potential market for Chinese companies who were now shut out of Western markets and could enter a new market in which there was no American competition. It was, in other words, a win-win situation for China.[5]

From Iran's point of view, and especially Rafsanjani's, a partner with China's stunning achievements in economic growth since 1978 would be able to provide guidance for a similar revival of its own languishing economy. In addition, there was the attraction of a friendly country which was powerful enough to offer diplomatic and military opposition to the United States, in particular China's power of veto on the Security Council of the United Nations. With the decline and dismemberment of Iran's once all-powerful northern neighbour the Soviet Union as a great power in the same period, China became the only country in the world which could provide this level of support for Iran.

For these reasons of mutual convenience China and Iran were drawn closer together than ever before, even more so after the American invasion of Iraq in 1991, when, paradoxically, the strong American presence in the Persian Gulf was counter-balanced by a huge increase in military support for a strongly anti-Communist regime. In the summer of 1995, President Clinton signed the Iran Sanctions Act (ISA), which banned both trade and investment in Iran by American companies, and in September of the same year the US Senate passed the Iran Foreign Oil Sanctions Act to prevent the export of energy technology to Iran. More recently, ISA has been extended to 2011.[6] With these sanctions in place, Iran looked to China for support, while China saw its role in Iran as a thorn in the side of American hegemonism. Chinese denial of America's right to interfere in domestic issues, such as human rights, could be applied by Iran to such matters as developing a nuclear programme. Yet while China's role in the Security Council made her a formidable ally in the international forum, she refused to participate in any discussion of a coalition with other Asian countries like India and Pakistan against the United States. Pragmatism reigned on both sides.

After the summer of 1989, Chinese ministerial visits to Iran intensified to unprecedented levels. Between August that year and September 1990 there were visits by no fewer than five Chinese ministers: the Minister of Energy, the Minister of Geology and Mineral Resources, the Minister for the Petroleum Industry, the Minister for Public Health, and the Minister of Ports, Telegraph and Telephones, each with its relative protocol exchange visit. The following year saw visits by Prime Minister Li Peng (July) and President Yang Shangkun (October).[7] During the same period there were many lower-level exchanges between military delegations. In fact, one of the tangible results of this hectic series of exchanges was that arms sales from China to Iran increased from $74 million in 1989 to $287 million in 1993, and then to $323 million in 1996, before dropping back sharply at the end of the decade.[8] The quid pro quo was increased and guaranteed supplies of oil to fuel dramatic Chinese economic growth.

China had supplied military equipment to the Islamic Republic of Iran since 1982, when – as so often in this story – there was what has been described as a 'serendipitous meshing of Iranian demand and Chinese supply'[9] as on the one hand the supply and replacement of American weapons which had been the basis of the Shah's extravagant armed forces dried up, and on the other hand China was ramping up industrial production as a result of reforms and incentives of Deng's new policies. Ironically, a virtuous circle was created in which massive sales of arms to Iran provided the cash for the modernisation of China's own forces. These supplies including large numbers of fighters and tanks and a number of cruise missiles – in particular the so-called Silkworm Missiles (the HY-2 Haiying, or 'Sea Eagle'), with a range of nearly 100 kilometres, which were used in an attack against an American-flagged tanker in 1987.[10] In fact in the 1980s, Iran was – together with its Muslim neighbour Pakistan – already the main recipient of Chinese military aid, with as much as twenty-two per cent of all its arms being supplied by China during the war with Iraq.[11] On one count, in the same decade China supplied 540 tanks, 300 armoured personnel carriers, 140 fighters and 7,500 anti-tank guided missiles,[12] sales which provided a valuable source of foreign currency for the PLA.

From 1989, there was a shift in emphasis as Iran began to concentrate on developing its own military technologies in areas such as missiles, chemical warfare and nuclear reactors. In these areas too, China provided the know-how which the United States had once provided to the Shah.[13] But it is also true that China itself benefited from such close collaboration with Iran by being able to study state-of-the-art Russian weapons captured during the war with Iraq and advanced American equipment like the F4 Phantoms which Iran owned. Yet weapons sales also continued, with surface-to-air missiles, mines and radar systems. Most importantly, they included new anti-ship missiles modelled on the Exocet (notorious in Britain after the Argentine Navy used one to sink HMS *Sheffield* in 1982 during the Falklands War) and known as the C-801 and C-802, the former powered by a solid-fuel rocket and the latter by a turbojet. Both these missiles could be launched either from an aircraft or from a submarine, and were later produced in Iran with Chinese assistance, the C-802 with the name of 'Karus' after American pressure on China brought an end to supplies. China also sold launch platforms and ten fast-attack boats each of which could carry four C-802 missiles, in addition to shore-based launchers. This attack boat, known as the 'Hudong', was later superseded by a faster attack catamaran known as the China Cat, which has a top speed of fifty knots. In fact, these sales were one of the most controversial aspects of arms sales to Iran – and perhaps a harbinger of the future blue-water policy. A conflict in the Persian Gulf with Iran using Chinese attack craft, launchers and missiles against American forces would be a safe and ideal test of China's real capabilities in the East China Sea. Be that as it may, according to the Stockholm International Peace Research

Institute the total sales of Chinese weapons to Iran between 1982 and 2004 amounted to $3.8 billion.

From China's point of view, such sales were one way of restricting American hegemony in the Middle East by creating a powerful military presence in a hostile country well-positioned in geographical terms to dominate the entire region. They were also important in China's strategy of guaranteeing supplies of oil and gas – a factor which for Iran's other major arms supplier in the 1990s, Russia, was obviously irrelevant. For Iran, Chinese supplies fulfilled a parallel role in circumventing sanctions on arms sales by the United States and the European Union, and also acted as a counter-balance to over-reliance on Russian supplies. It was in many ways a perfect solution to a wide array of problems for each country, and serves as an indicator for broader partnerships or alliances in the future.

Even more controversial than the sale of missiles and technological assistance in developing new weapons was China's assistance in nuclear technology. One of Iran's original partners in its nuclear programme was the French company Framatome, with which a contract to build two nuclear reactors at Darkhovin, south of Ahvaz, was signed in 1974. But they were still not operational when the Revolution came five years later and the contract was cancelled along with many others. This was when Iran turned to China, as well as the Soviet Union and India, as potential partners. On 10 September 1992, President Rafsanjani announced that the Qinshan Nuclear Power Company and the Shanghai Nuclear Research and Design Institute had agreed to build the reactors at Darkhovin as part of a broader nuclear cooperation agreement. This new contract was also plagued with difficulties: first the site was changed to Bushehr since Darkhovin was considered to be too close to Iraq, and then Iran's difficulty in raising the $2 billion needed for the reactors also stalled the project. In 1995 it was said to have been cancelled, while a year later the Chinese Foreign Minister stated that it had simply been postponed.[14] This project was interpreted by American experts in terms of a clandestine nuclear weapons program that remains controversial today. By 1996, China was openly selling uranium enrichment technology and other nuclear technology to Iran, and announced to the International Atomic Energy Authority that it wished to carry out the sale with IAEA approval and safeguards.[15] In similar fashion, the Nuclear Technology Center at Isfahan was founded in the mid-1970s with French assistance to provide training but was in the 1990s provided by China with a miniature neutron source reactor (MNSR), a heavy water, zero power, reactor, which went critical in 1995, and two sub-critical reactors.[16] Thus, while China was never the unique partner of Iran in its nuclear programmes, since most of the other nuclear powers were involved at some stage in their development, from 1985 to 1997, when American pressure and China's pragmatic need for good relations with the United States led China to retreat from this particular relationship, it was the most important of those partners. During the same period, to take just one example of many, the Beijing

Research Institute of Uranium Geology provided assistance in exploration for uranium deposits.[17]

Thus it was not merely a matter of straight weapons sales. China was seen in the late 1990s to have made 'significant contributions to Iran's indigenous military production capability through the provision of scientific expertise, technical cooperation, technology transfers, production technologies, blueprints, and dual-use transfers.'[18] But by that time the trend was already in reverse for reasons not directly linked to Iran.

After the rapid collapse of Saddam Hussein's well-regarded army in Iraq during the 1991 Gulf War, leading military planners in Beijing became aware of how vulnerable China would be in a modern war. The realisation that land-based forces would be of little use in an attack based on aerial supremacy was a big shock. New fears focused on Taiwan – large numbers of troops and weapons no longer needed along the Soviet frontier had been transferred to face that island and conventional missiles had been deployed in readiness for an anticipated local war. Missiles were launched during exercises in 1995 and 1996, one in the latter year landing in the sea just nineteen nautical miles from the northern port of Keelung.[19] The tensions caused by these operations, and fears of retaliation from American aircraft carriers or the nearby US base in Okinawa, drove the ever-pragmatic China to seek conciliation with America and allay the fears of neighbours like Japan which were important to the country's own development. This necessarily entailed downgrading of the relationship with the more distant and problematic Iran. In fact one specialist, Professor Avery Goldstein of the University of Pennsylvania, has detected a major shift of policy around 1996, since when 'Beijing has forged a diplomatic strategy with two broad purposes: to maintain the international conditions that will make it feasible for China to focus on the domestic development necessary if it is to increase its relative (not just absolute) capabilities; and to reduce the likelihood that the U.S. or others with its backing will exploit their current material advantage to abort China's ascent and frustrate its international aspirations.'[20] In other words, entering into conflict with the United States over Iran simply wasn't worth the trouble. To accept the constraints implicit with 'working in multilateral settings was preferable to the risk of isolation and encirclement and could help foster a reputation for responsible international behaviour.'[21] Put another way, it was more useful to sign a nuclear non-proliferation agreement that could also help with neighbouring Asian countries like North Korea than to continue to furnish technical assistance to a single aspiring nuclear power. The following year, China agreed with the United States to halt all forms of nuclear cooperation with Iran and also to stop sales of 'advanced anti-ship cruise missiles, the weapons most threatening to oil tankers and U.S. warships.'[22]

For the moment, Iran was sacrificed in order to stabilise relationships with the United States.

Notes

1. Constantine C. Menges, *China: The Gathering Threat*, Nashville: Nelson Current, 2005, pp. 367–417.
2. Bates Gill, 'Chinese Arms Exports to Iran', *Middle East Review of International Affairs*, Vol. 2, No. 2 (May 1998), pp. 55-70, p. 57.
3. 'Millionaire Mullahs', http://www.forbes.com/free_forbes/2003/0721/056.html.
4. Garver, *China and Iran*, p. 96.
5. In fact, writing these words in Beijing during the 2008 Olympics, it is worth noting that Iran was one of the first countries to endorse Beijing's Olympic ambitions for 2000, during the September 1990 Asian Games and before the official – but ultimately unsuccessful – first bid was launched.
6. CRS Report to Congress: The Iran Sactions Act (ISA), 12 October 2007.
7. Listed in Garver, *China and Iran*, Appendix, pp. 313–15.
8. See the Table 7.4 in Garver, *China and Iran*, p. 179, compiled using several sets of data; in fact the same table shows that sales under the Shah had reached much higher levels, at $546 and $625 million respectively in 1986–1987, before the boom in oil wealth tapered off.
9. Garver, *China and Iran*, p. 167.
10. Ibid., Table 7.4, p. 179.
11. Karl W. Eikenberry, 'Explaining and Influencing Chinese Arms Transfers', Washington DC: National Defense University, Institute for National Strategic Studies, McNair Paper No. 36, February, 1995, p. 38.
12. Eikenberry, 'Explaining and Influencing', Table 3, p. 12.
13. See the account with technical details in Garver, *China and Iran*, pp. 185–196; see also Bates Gill, 'Chinese Arms Exports to Iran', *Middle East Review of International Affairs*, Vol. 2, No. 2 (May 1998), pp. 55–70.
14. Andrew Koch and Jeanette Wolf, 'Iran's Nuclear Facilities: a Profile', Washington: Center for Nonproliferation Studies, 1998, pp. 4–5.
15. Gill, 'Chinese Arms Exports to Iran', p. 67.
16. Koch & Wolf, 'Iran's Nuclear Facilities', pp. 5–6.
17. Ibid., p. 17. See also the detailed review of Chinese assistance to Iran's nuclear programmes in the chapter with that title in Garver, *China and Iran*, pp. 139–65.
18. Shichor, *The Middle East*, p. 58.
19. Ng, *Interpreting China's Military Power*, p. 124.
20. Goldstein, 'The Diplomatic Face of China's Grand Strategy', p. 836.
21. Ibid., p. 843.
22. Garver, *China and Iran*, p. 115.

Chapter 6

Mutual Interest in the Twenty-first Century

In 1978, trade between China and Iran was almost non-existent: China had until that year been a virtually closed market, while Iran under the Shah had imported goods principally from Western nations, roughly half from the United States, Germany and Britain alone. In that year the United States provided 21 per cent of all imports to Iran, Germany 19 per cent, Britain 8 per cent and China a mere 1 per cent; not surprisingly, by 2003 these percentages had been substantially reversed, with 0 per cent, 11 per cent, 3 per cent and around 10 per cent respectively.[1]

In the same period, as is well known, China's GDP grew by an average of nine per cent every year. Apart from the problem of industrial energy consumption, one corollary of this astonishing growth – and the official objective of quadrupling GDP between 2000 and 2020 – is the justifiable ambition of its citizens to enjoy the benefits of warm homes, private cars, electronic gadgets and leisure travel on a par with those of Europe and the US. There are no longer only 'Eight Bigs', but several hundred. This is why in 2007 China accounted for as much as forty-three per cent of annual global oil consumption growth.[2]

China clearly needs oil now and in the future, and lots of it, but understands that it cannot simply purchase oil (and gas) from a country like Iran in exchange for cash. Iran has a large and rapidly growing population, and needs to develop its own industries to avoid excessive future reliance on its natural resources. There is ample space for development in industries such as the construction and automobile industry, where Iran previously looked to Germany and the United States and where China possesses growing knowledge and competence. Now China has overtaken Germany in terms of imports by Iran, while American imports currently stand at zero. There are at least 250 Chinese companies active in Iran, with activities ranging from vast projects like oil refineries and the Metro system in Tehran to smaller ventures like the construction of fish canneries, sugar refineries and paper mills.[3] But oil remains today the main item of trade from Iran to China.

Chinese Demand for Oil and Gas

Motor vehicles are one of the most significant drivers of the growth in oil demand, as China's production grew from 220,000 in 1993 to 2,340,000 in 2004. At present, car ownership in China is still at very low levels outside the major eastern cities, calculated a few years ago at twenty-four cars for each 1,000 people, compared to a global average of 120. This huge market potential is why twenty-five international brands are now *manufactured* in China, including from early 2009 a very new model like the Audi Q5, as well as cars from a similar number of Chinese car companies. Car and SUV sales in 2008 are expected to pass nine million, which would entail fourteen per cent market growth over 2007, and growth in line with increasing GDP is likely to continue for the foreseeable future. This renders extremely plausible the estimate in a detailed study by IBM and the Transportation Research Institute of the University of Michigan published three years ago that ownership would rise to 100 per 1,000 inhabitants by 2015 and to 400 per 1,000 inhabitants in 2050. This would mean an increase from thirty-three per cent of total Chinese petroleum demand today to around fifty-seven per cent by 2030.[4] Or, to put it in another, way, an average annual growth in overall primary energy consumption of 3.5 per cent between now and 2030.[5]

As the zest for tourism grows and more Chinese take holidays, the airline industry will also experience dramatic growth. A joint-venture factory to assemble the Airbus A320 in Tianjin was completed in September 2008, with delivery of aircraft expected to begin in 2009 and production planned to reach four A320s each month by 2011.[6] Expectations for the future market in passenger jets has also spurred the Chinese government to make plans for an indigenous large passenger aircraft to rival Boeing and Airbus models which Chinese airlines are currently obliged to purchase for lack of Asian competition. In March 2007 the State Council gave formal approval for a long-term plan to design and manufacture a wide-bodied jet for over 150 passengers, with 2018 given as a target date for the maiden flight.[7] This makes good business sense in a market for new aircraft estimated at around 1,600 large jets by 2020 (Airbus thinks 1,900), and as many as 3,000 more by the middle of the century.[8] But it also entails huge increases in energy consumption.

Planes fly, and most cars drive, on derivatives of oil; in fact ninety per cent of transport runs on oil. But that is not of course the only source of energy. At present, around sixty per cent of China's total energy requirements are met by coal; the country actually produces almost half of the world's coal (44.8 per cent),[9] and consumption of that fuel also increased by around seventy-five per cent in line with the overall increase. The IEA's chief economist has said that from 2007 to 2015 China will 'install, as new, as much energy generating plant as currently exists today in all of the twenty-five countries of the expanded European Union – a total of 800 gigawatts.' As much as ninety per cent of this energy would derive from coal.'[10] Yet while the basic source of China's energy will be coal for the foreseeable future, oil and gas remain essential and strategically important. Coal cannot propel cars on the road, except when converted to electrical power – which is unlikely to be a viable substitute for oil for many years.

There is one further interesting facet of oil. As Lester Brown has observed, large modern cities are a product of the oil age whose very metabolism 'depends on concentrating vast amounts of food and materials and then disposing of garbage and human waste.' In the past horse-drawn wagons, or in the case of China rickshaws and pedicabs, necessarily operated within a small urban area; then with the gradual introduction of lorries and vans using cheap petrol, it was possible to service a greater area with the facilities of a city. Now, with the vast spread of modern urban centres like Beijing, 'as cities grow ever larger and as nearby landfills reach capacity, garbage must be hauled longer distances to disposal sites.'[11] This is clearly a serious matter in terms of China's large number of cities, increasing urbanisation, and potentially decreasing supply of oil. Living costs in cities will obviously rise when oil prices increase; the giant shopping malls which the Chinese consumer loves, with their constant flow of new products (and rubbish), thrive on oil.

Industrial consumption in China presently accounts for around seventy per cent of oil use. To take one example, the number of steel factories doubled between 2002 and 2007, with a total number of 7,000 at the end of the latter year. Clearly, these factories dramatically increase the demand for electricity and hence for new power plants and transport infrastructure. Some of the companies are huge, such as Baosteel (the Shanghai Baosteel Group Corporation, created in 1998), which has twenty-two wholly-owned subsidiaries, shareholdings in twenty-four other companies, and fourteen holding companies (eleven are iron-and-steel companies), with a total production capacity of twenty million tons – which is alone twice that of Iran's.[12] Other Chinese producers like Tangshan Iron and Steel Co, Wuhan Iron and Steel, and Shougang in Beijing are not far behind (it is worth nothing that Baosteel is however still ninth in size in terms of *revenues* on the global scale, which are less than half those of the top two companies, Mittal and Thyssen). Given Beijing's ambitious infrastructure projects for coming decades, including new expressways and bridges and a high-speed railway network, demand for steel can only increase.

If we take into consideration the long-term growth of Chinese demand for both oil and natural gas since Deng's reforms and opening up in 1978, the ten-year increases are as follows:[13]

	1977	1987	1997	2007
Oil consumption (1000s barrels per day):	1638	2062	4179	7855
Gas consumption (billions cubic feet per day):	12.1	13.9	19.5	67.3

The 2007 consumption of oil, at nearly eight million barrels a day, represents a 4.1 per cent increase over 2006 and accounts for 9.3 per cent of total global consumption. Growth in consumption was fairly steady from 1977 until two or three years ago, when there was a substantial acceleration. If we consider that China's domestic oil production in 2007 was calculated as slightly less than four millions barrels a day (3.7 million), the increasing shortfall is obvious, and is estimated to increase in coming years. Where should China look to make up for this shortfall? Countries like Sudan, Angola and Venezuela are currently important suppliers, but Iran is closer in many ways and at present has a vastly superior share of proven reserves in the world at 11.2 per cent – second only to Saudi Arabia, with 21.3 per cent. China itself possesses 1.3 per cent; Venezuela has 7 per cent, but Sudan and Angola only have 0.5 per cent and 0.7 per cent respectively. Iran currently produces 4.4 million barrels a day, which is very close to half of China's total needs and would complement domestic production perfectly were China to be the only customer. In terms of natural gas, the sudden acceleration in consumption a few years ago is even more dramatic, nearly quadrupling over the past decade. Here too, Iran could be a formidable partner, since it possesses 15.7 per cent of proven global reserves of natural gas – in this case second to Russia, with 25.2 per cent, while China has only 1.1 per cent.

At the beginning of the 1990s, oil exports from Iran to China were very small, but then made a huge leap as bilateral trade developed, from 0.5 million barrels in 1992 to 16.87 barrels two years later, and on to 26.43 million barrels after two more years. By 2004, Iran supplied fourteen per cent of China's net imports and had become the second largest supplier of the nation's energy. In that year, two important long-term deals were made. In early 2004, Zhuhai Zhenrong, one of four state-owned crude oil importers, signed a deal to import 110 million tons of gas over a twenty-five year period, and in October an even bigger deal was struck between the China Petrochemical Corporation (Sinopec) and the National Iranian Gas Exporting Company (Nigec) which involved developing the Yadavaran oil-field in south-western Iran and guaranteeing the supply of 150,000 barrels of oil a day and also ten million tons of gas annually for a period of twenty-five years. In fact Sinopec is currently involved in around 120 oil and gas projects in the Middle East, while ten per cent of China's oil imports globally come from fields in which China's state-owned oil companies have an equity stake.[14] In a sense, China is seeking to replicate the equity model which British and American companies favoured in the first half of the twentieth century, a strategy which may fail but may also push her into deeper alliances with oil-producing countries in the future. But perhaps they are too late, since most oil reserves are now owned by the producing countries themselves.

In the same year another state-owned firm, the Chinese National Petroleum Corporation (CNPC) was awarded a contract to develop the Tabnak field and bought out the contractors of the Masjid-e Suleiman field, while the exploitation subsidiary of Sinopec drilled a new oil and gas well in the Kashan field and was invited to participate in bids for several other fields.[15] In China, at about the same time, yet another state-owned firm, China National Offshore Oil Corp (CNOOC) signed an agreement to build a new terminal in Zhejiang to handle three million tons of gas imports annually, while Sinopec agreed to build a similar terminal on the Caspian Sea. These long-term supply lines, and the corresponding pipeline network linking China with Turkestan and Iran, are part of a twenty-first century version of the ancient Silk Road known as the 'Pan Asian Global Energy Bridge'. As part of a deal allowing China to develop oilfields in Kazakhstan, it agreed to build a 1,800-mile pipeline to Xinjiang and a 170-mile pipeline through Turkmenistan to Iran. In mid-2008, the section from the oilfields to Shanshan in Xinjiang had been completed, and work was well-advanced on that from Shanshan to Luoyang (Henan province) and Pengzhou (in Sichuan). A parallel project to join China to the Caspian Sea, and eliminate the strategic weakness of sea transport, could lead to even stronger ties with Iran and decrease the risks of interruption to oil and gas supplies by future diplomatic sanctions or naval blockades. These initiatives tally perfectly with two significant current trends in the oil trade: the increasing relative importance of the Middle East as the world's dominant oil producer, since there are no new producers which can match the area's production, representing nearly fifty per cent of the world's total; and, second, an increase in the proportion of Middle East oil which is shipped to the Far East. Most of China's oil imports from the Middle East are shipped through the Strait of Malacca, the Lombok Strait and the Strait of Macassar, each of which could 'fairly' easily be blockaded by the US Navy,[16] which could also easily blockade the major Chinese ports (although bottlenecks equally vital for the United States such as the Suez and Panama canals are also vulnerable).

For these reasons, China is currently building a strategic oil reserve, but even this may not be enough in the event of a maritime blockade. At present, this reserve consists of twenty-five days' worth of net oil imports, or 100 million barrels; it will increase to 200 million barrels, roughly forty-two days supply for higher levels of consumption, by 2010, after which a third phase is planned to increase reserves to around 500 million barrels. But according to American analysts, this may not be enough because 'without significant improvements to China's transportation and distribution networks, gross storage capacity may prove insufficient to cushion severe disruptions.'[17] Hence the need to develop a long-term and comprehensive strategy with oil-producing countries. But while some suppliers, like Russia, are problematic and subject to sudden shifts of policy, others like Angola, Sudan and

Venezuela are widely dispersed and also unpredictable in the medium- to long-term. The supplier which fits the bill – not too distant, already with a substantial history of cooperation with China, with sufficient reserves, and above all with a parallel anti-hegemonic stance regarding the United States – is obviously Iran. America is itself concerned, since it feels that China's new relationships with such suppliers and also with countries which can facilitate and guarantee passage entail 'increased investment in a blue-water capable fleet and, potentially, a more activist military presence abroad'.[18]

But the real problem is that this increase in Chinese demand runs parallel to a predicted general decrease in global supply.

The Peak Oil Debate

Will there be enough oil to satisfy China's growing demand as well as that of existing developed countries? For some years now there has been a debate about the oil peak, that is to say in the clearest of definitions 'the midpoint of global hydrocarbon production',[19] or in other words the point at which proven supply of oil enters into permanent decline. More bluntly, when oil starts to run out.

As long ago as 1956, a geologist employed by Shell Oil, M. King Hubbert, predicted that the production of oil in the United States would peak at the end of the 1960s. No one believed him at the time, but after his prediction the graph which showed both discovery and consequently production peaking and declining became known as Hubbert's Peak. The problem is that according to this theory we are reaching, or have already reached, the point at which about half of all the oil that is available for use in the world has already been consumed. Expressed in another way, the world at present consumes between four and six times the amount that we discover. The gobal depletion rate is about four per cent a year, and this while Chinese demand is growing at around two per cent a year.

Current estimates on when the global oil peak will occur vary widely, and some experts think that it is in any case an unreliable prediction because more oil fields are being discovered and new techniques make it feasible to extract oil where previously it was difficult or impossible – in deep-sea oilfields, for example – and that alternative energy sources such as natural gas will resolve the problem. Chris Skrebowski, of the Oil Depletion Analysis Centre, asserted during a conference in late 2006 that peak oil is most likely to occur globally in 2011 at around 93 million barrels per day.[20] Another participant of the same conference, Jörg Schindler, suggested in his paper that the peak had already been reached in 2006, while the ex-BP geologist Colin Campbell, another key figure in the peak oil debate, had even argued for 2004. However, Campbell himself cautions on the website of the Association for the Study of Peak Oil and Gas (ASPO), which he founded, that these estimates are necessarily imprecise since solid data are unavailable: 'oil companies tended to report cautiously, being subject to strict Stock Exchange rules, whereas certain OPEC countries exaggerated during the 1980s when they were competing for quota based on reported reserves'.[21] A well-known paper by Robert Hirsch published in 2005 was conservative in its estimates, but in any case predicted that the peak would occur within twenty years of that date. He and his co-authors provide a list of eleven predictions ranging from Schindler's 2006 to Shell's '2025 and after', concluding that 'no one knows with certainty when world oil production will reach a peak, but geologists have no doubt that it will happen'[22] since there are few large oil fields left to be discovered. This seems to be confirmed in another paper by Schindler, who points out that while between 1960 and 1970 'the average size of new discoveries was 527 Mb [million barrels] per New Field Wildcat' from 200 to 2005 this had declined to '20 Mb per New Field Wildcat'. The pattern is repeated: 'To increase the supply of oil will be become more and more difficult, the growth rate will slow down and costs will increase until the point is reached where the industry is not anymore able to bring into production a sufficient number of new fields quick enough. At that point, production will stagnate temporarily and the eventually start to decline.'[23] The perfect example is the decline of Britain's North Sea oil, which on this analysis peaked in 1999, but oil-fields in Russia and Alaska are also seeing sharp decline. The 2008 edition of the authoritative annual *World Energy Outlook*, published by the International Energy Agency (IEA) at the end of that year, presented significant new data on global energy trends up to 2030. It argued that *global* oil production was already declining much more quickly than previously imagined. The average annual rate of decline over the next two decades was quantified as being 9.2 per cent without increased investment, and 6.4 per cent even with huge investments in exploration and infrastructure.[24]

This situation is made worse by the fact that although oil only represents thirty-six per cent of global energy supply, and even less in China, it provides fuel for around ninety per cent of all forms of transport and almost 100 per cent of food supplies reach their destination with the aid of oil. Given the fact, that transport in the form of cars and commercial vehicles, together with commercial aircraft, is likely to increase so much over the next half century, and that feasible substitutes for transport are not likely to be ready soon, this exacerbates the situation for China (from 2000 to 2007 China's extra consumption represented nearly a third of the increase in global oil demand).[25] At the conference mentioned above, a senior consultant with CRA International, Hugh Ebbutt, argued that China and India together would need an extra 10 billion barrels of oil a year by 2020 and observed that this is an enormous amount considering that current production is about 30 billion barrels a year (Schindler, in the paper mentioned above, estimated *total* production for 2030 at 39 billion barrels). There is also another problem, less often discussed: for if it is true that depletion is imminent, and that prices are likely to soar on the open market, then it would be much more rational from the producers' point of view to leave the oil underground and await dramatic price increases. Many countries are beginning to consider such an option; in 2006, for example, Algeria announced that it no longer wanted the extra revenue: 'Algeria's debt had been repaid and there was a fear that more revenues would simply induce an attack of "resource curse".'[26] There are also other problems, such as lack of investment or inadequate supplies of technicians and expert management. Whatever happens, there will be, perhaps by 2020 and certainly by 2030, a supply gap which nuclear or alternative energy sources will be unable to fill at that time. Something must give.

This again, from China's point of view, makes Iran an attractive prospective partner and ally.

Iran's Supply of Oil and Natural Gas

Iran has the opposite problem. The country has the second-largest oil reserves in the Middle East, after Saudi Arabia, and the second-largest natural gas reserves in the world, with hydrocarbons accounts for twenty-two per cent of GDP and eighty per cent of its total export earnings. Iran, which currently accounts for about fifteen per cent of China's oil imports, needs to find a customer to guarantee its exports in the presence of US-inspired sanctions and trade embargoes, and in exchange for oil obtain products that are increasingly difficult to purchase on the open market, such as advanced weapons. It also needs to exploit its proven oil reserves to develop an industrial economy or to emulate its successful southern neighbours like Dubai by inventing a new business model for the country before its oil and gas revenues enter into serious decline.

The production of oil in Iran is concentrated in a few very large fields which also have high rates of decline. According to official sources, production is expected to grow from the current 4.4 million barrels a day to 6.8 million in 2030, although this will require access to foreign technology and capital – which China not only can provide but is doing so through its various new ventures in Iran. The production of natural gas is expected to increase over the same period from the low current level of 10.8 billion cubic feet per day to 240 billion cubic feet by 2030, of which exports to Europe and Asia through new pipelines will be around 57 billion cubic feet per day. This also requires huge capital investment of around $85 billion over the same period.

Iran's problem is that while oil and gas together account for a similar level of GDP to most Middle Eastern producers, at twenty-two per cent, it has a much larger territory to develop and a much greater population. Worse still, exports of these two products accounted for around eighty-five per cent of total exports (the 2007 figure), so the biggest challenge is to reduce dependence on oil and gas production and exports, and use the revenues to promote growth and diversify the economy. To this end, the Iranian Parliament (Majlis)developed a five-year plan for the period 2005–2009 which aimed to privatise some industrial sectors and to introduce overall economic reforms. The plan aims to increase annual GDP to Chinese-style levels of 8 per cent, reduce unemployment from the current 10.4 per cent to 8 per cent, and also reduce inflation from 13 per cent in 2004 to 10 per cent in 2009. All this requires enormous investment, estimated by the government at around $356 billion from Iran itself and as much as $31 billion from overseas investors. Above all, it is planned to increase non-oil-related exports by as much as eleven per cent annually. This is one area in which China could be a vital financial and industrial partner, first through injecting capital by foreign direct investment, a process it understands perfectly, second in assisting Iran to develop new non-oil-related industries, and third by providing a potential export market for future products from Iran.

Industrial partnerships

Today, industrial partnerships are still in their infancy, but basically concern the idea of some kind of modern Silk Road system. In fact the model used for the special economic zone created by China in Lahore, the special textile zone in Faisalabad, and the free-trade zone currently being built by China in Kazakhstan, could easily be extended to Iran. For pan-Asian overland transport routes will also change dramatically in the next few years. At the eastern end, China has entered into several projects with Pakistan Railways; at the western end, in late 2006 President Musharraf of Pakistan called for such a link between Iran and Pakistan, to begin when a new line from Kerman to Zahedan enters into service in 2009. Thus it would be relatively simple to revive an old dream of connecting the Iranian railway network with Quetta in Pakistan and points further east, for in the late-nineteenth century the British rulers linked Quetta to the rest of Pakistan and also built a railway through Baluchistan to the Persian city of Zahedan. There is also another route, whose importance was emphasised by the Foreign Minister of Iran at the end of the tenth Iran-Kazakhstan joint economic commission in Astana in October 2008, that involves plans for a northward railway link from Iran to Turkmenistan and Kazakhstan;[27] since the former capital Almaty is already linked by rail to Urumqi, in Xinjiang, on a line which runs across Kazakhstan from Moscow, this new route could easily be extended into China. Either way, China would then be directly linked by rail to Iran, and the development of industrial sites in Iran would become simpler. One only has to see the unending goods trains with multiple locomotives and hundreds of wagons which wend their way slowly but surely across China to understand the implications of such a network.

In fact this is an old Chinese dream as well. In his book *The International Development of China,* which as we have seen was composed as a list of infrastructure projects, Sun Yat-sen referred to the 'Eurasian Railway System' as one of the key elements in his plan for China's future – with 100,000 miles of track for China alone. The terminus of this system would be his projected Great Northern Port – 'as large as New York' – to be constructed near the site of modern Tianjin.[28] The Chinese would build a 'trunk line' from the Great Northern Port to Urumqi and Ili, where it would connect with the then-projected Indo-European Line and on through Baghdad, Damascus and Cairo, and onwards to a future African system which would result in the Great Northern Port being linked to Capetown. There is, he wrote, 'no existing railway commanding such a world-important position as this.'[29] Language like this is reminiscent of Mackinder, and also looks prophetically forward to the Binhai project which will soon make Tianjin a financial and industrial hub in the north to rival Shanghai, just as Sun had intended.

In the near future, therefore, the infrastructure for commerce throughout Turkestan will be in place, both at a national and international level, with a completed railway network which avoids the need to traverse Russia added to the existing sea and air routes. Until comparatively recent times, within living memory of elderly inhabitants of Kashgar and the western oasis towns of China, travel along these routes had not advanced beyond the camels and donkeys of the medieval Silk Road. There is no better way to understand this than to read Owen Lattimore's extraordinary account of his journey across western China in the 1920s with a camel train. Now there are flights from Urumqi to Moscow, Islamabad, Jeddah, Tashkent and Almaty, and from Kashgar to Tashkent and Bishkek. International road connections include the Karakorum Highway, completed in 1986 following an ancient pilgrim and trade route which was part of the Silk Road system, linking Kashgar with Havelian in Pakistan and thence on to Islamabad. More modern infrastructure routes are formed by the oil and gas pipelines, difficult to construct but relatively impervious to the climatic conditions once built.

All this, in the Chinese view, is not before time, since other recent events have conspired to turn China's eyes once again towards Iran.

The Second Sino-Persian Anti-hegemony Partnership

The new century opened with, from the anti-hegemonistic point of view, significant signs of arrogance and interference on the part of the United States. The first omen was the missile hit on the Chinese Embassy in Belgrade on 8 May 1999. There were student protests against the United States all over the world, from Rome to Chicago, as well as within China. Those stationed outside the American Embassy in Beijing invoked antihegemony explicitly with the slogan: 'Down with hegemonic politics!'[30] China's past humiliations were recalled as the official Party newspaper *People's Daily* thundered: 'This is 1999, not 1899. This is not the age when people can barge about in the world just by sending a few gunboats.'[31] In fact the whole episode took place against a backdrop of Chinese anger about an American imperialistic assault on what was portrayed as 'innocent Serbia'.[32] The whole matter was reported in newspapers as a simplistic one of patriots against imperialists; the mistaken bombing was therefore manna for the newspapers.

Two years later, on 1 April 2001, a Chinese Shenyang J-8D fighter collided over the South China Sea with a much larger American spy plane based in Okinawa, technically an EP-3 maritime patrol aircraft, resulting in the death of the fighter pilot and an emergency landing by the Americans on the southern island of Hainan. The twenty-four man crew was briefly held in custody but released ten days later. Once again, America was perceived as arrogant because its representatives refused to apologise for the incident, indeed tried to push responsibility for the mid-air collision onto the dead Chinese fighter pilot. Indeed it was argued in the Chinese press that American 'rhetoric about Chinese culpability was more dangerous than the collision itself.'[33]

But these complaints and refuelling of the humiliation narrative were soon set aside by an even more dramatic event which temporarily brought about some sort of reconciliation and an apparent shared purpose. For, as we have briefly mentioned, the terrorist attack of 11 September 2001 at first brought sympathy and rapprochement from China, which immediately saw the possibility of creating a global anti-terrorist campaign which would suit its own ends and help to control separatist Muslim terrorist activities in Xinjiang and neighbouring countries. The addition of the East Turkestan Islamic Movement to the State Department list of terrorist organisations in exchange for China's support for President Bush's anti-terrorism drive 'helped to legitimize Beijing's often brutal treatment of the Uygur minority.'[34] For the Chinese leadership, the 'war on terror' was a marvellous distraction which absorbed the full attention of the new president and his advisors, and afforded their country precious time out of the international limelight. Unfortunately, however, all the consequences of the war against terror were not seen so positively, especially the decision to go to war again in Iraq with a multinational coalition under the leadership of the United States in the spring of 2003. For this instantly evoked the spectre of American imperialistic arrogance.

Indeed, towards the end of 2004 a vice-premier and former foreign minister, Qian Qichen, spoke openly of the 'cocksureness and arrogance' of the United States, arguing that 'the Iraq War has destroyed the hard-won global anti-terror coalition.'[35] For the invasion of a sovereign state was seen as an attempt to rule the world by means of unilateral military strength, while the Chinese instinctively seek a multilateral approach to such problems. It could be read as a dangerous precedent.

China turned again towards Iran. Three months after the Belgrade missile attack Ji Fengding, Vice Foreign Minister, visited Tehran and insisted to a clearly receptive audience on the need for greater cooperation between China and Iran as well as emphasising the fact that both countries were ancient civilistions.[36] A few months later, the Foreign Minister himself went to Iran, and within two years President Khatami travelled to Beijing, Vice-President Hu Jintao to Tehran, and later President Jiang Zemin himself to Tehran (in the spring of 2002). In a statement made after President Khatami's trip to Beijing in June 2000, during which his delegation also visited Urumqi and Kashgar, agreement was reached on several issues that were implicitly anti-American: on the need to foster 'world multipolarization', that the security of the Persian Gulf should be 'safeguarded by the countries in the region free from outside interference', on the need for a political and economic order that is 'free of hegemonism and power politics', and on opposition to 'interference in the internal affairs of other countries under the pretext of human rights'. In the words of the official communiqué, China and Iran 'reached common understanding on enhancing bilateral cooperation, opening up new prospects for the bilateral ties and establishing a 21st century-oriented long-term and wide-ranging relationship of friendship and cooperation in the strategic interests of the two countries on the basis of mutual respect for sovereignty and territorial integrity, equality and mutual benefit, and peaceful coexistence.'[37] While it is true that there is no mention of partnership or strategic partnership in the cautious language of this communiqué, such an agreement could easily serve as a blueprint for future initiatives which extend this implicit partnership into something stronger – when China decides that the time is ripe. For the moment, pragmatism still ruled. In 2000, oil imports to China jumped by eighty-four per cent and trade between China and Iran by seventy-three per cent. More generally, in the period from 1999 to 2006, when China's arms transfers to developing nations represented around twenty per cent of the global total, 28.9 per cent of this quantity was to the Middle East, and principally to Iran.[38]

In discussion of matters such as Iran's nuclear capability, China has been keen to avoid confrontation with the United States and to make a show of agreement within the United Nations. It has maintained dignified restraint. But it is also notable that China has resisted American pressure on three key issues concerning Iran over the past twenty years: first, in providing weapons during the 1980–89 war with Iraq and thereby thwarting attempts to cut off supplies with 'Operation Staunch'; second, in continuing to supply dual-use technologies and materials after agreeing in 1997 not to do so; and, thirdly, by opposing strong sanctions against Iran's nuclear programmes. The reason for these slights is that the relationship, and its role within China's Central Asia and Middle East policies, is so important that 'Beijing is especially loath to sacrifice Iran to Sino-U.S. cooperation.'[39] At the same time, however, China has continuously resisted Iran's entreaties to join in an Eurasian bloc against American hegemony. It is at present an unstable, shifting relationship whose success may be vital for the future of both countries.

Given their geographical position and geopolitical significance, China's rise to global superpower status and Iran's role as a non-Arab but Islamic regional power straddling the oil and gas wealth of the Middle East and Central Asia, their relationship is vital for the future both of Turkestan and the world. Already the cat-and-mouse diplomatic probing and experimental groupings of the new nations of Turkestan, and regional power-plays of great powers such as Russia and the United States, must necessarily involve both China and Russia. As this book was nearing completion, it was announced that Turkmenistan may have in the Yoloten-Osman deposits one of the world's four or five largest gas fields (with others yet to be fully explored). If the results of a survey by an independent consulting firm are verified, it would mean that Turkmenistan 'will have reserves just 20% lower than that of Russia and outstrip Iran by far'.[40] This is excellent news for China, which is already financing the Central Asia–China gas pipeline through a joint-venture between PetroChina and China National Oil and Gas Exploration and Development Company, the Trans-Asia Gas Pipeline Company. It would also mean that Russia's present domination of world oil reserves diminishes in comparison to those of Turkmenistan - enhancing the role of a potential future alliance.

Borromean Rings: the Strategic Interdependence of China, Turkestan and Iran

Borromean rings are rather like three-dimensional Venn Diagrams and consist of three interlocking rings, with the special property that if any one of them is removed, all three become separated. This metaphor will be used to explain the way in which these major strategic areas are so intertwined that they cannot be thought of separately, and the ways in which this fact will condition the future foreign policy and military strategy of each – with particular emphasis on China and Iran.

Between NATO to the west of Turkestan and SCO and ASEAN in the east, there are several international cooperation organisations which play an important role in regional stability, including SCO (Shanghai Cooperation Organisation), GUAM (from the initials of Georgia, Ukraine, Azerbaijan, and Moldova), CSTO (Collective Security Treaty Organization), ECO, the Economic Cooperation Organization, EurAsEC (Eurasian Economic Community) and BSEC (Organisation for Black Sea Economic Cooperation), which, in effect, are organisations or private members clubs which function as Borromean rings.

One of the earliest of these 'clubs' in its present form was the SCO, which we have mentioned earlier. It was founded in 2001 with the specific scope of limiting American power in Turkestan, and based on the earlier Shanghai Five (1996), composed of China, Russia, Kazakhstan, Kyrgystan and Tajikistan, with the later addition of Uzbekistan. As we have seen, Iran currently holds observer status in the SCO, but could soon become a full member.

The CSTO began life as the Commonwealth of Independent States Collective Security Treaty in 1994. It became known as the CSTO in 2002, when the presidents of Russia, Armenia, Belarus, Kazakhstan, Kyrgyzstan, and Tajikistan signed a new charter. As its name implies, unlike the other organisations discussed here the emphasis of the CSTO is on 'security' and its focus very strongly Russian; the headquarters is in Moscow and the official website exists only in a Russian version. The emphasis of the charter is on military matters, together with an interest in the drugs trade based on Afghanistan and terrorism, like its eastern counterpart the SCO. Article 7 of the Charter declares that the member states will create a military infrastructure and provide both training and equipment to make a regional security system. According to transcripts of discussions at the regular session of the CSTO held in Moscow in September 2008, most of the discussion concerned recent events in South Ossetia and Abkhazia – with obvious support for Russia's role. Its desire is to become the 'core institution of security' in the region, and one of the key decisions at that meeting was to strengthen the presence of its Collective Rapid Reaction Forces in what is effectively Turkestan.[41]

Since the beginning, Russia has offered other CSTO member countries special conditions for Russian military training and the chance to buy Russian weapons and equipment at internal Russian market prices. In 2003, it opened a military air base in Kant (Kyrgyzstan) which became a key component of the Collective Rapid Reaction Force. For members are bound by statute to provide military assistance to other members in time of need. In mid-decade a series of border exercises, or *rubezh*, were initiated: in 2004 in Kazakhstan and Kyrgyzstan, in 2005 in Tajikistan, in 2006 again in Kazakhstan and in 2007 in Tajikistan.[42] In 2006, after first adhering to GUAM, Uzbekistan joined CSTO.

Although the idea has always been denied by its member nations, it seems that GUAM, the result of a Summit meeting held in Yalta in June 2001, was created as a counterweight to CSTO. Certainly, those nations have generally maintained good relationships with Russia, but have also developed very close ties with the United States, partly in view of the fact that they offer an alternative corridor for pipelines bringing Caspian oil and gas to Europe. Evidence of the importance of Georgia for the United States was manifest in the South Ossetian crisis in the summer of 2008. This pro-American, westward-looking stance – reminiscent of the great Romanian novel *Westward Lies Heaven*, by Petru Dumitriu (1964) – may be the reason that Uzbekistan, which signed the original charter, later withdrew. In fact, in a more recent Summit meeting, in June 2007, the four members were joined by three European presidents, those of Lithuania, Poland and Romania, together with high-level representatives from Bulgaria, Estonia, Latvia, the United States and Japan.

The Economic Cooperation Organization is interesting in the context of this book because its present member countries correspond closely to Turkestan, with the single addition of Turkey on the Western end and the absence of any part of

China on the eastern end. The map of member states published on the website is an almost perfect graphic representation of Turkestan as defined in Chapter 1 above: a curving eastern extension from the border of Pakistan to the most easterly point of Kazakhstan to complete the basic slightly-tilted oval of the central bloc, minus Turkey, would include the most populated parts of Xinjiang/East Turkestan (see Map 6).

ECO was established in 1985 by Iran, Pakistan and Turkey to promote economic and technical cooperation, and in 1992 was enlarged by the addition of Afghanistan, Azerbaijan, Kazakhstan, Kyrgyzstan, Tajikistan, Turkmenistan, and Uzbekistan. In fact ECO succeeded the earlier Regional Cooperation for Development (RCD), founded in 1964, and the present structure, with the secretariat in Iran, an economic bureau in Turkey, and a scientific bureau in Pakistan, reflects the organisation's history. The basic idea of ECO is to establish a single market for goods and services, much like the European Union. This may be seen in its main objectives, which follow those of the RCD and include the achievement of sustainable economic development of member states' economic liberalisation and privatisation, the progressive removal of trade barriers and the promotion of intra-regional trade, and, to facilitate this, the development of a transport and communications infrastructure linking members of the rest of the world.[43] Interestingly, at the end of 2007 a memorandum of understanding was signed with SCO with the aim of 'effective and mutually beneficial cooperation'. China has observer status in the ECO, just as Iran does in the SCO.[44]

The Eurasian Economic Community was formally created in May 2001, when an earlier treaty was ratified by Belarus, Kazakhstan, Kyrgyzstan, Russia and Tajikistan May 2001, as a spin-off from the earlier CIS (Commonwealth of Independent States) Customs Union. Pulling together three former CIS states links along the northern edge of Turkestan, this will become a formal union between Belarus, Russia and Kazakhstan in 2011.

The most obvious problem even in such a brief review of these organisations is the ambiguous and shifting position of one of the most difficult countries of all, Uzbekistan, suggesting that all these groupings are essentially temporary and could easily be reshuffled when new political considerations appear on the horizon or dramatic changes occur in the global economic and military order.

Another intriguing problem is which way Turkey would turn in a crisis, west, east or north. A Muslim country, with a Romanised script but still speaking a language related to Arabic and Persian, its people once migrated from Turkestan to its present territory. Russia would like Turkey to join the CSTO – just as the United States would like its neighbour Georgia to join NATO – even though Turkey is already in fact a member of NATO and has formally applied to join the European Union. In fact it was Russia's desire to reassume its traditional role in the Caucasus and around the Black Sea, as well as control of oil and gas pipelines, which led to the attack on Georgia in the summer of 2008, while the new independence of South Ossetia and Abkhazia show how dynamic and flexible the entire region has become. Ancient rivalries and wars, including the Crimean War and a long fight over control of shipping lanes from the Black Sea into the Mediterranean, have meant constant tension in the past, while Turkey's role in the creation of the Baku-Tbilisi-Ceyhan pipeline (from Baku on the Caspian coast of Azerbaijan to Turkey, via Georgia) to deliver Caspian oil to Europe without traversing Russian territory brings this oil-less country to the heart of regional problems linked to energy resources. This pipeline was conceived of as a major blow, in particular, to Russia's longstanding domination of energy routes from the Caspian to the West. Turkey at present imports most of its natural gas from Russia, and the massive northern neighbour is her main trading partner; at the same time, Turkey is also a major trading partner with Georgia and Azerbaijan in the north-east. In the end, this growing series of alliances is effectively creating another bloc against American hegemony in the western part of Turkestan, even though the original idea of building a pipeline westwards from Baku – and by extension eastwards under the Caspian to Kazakhstan and Turkmenistan – was originally sponsored by the United States as a means of circumventing Russian control over energy supplies from the region.

In fact, yet another regional cooperation came into existence as the Black Sea Economic Cooperation in 1992, with its headquarters in Istanbul. It is now known as the Organization of the Black Sea Economic Cooperation (BSEC). The original eleven members, Albania, Armenia, Azerbaijan, Bulgaria, Georgia, Greece, Moldova, Romania, Russia, Turkey and Ukraine, were joined by Serbia and Montenegro in 2004. The aim of the BSEC members was to create a 'model of multilateral political and economic initiative aimed at fostering interaction and harmony among the Member States, as well as to ensure peace, stability and prosperity encouraging friendly and good-neighbourly relations in the Black Sea region.' All this, its Charter explicitly declares in an interesting recognition of the existence of the Borromean Rings, should be accomplished in a way which does not contravene the 'international obligations of the Member States including those deriving from their membership to international organizations or institutions of an integrative or other nature and not preventing the promotion of their relations with third parties.'[45] Together, as its web-site proclaims, its members represent the second-largest source of oil and natural gas after the Persian Gulf region, and will soon create an essential transport and energy transfer corridor for Europe.[46]

Last, naturally is the problem of Iran, which, like Uzbekistan, could be pulled east or west or north as the diplomatic sands shift. Here a new complication was introduced in 2007 when the Secretary-General of the CSTO, Nikolai Bordyuzha, remarked that the organisation would be willing to consider and accept an application for membership by Iran. Bordyuzha is both an ex-Soviet army general and an ex-KGB high-ranking official, and was once thought of as a potential president of Russia. He knows as well as anyone, including the Chinese leadership, that the ultimate position of Iran will be a vital tool for whichever power succeeds in future years in assuming control of Turkestan and its immense wealth of energy resources.

In effect, this is the Great Game once again, with Russia pushing eastward and southward, China pushing westward, and the United States assuming the role of Britain by pushing north from the Pacific Ocean and the Persian Gulf.

China and Iran as a Potential Bloc

There is another way of viewing this vast region, as a 'bloc' rotating on an axis between China and Iran, from which all the countries along the axis will gain advantages. Let us look briefly at two of them.

One such country is land-locked Turkmenistan, a predominantly Muslim country the size of California with only five million inhabitants which could eventually be drawn into an alliance. Culturally it has close ties to Iran, having once been part of Khorassan in the Persian Empire. Turkmenistan needs customers, but more than anything it needs pipelines to reach those customers – preferably without needing to submit to Russian control that amounts to a virtual monopoly on its gas exports. This problem is shared with other neighbours, and led to the American sponsored project, together with Azerbaijan, Georgia, and Turkey, for a Trans-Caspian Gas Pipeline which would enable Turkmenistan to send gas under the Caspian and therefore eliminate the possibility of Russian interference. To further this desire to 'escape' from Russia, after several failed attempts to create partnerships with its difficult neighbour Iran, with which it shares a 616-mile border, in the spring of 2006 President Saparmurat Niyazov (who died at the end of that year) travelled to China to meet Hu Jintao with a contract for a new pipeline to be built with Chinese assistance to Shanghai, which will pass through both Uzbekistan and Kazakhstan. With a self-serving flourish of rhetoric, he called this 2,500 mile pipeline the 'Great Silk Road of the 21st Century'.[47]

Another candidate could be Kazakhstan. Suppose, as we suggest in the scenarios at the end of this book, that immense country were to split into two natural and more or less equal parts, one Christian and Russian-speaking and the other part Muslim and Kazakh-speaking? Or suppose not. In either case, it is another land-locked country, with a border with Turkmenistan and a much longer border with China - which has a minority group of Kazaks. Links are close, so much so that the present Prime Minister, Karim Kajymqanuly Massimov, besides holding a doctorate in Economics, is a fluent Mandarin speaker and has degrees from both Beijing Language and Culture University and Wuhan Law School. In addition, he has previously held positions as his country's representative in both Urumqi and Hong Kong, and therefore has deep knowledge and understanding of China – probably one reason why he was made Prime Minister in January 2007 at the young age of forty-two.[48] Such political leaders, who will grow in number as China develops its soft power, may hold the key to future more solid alliances.

Closer links with such important gas producers would tally perfectly with China's declared objective of increasing the use of clean gas over dirty coal from the present three per cent of total primary energy consumption to twelve per cent in 2020,[49] although it must be said that bilateral trade is currently extremely small – partly in function of the tiny population of Turkmenistan, with a GDP per capita of $8,500 and twenty-seven per cent of the population under the poverty line.[50] Yet is an intriguing example of the way in which China, together with a strong Muslim partner in Iran, could simultaneously undermine American hegemony and weaken Russia by increasing its dealings with the emerging economies of 'Turkestan'. Already in 1979, the Israeli scholar Yitzhak Shichor, with another perspective, could write that 'China considers Iran to be one of the most serious obstacles to the expansion of Soviet influence and presence in the Persian Gulf, as well as a major contributor to organizing and uniting the members of OPEC and other Third World countries against "superpower hegemony".'[51] Until then, Iran had been a close ally of the United States. Today, Iran is engaged in its traditional but potentially dangerous game of playing the great powers against each other, namely the United States, Russia and China; sooner or later, it will need to make a choice.

The stability of the 'bloc' could also be the key to resolving subsidiary disputes and conflicts concerning its neighbours, which include some of the thorniest problems on the current global agenda. At the extremities of the bloc, for example, are two of the countries which have exercised the minds of the best foreign experts in the world for years without finding the perfect solution, namely Iraq to the west and North Korea to the east. It would be to the advantage of all, except possibly for that of American hegemony, if these two countries could be brought into the fold. Then there are two even more tetchy neighbours who share frontiers, historical connections and reasonably friendly relations with China and Iran, but whose policies and allegiances are today amongst the most convoluted on earth, namely Afghanistan and Pakistan. The former country, with a history of violence and various forms of civil war which now stretch back for thirty years, and its probable role as a haven for international terrorism, will at some time in the future require a radical permanent solution to its problems - perhaps dismemberment. The latter, also a potential candidate for dismemberment, maintains a delicate fraternal love-hate relationship with India to the east, and shares deep affinities to the Sunni nations of Islamic fundamentalism to the south-west. It is also true, however, that prominent politicians in Iran have begun to play down the Sunni/Shi'a divide. In a meeting in Bahrain in October 2008, for example, the Speaker of the Majlis, Ali Larijani, while discussing enhanced regional cooperation, emphasised that Shi'a and Sunni Muslims have been living side by side peacefully for centuries but that in recent years 'Americans and

Westerners have been trying to foment dissension and arouse [the sectarian sentiments of] some people about the issue'.[52]

One contention of this book is that the direction of the choices made by China and Iran will depend on new threats and opportunities which emerge in Turkestan in the coming decades. Another is that a mutual proactive strategy by these two nations would drive Turkestan rather than react to events within it, and therefore present a real future political and economic threat to the rest of the world.

Notes

1. Percentages from Figure 9.1 in Garver, *China and Iran*, p. 238.
2. EIA, 'Short-Term Energy Outlook', January 2008; available at http://www.eia.doe.gov/emeu/steo/pub/outlook.html.
3. Kamal Nazer Yasin, 'Iran and China: Unlikely Partners', *Eurasianet.org*, 4 April 2006; available at http://www.eurasianet.org/departments/business/articles/eav040406.shtml.
4. 'Inside China: The Chinese view their automotive future', IBM Institute for Business Values, 2005, p. 5 and p. 22.
5. International Energy Outlook 2007, Washington DC: U.S. Department of Energy (Energy Information Administration, office of Integrated Analysis and Forecasting), p. 83; available at www.eia.doe.gov/oiaf/aeo/.
6. http://v4.airbus.com/en/presscentre/pressreleases/pressreleases_items/07_06_28_tianjin_fal.html.
7. Estimate by Liu Gaozhuo, President of the China Aviation Industry Corporation, *China Daily*, 3 March 2004. CAIC already manufactures Embraer regional jets under license, and is developing its own 100-seat regional jet, the ARJ21; CAIC has produced missiles and military aircraft for the PLA for many years. (http://www.avic1.com.cn/English/EnglishIndex.asp).
8. *People's Daily*, 22 March 2007.
9. Key World Energy Statistics 2006, Paris: International Energy Agency, p. 28.
10. Reuters, 24 April 2007.
11. Brown, *Plan B 2.0*, p. 36.
12. http://www.baosteel.com/group_e/e02introduction_n/0201.htm ; it ranked No. 307 in the Fortune 500 for 2007.
13. All data in this and the next paragraph have been taken from the BP Statistical Review of World Energy 2008, published in June 2008 and available at http://www.bp.com/productlanding.do?categoryId=6929&contentId=7044622.
14. Alterman and Garver, *The Vital Triangle*, p. 6.
15. Howard, *Iran Oil*, p. 47 and pp. 95–96.
16. See the useful synthesis by Chas W. Freeman Jr, 'Energy as China's Achilles' Heel?', in Collins et al., *China's Energy Strategy*, pp. 13–20.

17. Annual Report to Congress: The Military Power of the People's Republic of China, Washington: Office of the Secretary of Defense, 2008, p. 10.
18. Annual Report to Congress: The Military Power of the People's Republic of China, 2005, p. 10.
19. Definition from the home page of http://www.peakoil.com.
20. Reported in *Five Minutes to Midnight*, Report on the Energy Institute's conference on Oil Depletion, 7 November 2006, by *Industrial Fuels and Power* (www.ifandp.com).
21. http://www.peakoil.net/about-peak-oil.
22. Robert L. Hirsch, Roger Bezdek and Robert Wendling, 'Peaking of World Oil Production: Impacts, Mitigation, & Risk Management', US Department of Energy, February 2005, p. 4 and p. 8.
23. Jörg Schindler and Dr. Werner Zittel, 'Crude Oil: The Supply Outlook', Report to the Energy Watch Group (EWG-Series No. 3/2007), October 2007, pp. 7, 9.
24. *World Energy Outlook 2008*, Paris: International Energy Agency, 12 November 2008; see the chapter on 'Oil Market Outlook', pp. 91-105.
25. Howard, *Iran Oil*, p. xi.
26. Paul Stevens, *The Coming Oil Supply Crunch*, London: Royal Institute of International Affairs (a Chatham House Report), 2008, p. 23.
27. 'Iran, Kazakhstan ink MOU to boost economic ties', *Tehran Times*, 18 October 2008; http://www.tehrantimes.com/index_View.asp?code=180322.
28. Sun, *International Development*, pp. 1 5-16. Interestingly, in public relations material for the new Binhai development area to the east of Tianjin, designed to create a northern counterpart to Shanghai and Shenzhen just as Sun envisaged, there is a contemporary echo of his words in 1922: 'Acting as the gateway to the three northern regions (China's northeast, central north and northwest), with the support from Beijing, Tianjin and Hebei Province, facing Northeast Asia, especially Japan and South Korea across the sea, the TBNA [Tianjin Binhai New Area] is the eastern terminus of the Eurasian Continental Bridge in the north of China, providing access to such neighboring inland countries as the Republic of Mongolia and Kazakhstan to the sea.' http://en.investteda.org/BinhaiNewArea/overview/t20060430_39712.htm
29. Ibid, pp. 18-21.
30. Reported in Gries, *China's New Nationalism*, p. 14.
31. Ibid., p. 17.
32. Terrill, *The New Chinese Empire*, p. 15.
33. Gries, *China's New Nationalism*, p. 111.
34. Gries, 'China Eyes the Hegemon', p. 407.
35. Reported in *China Daily*, 1 November 2004, and quoted here from Gries, 'China Eyes the Hegemon', p. 401. The comments were widely reported in mainstream newspapers in Britain and the USA.
36. Garver, *China and Iran*, pp. 117-8.
37. Ministry of Foreign Affairs of the People's Republic of China: 'Joint Communiqué Between The People's Republic of China and the Islamic Republic of Iran', 5 June 2002;

available at http://www1.fmprc.gov.cn/eng/wjb/zzjg/xybfs/gjlb/2818/2819/t16315.htm.

38. Figures from 'Conventional Arms Transfers to Developing Nations, 1999-2006', Washington: Congressional Research Service, September 26, 2007, pp. 23-4 and p. 28.

39. Alterman, Jon B. and Garver, John W., *The Vital Triangle*, p. 41.

40. 'UK Audit Firm Ranks New Turkmen Gas Field in World's Top Five', *Oil & Gas*, 14 October 2008, http://www.iqpc.com/News.aspx?id=122258873&IQ=oilgas; 'Energy superpower emerges in the Caspian', *Asia Times*, 17 October 2008; http://www.atimes.com/atimes/Central_Asia/JJ17Ag04.html.

41. http://www.dkb.gov.ru/start/index.htm.

42. Vladimir Paramonov and Aleksey Strokov, 'The Evolution of Russia's Central Asia Policy', Central Asia series, Defence Academy of the United Kingdom, June 2008, p. 14.

43. http://www.ecosecretariat.org/Detail_info/About_ECO_D.htm.

44. Signed at Ashgabat on 11 December, 2007 in English, Russian and Chinese; http://www.ecosecretariat.org/ftproot/Documents/MOUs/sco.htm.

45. http://www.bsec-organization.org/documents/LegalDocuments/statutory/charter/Pages/charter.aspx.

46. http://www.bsec-organization.org/Information/Pages/testt.aspx.

47. Hancock, 'Escaping Russia, Looking to China: Turkmenistan Pins Hopes on China's Thirst for Natural Gas', p. 77.

48. Biographical information from the government website: http://en.government.kz/structure/government.

49. Ibid., p. 78.

50. Data for 2006 from CIA *Factbook*, https://www.cia.gov/library/publications/the-world-factbook/geos/tx.html.

51. Shichor, *The Middle East in China's Foreign Policy* 1949–1977, p. 174.

52. 'Iran determined to expand ties with regional states', *Tehran Times*, 23 October 2008, http://www.tehrantimes.com/index_View.asp?code=180715.

Chapter 7

Future Threat

Many people, including Chinese friends of mine, would and do argue that the step from the first six chapters to the hypothesis of a combined threat to the world from China and Iran is absurd. For there is a dominant belief that China more than anything else seeks to emulate the United States – as it appeared to do in sporting terms during the recent Olympic Games – which therefore remains the true and permanent ally. Yet it might easily be argued otherwise. For example, D. S. Rajan, Director of the Chennai Centre for China Studies, has argued that the present pro-American stance is a short- and medium-term tactic to allay fears and create positive feelings about China's rise to global power status, while in the long-term the Party considers the United States to be an 'untrustworthy, duplicitous superpower'.[1] Moreover, Iran is potentially attractive to China as the only country which, by virtue of its geographical position, past history and present oil wealth and power, wishes to and can act as a double hegemon-blocker against two major powers, the United States and Russia – the former the only world superpower at present, the latter a once and potentially future superpower.

Perhaps the hypothesis *is* stretched, today. So far, in modern and contemporary history, China and Iran have been set on parallel but distinct courses – with the distance between the parallel lines maintained by China's apparent admiration for Iran's arch-enemy, the United States. Yet it would need little to bring them closer. The Byzantine fantasy of the Italian politician, Aldo Moro, who was assassinated by Red Brigade terrorists in 1978, invented the expression 'converging parallels' (*paralleli convergenti*) to describe the course of his own Christian Democrat Party and the opposing Italian Communist Party. The concept is logical nonsense, but it led pragmatically to Moro's so-called 'historic compromise' (*compromesso storico*) which effectively allowed two such disparate parties to govern the country. This ultimately enabled a former protégé of the Italian Communist Party founder Palmiro Togliatti and a leading member of the Party himself, Giorgio Napolitano, to become the first ex-communist president of a western nation. The concept of converging parallels is one useful way to consider the possible path or paths of China and Iran in the next half-century.

Such a convergence would require a powerful catalyst. But there are plenty of potential candidates around. Shortages of oil and natural gas, for example, can have immediate and dramatic effects on global equilibrium, as we saw once again in 2008. Several commentators would explain the present impasse of American foreign policy, and decline, with reference to decisions regarding Iraq, while Russia has seen a dramatic turnaround of its fortunes on the strength of its hydrocarbon reserves.

Suppose there is a ten per cent decline in world oil production by 2015, as many predict, with an equivalent increase in China's demand. Should China reduce its demand, and renounce its attempt to move its economy closer to First World standards and the 'harmonious society' of which its leaders speak? Why should it? No such powerful country has ever voluntarily reduced its expectations in favour of other, wealthier countries; certainly it is difficult to imagine the United States doing something similar. So, the question is, what will China do?

And one answer is: create a closer partnership or alliance with Iran. Already, since the last major signs of terrorist activity and separatism in 1997, when there was a large-scale uprising with hundreds of deaths in Yining (known to Uyghurs as Ghulja), near Kazahkstan, the majority of Uyghurs seem to have accepted that that violent resistance is no longer a viable path and now increasingly participate in the Chinese system. The words of one expert on the Xinjiang Uyghurs, and their sense that China itself is changing, might in fact be used of minorities anywhere in the country: 'People in their forties and older know that today is far better than the bad-old-days of the Great Leap Forward and the Cultural Revolution; and locals thirty and under feeling that youthful call-to-adventure see opportunities opening, slowly at first and maybe increasing over time.'[2] Thus, as the Muslims integrate ever more fully into the political and diplomatic system, and cross-border trade and interaction flourish, it is likely that their obvious cultural and linguistic advantages will be put to good use. Acceptance of deeper links with neighbouring Islamic countries, together with the coming oil crunch, will make closer links with Iran more feasible.

The Crucial Changing Role of China's Muslims

As we saw in the Introduction, Islam in China is far from homogeneous. There are in fact ten different Muslim minority groups, three of which are the largest and most visible: the Hui, distributed throughout China, and the so-called Uyghurs, who are concentrated in Xinjiang (the reason for the qualification will become clear later), and the Kazakhs in north-western Xinjiang. According to the 1990 census which assessed the number of practising Muslims, there were nine million Hui, over seven million Uyghurs and one million Kazakhs who together accounted for most of the Muslim population. The other seven groups, all restricted to the far western and north-western provinces, comprised less than a million together: the Dongxiang, Kyrgyz, Salar, Tajik, Uzbek, Bonan and Tatar minorities. But we should remember that the real figure is probably somewhere beyond 100 million.

There are important differences between these groups, first of all in religious practices. These vary from Shi'a to Sunni, and to different forms of Sufi practice, all of which are often subject to local influences from Chinese culture. This is often apparent in architectural style, for example in the Great Mosque of Xi'an which is laid out in a series of courtyards comparable to those of a great family compound or imperial palace, constructed according to Chinese principles of modular design based on the three elements of a foundation platform, a timber frame and a decorative roof, and replete with Chinese decorative motifs. In Kunming, the Great Mosque is designed like a single Chinese baronial hall, while in Lhasa there are two mosques built in pure Tibetan architectural style with the floors of their prayer halls covered in Tibetan carpets. There are also significant differences in language. The Hui speak a Sino-Tibetan language, the Tajiks in Xinjiang speak Farsi, while the remainder speak a variant of Altaic-Turkic.[3] More interestingly, the Hui have integrated with other minority groups and adopted their language, dress and customs, so that in Lhasa there is a community of Tibetan-Hui, in Mongolia small groups of Mongolian-Hui, and are several interesting combinations with the Bai and Dai peoples of Yunnan. One scholar noted extreme cases such as that of Hui woman in Yunnan who spoke only the Tibeto-Burman language of the important Bai minority group and were learning Arabic in order to study Islamic doctrine.[4]

Even within the Hui themselves, who are present in nearly all the cities and counties of China, there are important regional variations in belief and the level of integration into Chinese society. For this reason, one of the most renowned experts on Islam in China, Dru Gladwell, wrote in an anthropological study that he found there was no single voice that spoke for them: 'For the Hui, there is no "we". There is no community, nor individual, that even begins to represent all the Hui of China.'[5] There is, however, as Gladwell himself has shown, a distinctive 'Hui speech' (*Huihui hua*). They usually speak the language of the people amongst whom they live, Mandarin in the north, Cantonese in Guangdong, and minority languages in places like Yunnan. But their speech is coloured by words of Persian, Arabic and Turkish origin which provide strong markers of ethnic and cultural identity, especially since many of the words relate to religious practices.[6] Such words are often used between Hui rather than in conversation with Han people, thus conferring insider status on its users. One example is the use of Arabic words for numbers by shopkeepers and traders, who can thus discuss prices together in a Chinese language or dialect without non-Muslim Chinese listeners understanding them.

This 'Hui speech', together with distinctive dress, in particular the white *kefi* which is visible from a long way amidst a crowd of usually hatless Chinese, and the fact of not eating China's ubiquitous meat product, pork,[7] clearly differentiates the Muslim, as does the fact of living in quite distinct areas within the cities in which they are present, clustered around a mosque or in a distinctive urban neighbourhood. The large and concentrated Muslim population of Xi'an define themselves by their nearest mosque and live in what has been called an 'aural community' in which they can hear the call to prayer from their own mosque.[8] Yet many of the mosques are also discreet: the alley which leads to the main mosque of Kunming is distinctly uninviting from the street, its entrance flanked by a run-down noodle shop and rudimentary snack-bars, and the beautiful Chinese-style mosque itself is completely invisible; the main door to the Great Mosque in Xi'an is hidden away in the narrow lanes of a covered bazaar and quite easy to miss unless a visitor goes in search of it (few Chinese visitors seek out this huge and fascinating religious complex).

The feeling on visiting these mosques and Muslim quarters, whether in Beijing or further west in the provincial cities of Gansu and Xinjiang, and entering into conversations with their denizens in restaurants, is that of a strong but invisible bond between them. In the case of the smaller Muslim minorities, this bond is strongest with similar ethnic groups within the crescent of nations beyond China's western frontier. At present, unfortunately, such links tend to be expressed through revolutionary pan-Islamic organisations and terrorist networks, in the latter case especially westward into Afghanistan. But evidence of successful cross-border trade and commercial networks along the frontier between China and Kazakhstan augurs well for a different kind of network in the future.

Today, the terrorist threat is implicit in the air of cities like Urumqi and Kashgar, in the quick nervous eyes of Han security guards and in the uneasy segregation in restaurants and other public places; it regularly surfaces with violence as was seen during the build-up to the Olympic Games in Beijing. We will now look at the main revolutionary and terrorist organisations which are likely to have an impact on the future of Islamic politics in what we have described as Turkestan, and thus on the developing relationship between China and Iran: al-Qaida, the Islamic Movement of Turkestan, and Hizb-ut-Tahrir. We will also briefly consider the East Turkestan Islamic Movement in Xinjiang, the history of the Uyghurs, and how in the future they and other Islamic groups might coagulate and play a key role in a Sino-Persian alliance. For a cohesive Islamic force would be the decisive element in successfully creating such an alliance, which would on more than one level represent a huge threat to the Western world.

Al-Qaida

Al-Qaida (Qa'idat al-Jihad, 'the base of jihad'), has been in international terms the most notorious of Islamic terrorist groups since 2001. It consists of a more or less dispersive terrorist network which evolved from the integration of several mujahideen, or warrior, organisations with the Maktab al-Khidamat, or 'Bureau of Services', founded by Osama bin Laden in the 1980s.[9] As the *9/11 Commission Report* in the United States expressed it, 'a decade of conflict in Afghanistan, from 1979 to 1989, gave Islamic extremists a rallying point and training field,'[10] just as Khomeini's revolution had inspired them. Bin Laden's aim was to create a global pan-Islamic caliphate, with a focus on martyrdom for the cause and on the purification of Islam from Western influences. From the beginning it had an explicit anti-American bias, declaring the killing of American citizens to be a Muslim duty. In the summer of 2001 it merged with the Egyptian group al-Jihad led by Ayman al-Zawahiri. In fact both Bin-Laden and Zawahiri were followers of the Egyptian intellectual Sayyid Qutb (1906–66), who advocated a restoration to the original Muslim virtues based on the shari'a, the system of Islamic laws derived from the Koran, and was vehemently anti-American.

Al-Qaida's role in Afghanistan and broader Turkestan has necessarily brought contact and conflict with both China and Iran, for Kashgar is a short distance from the frontiers with Pakistan and Afghanistan where al-Qaida's leadership is thought to have been in hiding since 2001. Some intelligence sources believe that China actually provided training to members of the organisation in tandem with the Pakistani Inter-Services Intelligence (ISI), although, in the bizarre world of intelligence and counter-intelligence, even if that were true it may have been part of an effort to identify Uyghurs suspected of supporting al-Qaida. Although it is impossible to ascertain with any degree of certainty, it seems likely that some more or less loose forms of cross-border collaboration do exist. In the words of Robert Mueller, Director of the FBI, 'there certainly are individuals in China who could be described as having that same mindset as well as the desire to utilize terrorist acts to further their agenda, whether you would call it Al-Qaeda or a group loosely affiliated with Al-Qaeda and Al-Qaeda's leadership.'[11]

As yet, however, the followers of al-Qaida seem not to have made significant inroads into Xinjiang, although at least several hundred Chinese Muslims are thought to have undergone training in Afghanistan before September 2001 while some estimates run as high as 1,000.[12] Should these numbers seem small, we might remember that less than a hundred members of the Brigate Rosse were able to terrorize Italy for several years, and perhaps a third of that number constituted a similar threat to Germany in the form of the Baader-Meinhof gang. However, this relative lack of success may also be due to the fact that since the last large-scale religious protests in the region in 1997, the process of assimilation of Muslim minorities seems to have accelerated, partly as the result of economic growth and partly as the result of new economic opportunities and a certain freedom of movement deriving from the opening of frontiers with neighbouring Muslim countries.

Iran's relationship with al-Qaida is more ambiguous, since the Islamic Republic is widely believed to have sponsored several terrorist groups and engaged in mutual anti-American activities. In fact the *9/11 Commission Report* concluded that the relationship of al-Qaida with Iran was long-standing and included allowing known terrorists, including some of those implicated in the New York attack, to travel to the West from Afghanistan without stamping their passports. A government official even told *Time* magazine that 'Iranian officials approached the al-Qaeda leadership after the bombing of the USS *Cole* and proposed a collaborative relationship in future attacks on the U.S., but the offer was turned down by bin Laden because he did not want to alienate his supporters in Saudi Arabia.'[13] There is also tentative evidence of collaboration in other terrorist attacks, for example in Saudi Arabia itself in 1996.[14] For while the predominantly Shi'a clergy of Iran are not natural allies of a Sunni organisation, some of its objectives tally with those of al-Qaida and temporary tactical alliances between them are entirely possible. Several leading members of the terrorist organisation were thought to be living freely and openly in Iran a few years ago, including Osama bin Laden's own son Saad bin Laden.[15]

Islamic Movement of Turkestan (IMT)

This movement, formerly known as the Islamic Movement of Uzbekistan (IMU), is the most extreme terrorist group formed by ethnic Uzbeks with a strong presence focused on the region around Uzbekistan. It is an organisation of young and violent men, strongly opposed to the authoritarian rule of President Islom Karimov, 'deeply ideological, steeped in the theories and techniques of jihadism', who could be regarded as the 'Taliban of the Pamirs.'[16] Like al-Qaida, with which its origins in Kabul in 1998 are linked, its primary declared aim is to build an Islamic state which abides by the law of shari'a – perhaps more plausible in a state in which nearly 90 per cent of the population are Sunni Muslims (as is the case in Saudi Arabia). As the IMU this group acted mainly in Uzbekistan, but since a change of name to Islamic Movement of Turkestan in 2001 it has branched out with terrorist attacks in neighbouring countries. It also maintains close contacts with al-Qaida in Afghanistan, and the East Turkestan Islamic Movement (ETIM) in Xinjiang.

Led by an incongruous couple formed by a deeply religious imam, Tohir Abdoulalilovitch Yuldeshev, and a former Soviet paratrooper and veteran of the war in Afghanistan, Juma Namangani, the IMU began with the premise of violent and bloody overthrow of the existing regime in order to create a genuinely

Islamic state. Yuldeshev has been an opponent of Karimov since the independence of Uzbekistan in 1991, and has with financial support from Saudi Arabia and Pakistan built up a network of mosques and Madrasah, and arranged for his own jihadists to train in terrorist tactics in Afghanistan. In speeches given during visits to Turkey he has advocated the creation of a 'pan-Turkic Caliphate' in Central Asia.[17] Namangani is a born guerrilla who refused to accept a compromise peace at the end of the Tajik civil war in 1997 and chose to live with a group of militants and his Tajik wife in the mountains as a 'bandit in waiting', earning his living from farming and the transport of heroin with his own haulage business.[18] His military experience, deep knowledge of guerrilla tactics, and the personal bravery he exhibited in action, made him an explosive addition to this powerful ideology. It led to a spate of car-bombings in Tashkent and shoot-outs in 1999 and an offensive in Kyrgyzstan, which created the myth of Namangani as an Islamic freedom fighter. The IMT became closely involved with the Taliban, and received funding from Osama bin Laden, and over the next two years attacked both Kyrgyzstan and Uzbekistan, but they suffered huge losses after 11 September, when the full force of America and its partners against terrorism was felt. This is one reason the name was changed, from Uzbekistan to Turkestan, to disassociate itself from the former organisation and widen its appeal to non-Uzbeks. There were fresh terrorist actions, and since 2003 the IMT 'has been able to recover some of their strength and organisation.'[19]

The IMT remains important, and Uzbekistan is the country which many regard as most likely to become an Islamic State in the shari'a sense, because that populous republic lies at the heart of Turkestan. In the words of a scholar of the region: 'the core of Uzbekistan, the Zerafshan Valley with the cities of Samarkand and Bukhara, is the ancient Sogdia and the centre of gravity of Central Asian Civilization, both pre-Islamic and Islamic.' Its future could play a centrifugal role, with the significant minority Uzbek groups in neighbouring countries extending its influence outward: in Tajikistan the Uzbeks represent 24 per cent of the population, in Afghanistan, mainly along the northern frontier, 9 per cent, in Kyrgyzstan 12.9 per cent, in Turkmenistan 9 per cent, and in Kazakhstan 2.2 per cent. While in China, the Uzbek minority is much smaller, only around 15,000 people, they have a strong cultural affinity with the Uyghurs as a result of the similarity of their languages, which both belong to the Karluk or Chaghatay group of Turkic languages.

Hizb ut-Tahrir

Hizb ut-Tahrir was founded in Palestine in 1953 but has now become a global movement. Based on the tenets of Islam, and frequent recourse to the life and times of Mohammad and the original diffusion of Islam this political party's objective is 'to resume the Islamic way of life by establishing an Islamic State that executes the systems of Islam and carries its call to the world.' By this it means literally to create a new caliphate which would extend across all the lands of Islam, and thus, recalling our definitions in Chapter 1, from the Near East to the Far East, with Turkestan at its heart. Hizb ut-Tahrir would be far more insidious than any terrorist group if it were to be successful in its avowedly peaceful aims, since it 'calls for Islam in its quality as an intellectual leadership from which emanate the systems that deal with all man's problems, political, economic, cultural and social among others.'[20] For many in existing secularised Muslim states, its doctrines can be attractive and are far more articulate than most of the more radical movements. For instance, it is essentially anti-colonial in its outlook, viewing the colonial expansion of the nineteenth century in terms similar to Chinese and Persian politicians, recalling the time 'when the colonialists managed to lure a number of Muslims, and talk them into establishing party structures inside the Islamic state, built on the basis of independence and separation'.[21] This western 'poisoning' is the element to be overcome in establishing a new Caliphate comprising the Muslim nations.

For their model, the leaders of Hizb ut-Tahrir look back to the earliest and pure form of Islam, to what is known as the *Khilafat-i Rashida* (literally, the 'orthodox caliphates'), believing that the mass movement they are creating will 'eventually overwhelm one of the regimes of Central Asia or the Middle East'.[22] For the '*rashida*' here refers to the four 'orthodox' or *rashidun* caliphs, Abu-Bakr, 'Umar, 'Uthman and 'Ali, who were all relatives of Muhammad. These four men oversaw the militant and rapid spread of Islam from 632 to 661, in what has been described by a leading Arab historian as 'the period in which the lustre of the Prophet's life had not ceased to shed its light and influence over the thoughts and acts of the caliphs'.[23] It is worth noting here that under these caliphs the armies of Islam conquered Persepolis and the Makran (649–50 and 643),[24] which means they took Persia and reached the borders of modern Pakistan. Ominously, in terms of a future repetition of this success, in the first decade of the next century they reached Balkh, today in northern Afghanistan, close to the Russian frontier, Samarkand and Khiwa, in modern Uzbekistan, and occupied the province of Ferghana at the very heart of Mackinder's pivot and our Western Turkestan.[25]

Today, Hizb ut-Tahrir claims to be an essentially peaceful party, which publishes documents of extreme and sometimes surprising rationality, yet it emphasises the duty of all Muslims to go to jihad or 'holy war' in the precise sense of 'an obligation – imposed by Allah on all Muslims – to strive unceasingly to convert or to subjugate non-Muslims'.[26] A prominent expert on jihad has identified Hizb ut-Tahrir as a key factor threatening Kazakhstan, Kyrgyzstan, Tajikistan, Turkmenistan, Uzbekistan and even Pakistan in future years.[27] It is also interesting to note that there is widespread sympathy towards Osama bin Laden, by whom many of the jihadists are inspired and whom some of the leaders have met in person in Kabul in the past.[28] The portents are inauspicious indeed as far as China is concerned. Indeed, this organisation was thought to have been behind protests held in Khotan – a predominantly Uyghur town on the southern branch of the Silk Road in Xinjiang – in March 2008.

East Turkestan Islamic Movement (ETIM)

As we have seen, China quickly joined the ranks of supporters of the American campaign against terrorism after September 2001 (together with Uzbekistan), and voted in favour of the Security Council resolution which authorised military action against the Taliban, as it saw a chance to gain America's reciprocal support against the East Turkestan Islamic Movement. Furthermore, China closed its frontier with Afghanistan so that Taliban or al-Qaida supporters could not escape the country. It also offered financial assistance to the Afghans.[29] As a direct result, China was supported by the United States in its bid to have ETIM, an Uyghur group, listed at the United Nations as a terrorist organisation; an indirect result of this was the arrest of seventeen Uyghurs in Afghanistan in 2002, and their imprisonment in the notorious prison at Guantánamo Bay in Cuba until they were released without charge six years later (altogether there were twenty-two Uyghurs in Guantánamo, seven of whom were said to be members of al-Qaida).[30] There were also concerns about widespread dreams of setting up a trans-border independent 'Turkestan' of some form which China shared with other central Asian states. For this extremist group, which seems to be supported by a very small number of Uyghurs, has for its objective the creation of an independent state called East Turkestan. Other groups with similar aims include the East Turkistan Liberation Organisation (ETLO), the United Revolutionary Front of East Turkistan (URFET), and the Uyghur Liberation Organisation (ULO). While the first of these has links to the Islamic Movement of Uzbekistan, in 2001 the last two joined forces to create the Uyghuristan People's Party.

In the last decade of the twentieth century, some two hundred terrorist incidents in Xinjiang led to the death of nearly as many people, but extremism does not enjoy popular support and has been on the decrease since the founder of ETIM, Hasan Mahsum, was killed in 2003 by Pakistani forces in the mountains between Afghanistan and Pakistan where the leaders of al-Qaida are thought to have taken refuge. The Chinese support for American anti-terrorist initiatives made it more difficult for the members of ETIM to gain traction. In the spring of 2007, a training camp was captured and destroyed, while Husein Celil, of the East Turkestan Liberation Organisation (ETLO) which acted together with ETIM, was sentenced to life imprisonment after being captured in Uzbekistan.[31] At the beginning of 2008 there was an attempt to hijack a China Southern Boeing 757 *en route* from Urumqi to Beijing, which culminated in an emergency landing at Lanzhou (about half-way through the planned flight) and the arrest of four Ughyurs, including one young woman.[32] During the run-up to the Olympic Games in August, there were several rumours of the capture of terrorists and thwarted plots, and the central government even offered substantial bounties for information as well as checking all vehicles entering Beijing. There was a general feeling that should there be a terrorist attack it would be inspired by Uyghur separatists. Fortunately, no such attack occurred in Beijing or in the other Olympic cities.

Three separate incidents did occur in Xinjiang itself during the early phase of the Olympics, including the killing of sixteen Chinese policemen in Kashgar, three border guards stabbed to death at a frontier crossing near the same city, and attacks on a police station and government building in Kuqa. A Chinese terrorism expert noted in August that the terrorists had shifted strategy from random bomb attacks that might also involved innocent civilians to more precisely targeted attacks against police, army personnel and government officials.[33] This was in fact a strategy likely to be more acceptable to ordinary people. More worryingly, videos which threatened attacks against the Olympic Games bore the obvious influence of Bin Laden, and the Turkestan Islamic Party which is thought to have made them is believed to have direct contact with al-Qaida. It should be remembered that the frontier with Pakistan lies just 300 miles south of Kashgar, and that with Afghanistan slightly less, a fact which could easily bring disaffected Uyghurs into contact with ample supplies of arms and manpower.

But economic development in the Muslim states of Turkestan, including the construction of roads, railways, airports and pipelines, had already to a certain extent defused potential separatist movements in China by spreading benefits throughout the western provinces. At the same time, China increased cooperation with non-terrorist Muslim organisations. Thus, in 2005, Ekmeleddin Ihsanoglu, the Secretary-General of the Organization of Islamic Conference, the only international body uniting Muslim countries which comprises fifty-six Muslim states (Iran and Afghanistan were founding members in 1969, while the Central Asian members joined after the collapse of the Soviet Union[34]) travelled to Beijing at the invitation of the Chinese government. It was an uncontroversial meeting, with the routine declarations about historical links between Islam and China. But the diplomatic niceties were followed up the next year by a resolution which 'calls on the Secretary General to give special attention to the conditions of Muslims in East Turkistan (Senkiang [Xinjiang]) in China and to examine the possibility of working out a formula for cooperation with the Chinese Government to evolve appropriate solutions for their difficulties and causes, and most particularly their civil and religious freedoms.'[35] At about the same time there was also a conference in Yinchuan, capital of the Ningxia Hui Autonomous Region, at which Chinese and Iranian Muslims discussed how to promote Sino-Iranian Islamic cooperation and collaboration. But these were perceived as occurring within China, with no hint of separatism or even greater autonomy.

Thus we should not confuse the issue of Uyghur separatism with Hizb ut-Tahrir and other Islamist organisations, or with the better integrated and peaceable Muslims who live in other regions of China. For the nine other Islamic communities are neither particularly interested in nor support the issue of separatism. Neither is there any political consensus or unity between the ten minority groups. Dru Gladney, *concluded* an article in its first paragraph when he asserted that 'the people known as Uyghur will most likely be in the same situation at the beginning of the next millennium as they have been for most of this one: an internally colonised people, subject to the Chinese nation-state.'[36]

Holy War in China in the Past

There was however one example of Islam as a catalyst for bringing together the competitive tribal leaders in the near vacuum between Iran in the west and China in the east, and between India in the south and Russia in the north, when for thirteen years in the nineteenth century a single Muslim state centred on Kashgar was created in what the title of one authoritative study called the *Holy War in China.*[37] The author, Kim Hodong, writes of its adherents that 'at least in its initial stage, they saw themselves as engaged in a movement designed to revitalise a living Islamic spirit that would return their land to the *Dār al-Islām* [Abode of Islam]'.[38]

The key figure was Ya'qub Beg, the son of a minor official in the Khanate of Khokand and probably of Tajik origins, who created a unified power from the many rebel groups. He himself was therefore a foreigner, having risen to military power in Khokand rather than within Greater China; as Charles Boulger expressed it in the preface to his 1878 biography, 'a soldier of fortune, who, without birth, power, or even any great amount of genius, constructed an independent rule on Central Asia, and maintained it against many adversaries during the space of twelve years.'[39] Yet, as Boulger himself later states, Ya'qub Beg was not without influential connections, since his sister married the governor of Tashkent.[40] Unloved by his subjects, he sounds in Boulger's near-contemporary description like a fascinating man:

> He had, during the vicissitudes of his career in Khokand, been so often near assassination, or execution, that the result of the morrow had, to all external appearance, become a matter of secondary consideration to him, and his features, schooled to immobility by a long career of court intrigue, appeared to the casual observer dull and uninteresting. When, however, the conversation turned on subjects that specially interested him, such as the advance of Russia, the future of Islam, or the policy of England, he threw aside his mask, and became at once a man whose views, with some merit in themselves, were rendered almost convincing by the singular charm of his voice and manner.[41]

This portrait also brings out his devotion, linking obvious *political* threats to his *religious* devotion. For above all, he was a sincere Muslim, who often declared his wish to go on pilgrimage to Mecca, although he was forced by circumstances to do so by proxy.

At a time when the Chinese state was weakened by the Taiping rebellion in the east, and other Muslim rebellions in Yunnan and Shanxi, Ya'qub Beg managed to carve out for himself the new state of Kashgaria, which comprised much of East Turkestan, with his capital in the city of Kashgar itself. It endured from 1865 until his death in 1877, soon after which the Qing re-conquered the entire area.

The most curious aspect about this 'holy war' is how it became holy. For, exactly as in Iran in 1978, a rag-bag of reasons and resentments including excessive taxes, Chinese rule, regional rivalries and the possibility of obtaining economic benefit, led to religion becoming the unifier of what was not initially a religious war. In Kim's words, 'in spite of all these internal conflicts, we can find one common feature shared by them all: the emergence of religious figures as the formal leaders of the rebellion.' Some of the leaders referred to themselves as holy warriors, and a rebel government in Urumqi was called the Kingdom of Islam (*Qingzhenquo*).[42] This may seem a long time ago, but the memories of both Chinese and Muslims are long, and the case of Ya'qub Beg set a precedent which is still referred to in conversations in Kashgar.

Uyghurs

It is commonplace to say that the Turkic-speaking Uyghurs, who the Chinese know as *Weiwu'er*, once formed the majority of the population of the modern Chinese province of Xinjiang (the capital Urumqi, so called since 1954, is known by the Chinese as Wulumuqi). But in the past they were much more powerful: for a hundred years from 744 to 840 the Uyghurs ruled over an empire based on Mongolia which dominated Central Asia and were a significant military ally to the Tang dynasty in Xi'an. They converted to Manichaeism in the middle of the eighth century, and were allied to the Sogdians in the west whose missionaries had converted them, so that their empire stretched as far as the Caspian Sea. Their capital was Karabalghasun (Ordu-Baliq), north of the Gobi desert about two hundred miles west of Ulan Bator.[43] This great walled city, sited on a northern extension of the Silk Road, was said by an Arab traveller who visited in 821 to have twelve huge iron gates, a royal castle, and busy markets peopled by artisans and merchants.[44] The Uyghur emperors of the time often married imperial Chinese princesses, and there was a sizeable community of Uyghurs and Uyghur-Sogdian merchants resident in the Tang capital of Xi'an, successful and wealthy men who married Chinese women and often adopted Chinese dress. At the apogee of their furthest extension, the Tang extended their sphere of influence as far as Persia itself. After defeating the western Turks in 657 at Issyk Kul (today in Kyrgyzstan), their allies the Uyghurs created protectorates and garrisons in Tashkent, Samarkand, Bokhara, Kabul, Herat and as far as Zarang in modern Iran.[45] For centuries, the main trade along the roads between these cities involved the exchange of Chinese silk for Uyghur horses, sometimes tens of thousands each year. In 773, for example, 6,000 horses were sold in Xi'an for forty pieces of silk each, silk then being used by the Uyghurs as a form of currency. They even developed a secondary business as money-lenders, a business which together with horse-trading continued after the demise of the Tang dynasty.[46]

As well as being trading partners and military allies in times of need, however, the Uyghurs engendered fear, frequently attacking Chinese cities. It was relatively easy for them, as a Tang minister, the perceptive Li Chiang, observed to his emperor in 814. Since the Uyghurs had been allies in the past, they knew the 'natural layout of the mountains and rivers, and which frontier defence is manned and which not.'[47] One example occurred at the Tang's eastern capital at Luoyang in 757. A contemporary chronicle informs us that it was only when the city 'bribed the elders with enormous quantities of silken fabric and embroidery' that the Uyghurs discontinued the pillage after three days.[48] Five years later, they were back again claiming what they thought of as just payment for their assistance in subduing rebels against the Tang. This time, thousands of people died, some who sought to escape by hiding in the towers of two temples. They burned to death when the Uyghurs set fire to the buildings; it was said that the fires lasted for 'several weeks'. The destruction was such that 'everybody was reduced to using paper for clothing, and there were even some who used the Chinese classics as clothes.'[49] There were similar, but minor, incidents in Taiyuan and Xi'an, where in 762 even Chinese chronicles admit of their own people that everyone was 'very afraid'.[50] But after this period of equal and sometimes superior strength the power of this Uyghur Empire gradually diminished and in 840 it was extinguished by the Kirghiz – fellow Turkic people. The survivors moved west, some to Gansu where they were known as Yellow Uyghurs, and some to Xinjiang where they founded the Uyghur kingdom of Gaochang (or Qocho).[51]

These Uyghurs turkicised the local language but absorbed local religious influences such as Buddhism and Manichaeism. They were centred on Gaochang, at that time a key hub on the Silk Road thirty miles east of the present town of Turpan, now fifty per cent Uyghur and a sleepy place producing grapes, wine and sultanas. The massive city walls and a ruined monastery can still be seen at Gaochang, while in the torrid summers the kings moved to a now-disappeared higher city called Bishbalik, or in Chinese Peiting (a variant of Beijing), 'northern capital'. But even in Gaochang, as in most cities of Islamic culture, there was an excellent irrigation system which enabled a plentiful food supply. Interestingly, according to an envoy from the Song court who visited the city in 982, in addition to around fifty Buddhist monasteries there was a Manichean temple, the

Temple of the Pearl, in which 'the priests are from Persia, they strictly observe their own rites and qualify the Buddhist books as *wai-tao* ('alien doctrine').'[52] The envoy, Wang Yang-Ti, also noted that it was a wealthy kingdom, with no 'destitute people', where inhabitants lived to old age and 'those who cannot provide for themselves are cared for by public welfare.'[53] This mostly forgotten kingdom, with its extraordinary mélange of languages, cultures and customs, and a key role in trade along the Silk Road, endured for four centuries until it became part of the Mongol kingdom in 1240.

The problem is that there is little real connection between that empire and the present-day Ughyurs: the most striking instance of this being the fact that the 'imperial' Ughyurs were not even Muslims, a feature which is today their most distinctive characteristic. They were a religious hodgepodge of Zoroastrians and Nestorian Christians, together with the Buddhists and Manicheans mentioned above. In fact, after the empire, Uyghurs settled in three regions: in the Tianshan Mountains, in the Turfan area of Xinjiang, and in Gansu. Only in the first and most western of these three regions were the Uyghurs early converts to Islam, in 934; later they made their capital in Kashgar, where even today in the sprawling Sunday market something may be found of the atmosphere of other traditional Muslim markets, like the Turcoman market at Pahlavi Dezh in northern Iran (now known as Aq Qal'eh) or that at Mazar-e Sharif in northern Afghanistan. The second group was also initially mainly Buddhist, with its capital in Turfan, and only converted to Islam in the fifteenth century under the Yarkand Khanate, which was of Turko-Mongol origins. The third group, the 'Yellow Uyghurs' became, and remain, Buddhist.

In effect, the Uyghurs were assimilated into other cultures, but not without some resistance. Conquered by Qianlong in 1759, the region of modern Xinjiang was in theory part of the Manchu Empire, but after dozens of minor revolts became in 1864 the independent kingdom of Kashgaria under Ya'qub Beg. It was recognised by both Britain and Russia, both of whom established diplomatic missions in Kashgar, as a key command post in the Great Game. The distinguished Sir Douglas Forsyth (1827–1886) of the Indian Civil Service was sent to survey the region and obtain detailed information about Ya'qub Beg in 1870 and 1873. He does not mention the Uyghurs in his very detailed description of Yarkund and Kashgar. He divided the population into two parts: first, the 'Mongolian or Tartar', which included the 'Manjhu, the Moghol or Mongol, the Kalmák, the Kirghiz, the Noghav, the Kapchak, and the Uzbak, together with the Kara Khitay, the Khitay, and the Tuirani, who are excluded from that category'; and, second, the 'Caucasian, which included the 'Tajik of Hindu Kush, represented by the Wakhi, Badakhshi, Shighni, &c., the Kasiimiri, the Kabuli, and the Punjabi, all of whom are included in the appellation Aryan, together with the Syad and the Arab, who are not so included.'[54] He only referred to the Uyghurs as an ancient people, the 'Hiungral or Uighur, the Hun of Hyatila or Attila's invading armies'. Forsyth also observed that 'time and circumstances have completely changed their personality, and now they differ but little in external appearance from their cousins, the heirs of the Saljuk conquest of Asia Minor and Byzantium, where, in the west as in the east, they have given their name to the country of their adoption; Turkey on the one side, and Turkistan on the other.'[55]

The Russian colonel (later a general and Minister of War) Aleksei Nikolaevich Kuropatkin (1848–1925), who was sent at the head of an embassy to survey Kashgaria in 1876, confirmed Forsyth's observations. He referred to 'Uighurs' only in the historical sense of the medieval empire,[56] and recalled that after the suppression of this empire by the Chinese in the ninth century these medieval Uyghurs were deported to their deserted western provinces. 'In course of time,' he wrote, 'these Uighurs embraced the Mussulman faith, lost, through intermarriage with Chinese damsels, their primitive type, and now but little resemble their kinsmen who remained in Kashgaria.'[57] But these too have changed. Kuropatkin writes of the contemporary inhabitants of Kashgaria, a total of 1.2 million in his estimate, as a Turkish speaking admixture of Mongol and Turk who occupy the oases in the region and 'have adopted for their tribal designations the names of these oases': hence, in his spelling, Kashgarians, Yarkendians, Khotanese, Aksutians, Koochayans and Toorfantians.[58] So their names are derived from locations rather than their ethnic origins.

In the same year as his visit, Kashgaria was formally annexed by China and Ya'qub Beg was defeated in battles at Turfan and Urumqi by a Chinese general, who gave the former independent state the name Xinjiang, meaning 'new territory'. It was always distant from coastal China, so much so that the first Governor of Xinjiang under the Republic of China, Yang Chen Xin (Governor, 1912–28) used to refer to the eighteen stages of the desert journey to Gansu as the 'eighteen ten thousands of loyal troops' which protected his dominions from the warlord conflicts and civil wars further east.[59] In fact it was only during the throes of revolution that Yang succeeded, in Lattimore's phrase, in 'effecting what was virtually a confirmation of the status quo'[60] and brought stability to the region with strong Chinese governance. That, in turn, led to memories of the ancient empire coming back into play. For after a conference held by Central Asian Turkic Muslims in Tashkent in 1921, and the first modern episodes of Muslim separatism, Muslims in search of a common denominator for their resurgent nationalism recovered the long extinct name Uyghur. Thus the modern Uyghur identity is less than a century old. Their problem, as one scholar has written, was and is 'how to formulate their newly formulated Uighur identity under the Chinese government's watchful eye.'[61] Two attempts were made in the following decades to set up an Uyghur Republic, in 1933 at Kashgar and in 1944 at Kulja (known to Uyghurs as the First and Second Revolutions); but an end to these attempts came with the establishment of the People's Republic of China in 1949. The creation of the new cultural identity was also a slow process, as can be seen in the fact that an Arabic script for the Uyghur language was only introduced as late as 1987 (previously it was written with Roman or Cyrillic scripts, the latter mainly in Kazahkstan). In the meantime, the majority of the population of Xinjiang had become ethnic Chinese.

Other things are changing. An increasing number of Chinese Muslims go on pilgrimage to Mecca, and are involved in major projects in the Middle East and Africa, especially since many of them speak Arabic. Chinese Muslims were vociferous in their condemnation of the 2003 American-led invasion of Iraq, and there were numerous protests – with government permission – in cities with a large Muslim population. Dru Gladwell commented soon afterwards that 'China's Muslim subalterns have clearly grown into a more prominent position in China's domestic and international relations.'[62] For local factionalism and even terrorism, or legitimate political protest, must now be set against the new geopolitical ambitions and energy needs of China. As the late Imam Shi Kunbing, of the oldest mosque in Beijing and not a Uyghur, argued, 'with so much now at stake in the Middle East, the government cannot risk antagonizing its Muslim minorities.'[63] To this end, the Chinese government has consciously sought for some time to curry favour with wealthy Muslim nations, such as Iran, by restoring the historic tombs of Arab and Persian ancestors of today's Chinese Muslims, with specific actions such as that in 1979 of declaring the eleventh-century Ashab Mosque in Quanzhou and the Lingshan Muslim tombs outside the city to be historic monuments.[64]

One key element of this new atmosphere has been the building and restoration of large numbers of mosques and Madrasah in China over the last two decades. In Beijing, for example, the historic Niuje Mosque has been restored and a massive, bright green domed Islamic training college has been built just down the road. Tens of thousands of Muslim children study the Koran and Islamic theology in their schools, both publicly- and privately-owned, and many continue advanced studies abroad in countries such as Iran, Pakistan, Saudi Arabia and Turkey, which each offer different religious and learning experiences. Interestingly, in terms of our hypothesis, in one detailed study based on extensive interviews it was found that 'students who studied in Iran were among the most satisfied, even though their studies and training proved to be more rigorous than that offered anywhere else' since they must study Persian as well as Arabic, and the Shi'a school of law in addition to the four classic Sunni schools of law (most Muslims in China follow the Hanafi school of law).[65] Clearly the double impact of these schools and the increasing openness of China in general means that Muslim communities even in the most remote areas belong to a powerful network whose ramifications are both national and international. The Chinese Muslim has never been so well-informed.

At the fringes, the opening of the frontiers in recent years is also creating a new sense of belonging to an extra-territorial community in which Islam is the unifying force. In the border town of Yining, for example, which is roughly fifty per cent Uyghur and fifty per cent Han (unlike Urumqi, eighty per cent Han, and Kashgar, ninety per cent Uyghur), which is part of a Kazakh autonomous area, one Western observer reports that 'many Chinese Kazakhs feel at least mildly positive about Chinese rule, and many described Han-Kazakh relations and Uyghur-Kazakh as both being generally good.'[66] Thus the Ughyurs, who number at least 200,000 in Kazakhstan, for ethnic, linguistic and religious reasons are the ideal intermediaries for the new cross-border trading with Turkestan's most important country – and ultimately for more developed relations with other countries in the region.

A Third Sino-Persian Anti-hegemony Partnership?

At some time in China's imminent development, when these tectonic tensions between the three new regional great powers, possibly with an expanded European Union presence in Turkey and last of all the wildcat energies of India and Pakistan, force dramatic initiative, when the Borromean Rings we have discussed break up or spin out of control, China will offer a closer alliance to Iran. Together, they will create a sphere of influence greater than any previous empire since the Mongols. This alliance is likely to evolve from pre-existing cooperation agreements as demand for oil begins to exceed supply and forces tighter relationships, sometime around 2020–2030, or possibly earlier as the result of a global supply war.

The first event which forced a reconsideration of Turkestan and its alliances from the Chinese point of view was the break-up of the Soviet Union. Perhaps the first country to capitalise on this was Turkey, whose then president Turgut Özal – who entered office in the same year as the collapse – sought alliances with the so-called 'external Turks' in Azerbaijan, Kazakhstan, Kyrgyzstan, Turkmenistan and Uzbekistan. The Turkish government provided loans and aid, encouraged the setting up of joint ventures in these countries with Turkish companies, and established new air routes to facilitate both commerce and cultural links. In an obvious attempt to create soft power, Turkish language teaching programmes were set up in the five countries, while students were sent to Turkey on scholarships for more specialised training.

The second event was the terrorist attack on New York in September 2001, for until then the American presence in Turkestan was pacific and mercantile in nature. Now, suddenly, it was perceived by the United States as a nursery of terrorism and required immediate attention. But American forces stationed even temporarily in countries so close to China's western frontier and strategic nuclear facilities as Afghanistan, Kyrgyzstan and Uzbekistan disturbed the Chinese. So did growing financial support and economic interest in the oil and gas reserves, and American sponsorship of new pipelines towards Turkey and Europe. This had been happening before, but saw a rapid acceleration with the 'war on terror', and led to misgivings on the part of China. It feared that later, after 'having gained a foothold in Central Asia and relying on its economic might, the United States would … through the injection of finance acquire the ability to influence the political and economic situation in this segment of post-Soviet space to its own advantage.'[67]

As far as Iran is concerned, the signs have been there since the same time. It has always looked on Afghanistan as a lost territory, and seemed happy to sit out the series of wars which have occurred since the coup d'état of 27 April 1978 and the Soviet invasion a year later, perhaps thinking that sooner or later the spoils will be there for the taking (I recall on being driven south through the Salang tunnel under the Hindu Kush a month before the coup how the Afghan driver constantly praised the Russians for building such a magnificent tunnel, not realising that soon they would drive tanks through it). President Ahmadinejad has been noticeably more cautious about pronouncements concerning countries to the east than about Western 'enemies' like Iraq and Israel, the latter of which is more or less the same distance as China from its frontier. Already in the mid-90s, the then President Rafsanjani spoke of the need for an alliance with China and India to create a powerful balance against the United States.

From the point of view of a Chinese oil company, the prospect is rosy. In 2005, the deputy managing director of a key subsidiary of NIOC stated that 'China and Iran are perfectly matched for each other',[68] moving towards a win-win situation in which the energy needs of the former match the foreign currency needs of the latter. Such sentiments might be read as a harbinger of the converging parallels coming together.

Notes

1. In Rasgotra (Ed), *The New Asian Power Dynamic*, p. 85.

2. Wayne, *China's War on Terrorism*, p. 9.

3. Gladney, *Muslim Chinese*, p. 20.

4. Gladney, *Ethnic Identity in China: The Making of a Muslim Minority Nationality*, p. 38.

5. Ibid., p. 5.

6. See the Glossary in Gladney, *Muslim Chinese*, pp. 395–421.

7. Lattimore writes of a Chinese proverb to the effect that 'Three Mohammedans are one; two Mohammedans are half a Mohammedan; one Mohammedan is no Mohammedan.' In other words, when there were no others around to see them they were happy enough to eat pork and drink alcohol (*The Desert Road to Turkestan*, p. 204).

8. Maris Boyd Gillette, *Between Mecca and Beijing: Modernization and Consumption Among Young Urban Chinese Muslims*, p. 25.

9. Interestingly *mujahideen* and *jihad* both derive from the same Arabic root. The notion

of achieving martyrdom – the promise of access to paradise as a reward for political assassination – through suicidal acts has a long history in Islam, dating at least to the rule of Hassan-i Sabbah, founder of the sect of the Assassins at Alamut. It is fascinating to note that he was born in 1060 in the holy city of Qom, notorious much later as Khomeini's base. The total obedience and loyalty of the Assassins were remarked on by several medieval European authors. See the account in my book *The Assassins: Holy Killers of Islam*, Wellingborough: Crucible, 1987, pp. 133–43.

10. *The 9/11 Commission Report: Final Report of the National Commission on Terrorist Attacks upon the United States*, Washington, DC: U.S. Government Printing Office, 2004, p. 55.

11. In an interview with Reuters, 21 April 2004.

12. For example Wayne, *China's War on Terrorism*, p. 51.

13. *Time*, 16 July 2004; http://www.time.com/time/nation/article/0,8599,664967,00.html; see also 9/11 Commission Report, p. 169 and p. 240.

14. *9/11 Commission Report*, p. 60.

15. See Bill Gertz, *Washington Times*, 10 June 2003.

16. Johnson, *Oil, Islam and Conflict*, p. 114.

17. See the excellent chapter on the IMU/IMT in Johnson, *Oil, Islam and Conflict*, pp. 114-137.

18. Johnson's phrase, because of his brigand-like activities and drug-dealing; *Oil, Islam and Conflict*, p. 120.

19. Johnson, *Oil, Islam and Conflict*, pp. 135.

20. From the official website at http://www.hizbuttahrir.org/.

21. Taqiyuddin An-Nabahani, *At-Takattul Al-Hizbi* (Party Structure), Hizb-ut-Tahrir Publications, 1953, available at http://www.hizbuttahrir.org/modules.php?op=modload&name=Sections&file=index&req=viewarticle&artid=7&page=1.

22. See the account in Johnson, *Oil, Islam and Conflict*, pp. 67–73.

23. Hitti, *History of the Arabs from the Earliest Times to the Present*, p. 140.

24. Ibid., pp. 157–8.

25. Ibid., p. 209. Ferghana was already known to the Chinese at this time for the fine stallions which arrived at the imperial court in the form of tribute.

26. Definition at the bottom of the web page http://www.hizb.org.uk/hizb/reports/.

27. Rashid, in *The Rise of Militant Islam in Central Asia.*

28. Johnson, *Oil, Islam and Conflict*, p. 77–78.

29. Gill, *Rising Star*, p. 129.

30. Wayne, *China's War on Terrorism*, p. 52.

31. Xinhua, 19 April 2007

32. 7 March 2008. For a factual report and example of news coverage, see http://aviation-safety.net/database/record.php?id=20080307-0 and http://www.nytimes.com/2008/03/10/world/asia/10terror.html?ref=world&pagewanted=all.

33. Professor Chu Shulong, from the Institute for International Strategic Studies at Tsinghua University, quoted in *Asia Times Online* (at http://www.atimes.com/atimes/China/JH15Ad01.html).

34. http://www.oic-oci.org/.
35. Paragraph 9 of Resolution No. 1/33-MM, *On Safeguarding the Rights of Muslim Communities and Minorities in Non-OIC Member States*, Baku, 19–21 June 2006 http://www.oic-oci.org/baku2006/english/33-icfm-mm-en.htm#RESOLUTION per cent20No. per cent201/33-MM.
36. Gladney, 'China's Indigenous Peoples and the Politics of Internal Colonialism', p. 1.
37. Kim Hodong's *Holy War in China: The Muslim Rebellion and State in Chinese Central Asia, 1864–1877*, Stanford: Stanford University Press, 2004.
38. Ibid., p. xvi.
39. Boulger, *The Life of Yakoob Beg; Athalik Ghazi, and Badaulet, Ameer of Kashgar*, p. vii.
40. Ibid., p. 77.
41. Ibid., p. 90.
42. Ibid., p. 181.
43. Soucek, *A History of Inner Asia*, p. 66–7.
44. See Minorsky, 'Tamim ibn Bahr's Journey', p. 268.
45. Ibid., p. 33.
46. Mackerras, *The Uighur Empire, According to the T'ang Dynastic Histories*, pp. 47–49; see the section on this strained relationship in his Introduction, pp. 14–36.
47. Hsin T'ang-shu, in Mackerras, *The Uighur Empire*, p. 111.
48. Ibid., p. 59.
49. Chiu T'ang-shu, in Mackerras, *The Uighur Empire*, p. 76.
50. Ibid., p. 70.
51. Soucek, *A History of Inner Asia*, p. 77.
52. Quoted from Soucek, *A History of Inner Asia*, p. 79.
53. Ibid.
54. Forsyth, T.D. (Ed), *Report of a Mission to Yarkund in 1873*, p. 80.
55. Ibid., p.83
56. Kuropatkin, *Kashgaria*, pp. 89–95.
57. Ibid., pp. 153–54.
58. Ibid., pp. 33–34. He repeats the same formulations on his brief section on Muslims in the region, pp. 153–4.
59. Lattimore, *Studies in Frontier History*, p. 191.
60. Ibid., p. 184.
61. Soucek, *A History*, p. 270.
62. Gladney, *Dislocating China: Muslims, Minorities, and Other Subaltern Subjects*, p. 314.
63. Quoted in Gladney, *Dislocating China*, p. 313.
64. Dru C. Gladney, 'Muslim Tombs and Ethnic Folklore: Charters for Hui Identity', *Journal of Asian Studies*, Vol 3 (August 1987), pp. 495–532, p. 498.
65. Jackie Armijo, 'Islamic Education in China', Harvard Asia Quarterly, Volume X, Number 1, Winter 2006, http://www.asiaquarterly.com/content/view/166/.
66. Perlin, 'Where Four World Meet', p. 24.
67. Vladimir Paramonov and Oleg Stolpovski, 'Chinese Security Interests in Central Asia',

Central Asian Series, Defence Academy of the United Kingdom, May 2008, pp. 8-9.
68. Ali Akhbar Vahidi Ale-Agha, Petroleum Engineering & Development, in an interview with *Fortune*, 'Iran Looks East', *Fortune*, 21 February 2005.

Part III

Scenarios 2030–2050

China evinces no interest in confronting the United States … Still, it is not hard to imagine a set of circumstances in which U.S. officials would see Chinese actions as threatening vital U.S. interests and act accordingly. Iran is the most immediate flashpoint in this regard…
Alterman & Garver, *Vital Triangle,* 2008

Chapter 8

Drivers of Future Alliances

The most successful scenarios are those which at first sight seem absurd, but which then provoke us to try to imagine the unimaginable and understand its real-life implications. In fact it is often only with hindsight that strange events and concomitances lose their apparent absurdity. The future is necessarily unknown and major changes are often driven by apparently unrelated events, or at least events which appear to be unrelated until future historians have the relatively easy task of illustrating their causes *a posteriori*. Reasoning from present causes to possible future effects is a far harder task, but essential for long-term planning in areas such as national infrastructure or an anti-missile defence shield which cannot be improvised or built up in a few years.

Let us begin by providing an example, recalling an event which changed the course of world history in ways that were quite literally unimaginable to those who observed its immediate consequences. It was in fact a rare instance in which hype about a single small event changing the world was more than justified.

Slightly less than a century ago, a war began that not only set Britain and Germany against each other, but brought in Russia, the United States and most European countries, and eventually led, to cite a few random consequences, to the acquisition of Qingdao in China by Japan, the fall of the Ottoman Empire, and the invention of Iraq – among many other new nations. What happened to bring about these cataclysmic changes? The Archduke Franz Ferdinand of Austria, semi-ostracised nephew and undesired heir to the Emperor Franz Joseph, was assassinated by the son of a Serbian village postman in a risibly inept attack: after an initial failed attempt the putative assassin had gone into a café for a sandwich, happened to see the Archduke's car pass by, and even then only managed to fire at him and his wife again because the car stalled just outside the café. Who could have imagined that morning that such an amateurish killing in a recently-annexed provincial town of the Austro-Hungarian Empire would lead to the deployment of Chinese troops in a war on French soil? It would have been too far-fetched for a plausible plot in fiction.

We have seen above how in Tehran in 1978 and Beijing in 1989 once again the unimaginable *suddenly* became reality, with dramatic consequences and global impact. For in both cases even the best intelligence services failed to see what was coming. Yet there is one surprising similarity between China and Muslim states, as Huntington controversially pointed out. He observed that over the period from 1928 to 1979 Muslim states resorted to violence in order to resolve international crises no fewer than 76 times out of 142, and that when they did so it was 'high-intensity violence'. The average of use of violence, in 53.5 per cent of the crises surveyed, compares with 17.9 per cent in cases involving the United States and 11.5 per cent in those involving Britain. Among the major powers, he observed, 'only China's violence propensity exceeded that of the Muslim states: it employed violence in 76.9 per cent of its crises.'[1] Unfortunately, there will be more international crises, and more violence, in the twenty-first century, since war may be interpreted as a natural condition of the State, which was itself 'organized to be an effective instrument of violence on behalf of the society.'[2] Both China and Iran achieved their present political form through war and violence, and both will play a key role in future conflicts in Turkestan either as combatants or as peacemakers.

In the next chapter, we will now look at five scenarios which could emerge from what might appear today an improbable alliance between China and Iran around 2030–2050, based on current forecasts for economic and social change over coming decades. But first we will consider the main drivers of change.

The scenarios and hypotheses below are based on the assumption that China will not disintegrate in the first half of the twenty-first century, that Tibet and Xinjiang will remain an integral part of the country under a modified form of autocratic government, and that Taiwan will not yet be a fully integrated part of the country as Hong Kong and Macao are (although special permits are still needed for Chinese citizens to visit those cities, and flights from Beijing are considered international, as is investment). They also fit within a general framework of ideas about the coming decades in expert sources, without however imitating them since many predictions and forecasts emanate from an essentially American world view which the two countries studied in this book explicitly repudiate. For example, a report on *Mapping the Future to 2020* prepared by the National Intelligence Council in the United States (i.e. the CIA) opened with a summary of what its contributors considered the 'relative certainties' and 'key uncertainties' concerning that date. The *certainties* relevant to our argument include the fact that globalisation will become less Westernised, that we will witness the rise of Asia and possible new 'economic middle-weights', that political Islam will remain a potent force, and that there will be what it describes as an 'arc of instability' spanning the Middle East,

Asia and Africa. The *uncertainties* include the degree to which Asian countries will set the new 'rules of the game', whether the rise of China and India will evolve smoothly, possible political instability in energy-producing countries, the impact of religiosity on states and the consequent potential for conflict, the growth of jihadist ideology, whether there will be more or fewer nuclear bombs, the possibility of precipitating events leading to the overthrow of regimes in the Middle East, Asia and Africa, competition for resources, and whether other countries will more openly challenge the United States. [3] These concerns *all* tally perfectly with the arguments above and with the scenarios we are about to propose. But *all* are viewed from a different angle in Beijing and Tehran.

But even these relative certainties could be obviously be disrupted by a totally unexpected event, such as a regional nuclear conflict arising over a dispute which is as yet unimaginable. And there are many other possible problems which will only be visible with hindsight, as the dramatically changed situation after the collapse of the Soviet Union and a new American presence in Turkestan evinced. China is increasingly driven to seek novel and often asymmetrical solutions to old problems, and to face entirely new problems like an oil (or gas) crisis or what it calls peripheral warfare. No one can be certain how the complex relationships within and around the area we have defined as Turkestan will pan out over the next century, but the drivers which might initiate change and lead to the creation of new alliances are becoming visible.

Main Drivers of Change

China and Iran, in different ways and for different reasons, both enjoyed extraordinary growth and change as they recovered from their respective centuries of humiliation over the past twenty-five years. Sustained by major manufacturing capacity and government infrastructure expenditure in the first case, and wealth generated from oil and gas in the second, their climb from third world to first world status is likely to continue over the next quarter of a century – to the dismay of their many detractors. They will experience even greater social change as still large numbers of poor and disadvantaged citizens come to enjoy a greater stake of national wealth, with some predictable and other unpredictable consequences. In order to prepare for the future scenarios, we will first look at four aspects of national development which will be the greatest drivers of change over that period: plans for continuing economic growth, the role of military power, population growth, and energy (drivers often used in future scenarios, such as environmental protection, human rights or water scarcity, are – alas – less likely to have an impact on the China-Iran relationship).

Plans for Economic Growth: China

In the midst of the difficult market conditions of 2008 and 2009, it might seem that China's high growth rate, averaging nine per cent annually since 1978, is likely to slow. But in the longer term there is no good reason to doubt continued expansion. The Nobel-prize winning economist Robert W. Fogel has estimated that in terms of purchasing power parity China's GDP, which in 2000 was $5 trillion compared to $10 trillion for the USA, will in 2040 be three times that of the USA ($123 trillion against $42 trillion).[4] He also sees annual growth in China maintaining an average of around 8.4 per cent until that time, compared with an average of 3.8 per cent for the United States.

In 2007, the Chinese government published a twenty-volume work compiled by nearly two hundred experts under the title *An Outline of Sustainable Development in China*, in which strategic objectives until 2050 were outlined. It confidently predicts such things as an increase in the average length of the formal education process (from 8.2 years today to 14 years) and the contribution of scientific development to the national economy (seventy-five per cent). It also predicts zero growth in the natural growth rate of the population by 2030; zero growth in the consumption rate of energy and resources by 2040; and zero growth in the degeneration rate of the environment by 2050. The same work asserts that Shanghai will reach the level of 'moderately developed countries' in 2015, Beijing in 2018, and thirteen other major cities before 2050.

If Fogel's prediction concerning the overtaking of the United States and the Chinese government's plans for achieving such ambitious objectives are both verified, one of the key issues will be China's relationship with its erstwhile sponsor and ex-superpower neighbour Russia. Indeed one brief study concluded that 'the most realistic scenario foreseeable is the gradual economic absorption by China of the Asiatic part of Russia',[5] which could have significant impact on the entire region of Turkestan. The real problem is that such a massive collision of interests would not be merely economic, but between two powers 'occupying important positions in the global system of international and economic relations and both possessing powerful nuclear missile-equipped armed forces.' Such change will necessitate the formation of new groupings and alliances of regional powers.

Plans for Economic Growth: Iran

In the past twenty years Iran has enjoyed moderate GDP growth, increasing to an average of nearly six per cent in the past few years. In 2007, according to American sources, GDP in Iran grew by 6.2 per cent, of which agriculture represented 10.4 per cent, industry 33 per cent and services 48.8 per cent. Per capita income was estimated as $12,300.[6]

One major problem is the excessive reliance on hydrocarbon products. According to the latest figures provided by the government of Iran, as much as 82.5 per cent of its exports consist of crude oil and gas.[7] Yet Iran also has vast mineral resources, and is ranked between fourth and ninth in the world in terms of production of zinc, lead, cobalt, aluminium, manganese and copper. These were discovered and mapped by the Geological Survey of Iran before the Revolution, but have not yet been fully exploited. Another problem is the over-staffed and inefficient public sector, which still controls most of the economy in spite of an aim to privatise eighty per cent of state-owned enterprises in the current Five-Year Plan (2004-2009).[8] In fact this so-called privatisation is a semi-privatisation, in the sense that the government leases the state-owned enterprise and receives an annual rent while retaining ownership.[9]

Iran badly needs foreign investment and non oil-related industrial development. These are two areas in which China has vast experience. In fact one sector in which Chinese companies have been successful in Iran, apart from the oil and gas industries, is the car industry. In February 2003, the Chinese car company Chery Automobile, which was only founded in 1997, signed an agreement with a component manufacturer, Sanabad Khodro Tus, to produce Chery cars in Iran, initially aiming at 30,000 cars a year but gradually raising production to 50,000. In the following year, Geely Automobile announced plans to produce 30,000 cars a year in Iran. Then, in 2007, Chery entered into a further joint-venture with Iran Khodro, the largest car manufacturer in Iran and maker of the *Paykan* and its successor the *Samand*. In this venture, Chery has a thirty per cent stake, while Iran Khodro has forty-nine per cent and a small and rather obscure Canadian company called Solitac has twenty-one per cent (although Solitac is Canadian, its president Hossein Bavafa was born in Tehran and seems to have brokered the deal).[10] The new company will set up a $370-million plant in Babol in northern Iran to produce 200,000 models a year of the small and cheap Chery QQ, which is popular with young first-time buyers in China.[11] In Iran, its is known as the MVM 110, and is assembled as a 'Complete Knock Down', or kit, by Khodro's subsidiary Modiran Vehicle Manufacturing Company, whose website is entirely devoted to the model.[12] This is ironic because from 2000 to 2002, when Daewoo was acquired by GM, the Modiran plant was used to assemble the Matiz, after which sanctions made it impossible to export the kits to Iran. In fact the car became the subject of a lawsuit over patent infringement when General Motors claimed it was a copy of the Chevrolet Spark/Daewoo Matiz – a fact that can only make it more attractive to the market in Iran by cocking a snook at its nemesis. It is a tiny but fascinating example of the success of the anti-hegemonic alliance.

There was in the Five-Year Plan a strong focus on completing and improving existing infrastructure of airports and railways - and of course improved roads for the new cars. The emphasis is on a 'Proactive Interaction with the Global Economy', as one chapter title has it, with more than a fashionable nod towards 'knowledge-based development' and the corresponding reinforcement of knowledge transfer, intellectual property protection, and improvements in the educational system.[13] While there is an entire section in the *Plan* devoted to spiritual values and the 'preservation of the Islamic-Iranian identity', and seventeen specific ways to preserve and develop them (Article 106), there is a strong emphasis on economic and technological development by the always pragmatic leadership which might surprise a Western reader. In fact, in a key document concerning Iran's medium-term future, the *20-Year Perspective* published in 2004 (and later renamed *20-Year Vision*), there was the declared ambition to make Iran the leading regional power in terms of economic, scientific, and technological capabilities.

It is in the extreme pragmatism of leaders like Rafsanjani, and the need to resolve pressing problems of industrial development, housing and unemployment, that Iran will eventually find the raison d'être for a closer relationship with China.

Military Power: China

Given the expected sustained economic growth and desire to regain what it considers its rightful place in the world order, it is evident that China will continue to invest heavily in its military forces. For both the role of the PLA and foreign policy are changing rapidly with the new geopolitical circumstances.

One index of these changes is the well-informed *Annual Report* on the military situation in China which is prepared for the Congress of the United States. In the 2005 *Report*, the PLA was said to be 'emphasizing preparations to fight and win short-duration, high-intensity conflicts along China's periphery.'[14] This, translated, of course meant Taiwan, together with minor and limited conflicts concerning border disputes – with India, for example. But just two years later the tone had been raised and the emphasis switched, with the PLA said in the 2007 *Report* to be 'pursuing comprehensive transformation from a mass army designed for protracted wars of attrition on its territory to one capable of fighting and winning short-duration, high intensity conflicts against high-tech adversaries.'[15] This, translated, meant the United States in its local, or Pacific Ocean, ramifications in bases such as Okinawa in Japan, temporary airfields in Turkestan, or aircraft carriers standing offshore in the East China Sea. Ominously, in the 2008 *Report*, we read that 'China's expanding and improving military capabilities are changing East Asian military balances; improvements in China's strategic capabilities have implications beyond the Asia-Pacific region.'[16] This would seem to indicate Turkestan and the Middle East, or perhaps the Strait of Malacca, and represents a significant modification of policy in just three years.

In fact, since leading military planners realised how vulnerable China would be in a modern war after the collapse of Iraq during the 1991 Gulf War and the 1998 Desert Fox operation in Iraq, the PLA has been rapidly updating and modernising for air and sea warfare. For a country whose traditional power has been land-based, this required a major shift in thinking, and being China this thinking was articulated in a long-term plan. According to a government White Paper on defence, China's development and modernisation strategy for the PLA is articulated in three steps: first, 'to lay a solid foundation by 2010'; second, 'to make major progress around 2020'; and third, to 'reach the strategic goal of building informationised armed forces and being capable of winning informationised wars by the mid-21st century.'[17] While these intentions have led to a focus on air and sea forces, land warfare is not being forgotten. There is at present a programme to build 6,000 armoured vehicles including a 'very advanced armoured package' of T99 tanks and an eight-wheeled vehicle armed with a 100mm gun, 30mm canon and 7.62mm machine gun.[18]

Although the PLA is unlikely to be a threat far beyond its own territory for some time, that may not be the case in the period from 2030 to 2050. Long before that time, probably within a few years, oil and gas from the Middle East will account for over eighty per cent of total energy imports, so that the much-feared American hegemony in the Persian Gulf and Indian Ocean will be an ever-greater threat. Hence the pressing need, in China's view, to develop a fully operational and professional blue-water navy.

One essential tool for such a navy would be aircraft carriers. Here, given the secrecy of Chinese military planning, there is some uncertainty. In the 2008 *Report to Congress* it was suggested that some experts believe a carrier is already under construction, that certainly a research programme exists, and that if 'the leadership were to so choose, the PRC shipbuilding industry could start construction of an indigenous platform by the end of this decade.'[19] Later in the same year, military analysts at a conference in London asserted that within the next year the first navy pilots will begin training for aircraft carrier operations and are expected to be operational early in the next decade. It also seems that new refuelling planes now being delivered will double the range of the Chinese fighter aircraft. Such innovations will obviously make operations far from the mainland much more straightforward and pave the way towards a truly global force, especially when linked to the intelligence that China is developing an advanced fighter called the J-XX that could be as good as American planes.[20]

At present, the PLA Navy fleet comprises over twenty destroyers, over forty frigates, and between sixty and seventy attack submarines, including four Han-class nuclear-powered vessels and three new nuclear models currently being delivered. New models are in the pipeline. This makes China's submarine fleet the most important in the world in terms of quantity, and it is already a key player in the waters surrounding Taiwan and Japan.[21] The most recent submarines are equipped with both land-attack and anti-ship cruise missiles. In addition, there are more than forty medium and heavy amphibious transport ships, and around fifty coastal missile patrol craft. Although Chinese ships already venture into the open ocean – or blue water, as the specialists call it – the development of the

PLA Navy is still at present envisaged in terms of dominating coastal territorial waters up to 200 nautical miles and assisting in intelligence gathering, rather than attacking targets further away. For the imminent future, its main focus is likely to remain Taiwan. Yet some experts believe that by around 2020 China will be able to focus on 'the greater periphery', meaning the Strait of Malacca, the Indian Ocean, and the Persian Gulf.[22] That will require both a more extensive blue-water fleet, and investment in naval bases well beyond the Chinese coast. But it may not be necessary to sail too far: by 2015 China is expected to have six Jin-class submarines capable of firing the JL2 ballistic nuclear missile that could threaten both the western and eastern American seaboards.[23] In any case, further into the future, when the Taiwan issue is resolved, probably within the first half of this century, and energy issues come to dominate the PLA's military strategy, such investments will be feasible.

The first of the deep-sea ports is currently under construction at Gwadar, on the Gulf of Oman in western Pakistan, located less than fifty miles from the border with Iran and 250 miles from the Strait of Hormuz. It is perfect example of the way in which China can be moved to act rapidly in retaliation to US initiatives – often in a surreptitious way below the radar of the Western press. Hence when American forces invaded Afghanistan and entered into military action not far from the Chinese border, a project long in gestation was accelerated and the port complex was inaugurated by Wu Bangguo, who entered the Politburo in that year, on 22 March 2002. In fact, China demanded 'sovereign guarantees' to use the new port in retaliation for Pakistan having allowed the United States the use of Jacobabad and Pasni airbases (in Sind and Baluchistan respectively) during the Afghanistan invasion, and permitting posts near to the borders with Xinjiang and Tibet.[24] Following Chinese practice, Gwadar has been granted the status of a special economic zone (SEZ) and describes itself as the 'first free port city of the new millennium', seeing itself as a trading hub between Central Asia and the Gulf states, in particular Dubai. As its official website puts it, 'Gwadar is now destined to be the most important upcoming coastal town located on the junction of the three most strategically and economically important regions of the world that are oil rich Middle East, South Asia where one-fifth of world population lives and the Central Asian Republics'[25] (see Map 5).

This new project also offers a foretaste of how the alliance we are postulating could develop, given Gwadar's strategic position as a maritime pivot of Turkestan - as we saw in Chapter 1. Indeed some Indian newspapers, with a fine knowledge of British history, refer to it as 'a Chinese Gibraltar'.[26] Certainly it brings together four powerful nations, including China and Iran, and a leading regional bank, in a project that was unimaginable just a few years ago. Managed by the Port of Singapore Authority, the first phase of $250 million, which began in 2001, was roughly eighty per cent financed by China, and when the second phase is completed in 2010 Gwadar will become a key regional and international port.

There will be twelve large berths, suitable for warships and submarines as well as merchant vessels, ample warehousing space, and trans-shipment and trade facilities. It will be ideally situated to stimulate trade between the Persian Gulf, Iran, Pakistan and China, and in addition will be the closest major sea-port for nearly all the countries of Turkestan. To encourage this latter function, the Asian Development Bank will provide up to $1 billion for a national trade corridor (NTC) which 'will connect Karachi Port and the upcoming deep sea port of Gwadar through improved road networks in Balochistan and NWFP [ie north-west frontier province] to Afghanistan and Central Asia.'[27] In other words, it will link Gwadar by road to the Karakorum Highway, and thence to China as well as Afghanistan and Central Asia (in 2007, China and Pakistan also held feasibility talks on a future railway link parallel to the highway). To complete the picture, electricity for the massive project and its industrial infrastructure will be supplied by Iran, which will bear about one third of the cost of the initial investment, and provide the service from one power station located in Pakistan and one inside Iran itself. In fact, on a large-scale map Gwadar can be seen as the lowest point of an inverted equilateral triangle whose other points are Tehran and the Pakistan-China frontier.

Gwadar is at present the furthest of the so-called 'string of pearls' that China has been laying from its own coast through the sea-lanes of the East – which is itself no more than a variant on the use of strategic harbours for the extension of naval power by maritime nations like Britain, for example in Aden, or remote island bases like Diego Garcia in the Indian Ocean, used for American air strikes against both Iraq and Afghanistan. There are projects, in various stages of completion, for a container port and naval base at Chittagong in Bangladesh, and radar systems and refuelling bases at Sittwe, Coco, Hianggyi, Khaukphyu, Mergui and Zadetkyi Kyun in Myanmar. The most recent project is a contract signed in 2007 to develop a port at Hambantota on the southern tip of Sri Lanka (where China is currently financing new railway building). With increased blue-water capacity, the PLA navy will soon be capable of protecting and supplying the key sea-routes in the national energy supply chain, from the Gulf of Oman past Sri Lanka and through the Strait of Malacca to the home waters of the South China Sea - or from Sri Lanka straight up the Bay of Bengal to Rangoon, and the overland route by road or pipeline. This would require acceptance by India, with vastly superior forces available in the region. One naval expert has suggested that the PLA Navy could implement a more simple and less expensive strategy based on a Soviet policy in the 1970s and 1980s, which 'stationed a repair ship and a two-four ship task group at distant locations, such as Socotra, in the mouth of the Gulf of Aden.'[28]

This prompts one obvious question: how long will it be before China finances, leases or otherwise obtains its own port in Iran, inside the Strait of Hormuz, for example, on Qeshm Island or near Bandar Abbas, and thus extends its string of pearls into the Persian Gulf? Such a base might soon become a necessity, since the port at Gwadar is built on a small peninsula linked the mainland by a narrow strip which would be hard to defend against superior naval forces in the area – either from cruise missile attacks or from strikes launched from aircraft carriers. Thus its strategic value is limited unless, or until, the PLA 'manages to amass enough military power in its vicinity to defend it against nearby U.S. forces.'[29] One of the scenarios at the end of this book considers just such a possibility in the medium-term future.

In a table reviewing the past and future of China's primary alliance patterns and military strategy, Michael L. Levin of the Thunderbird School of Global Management summarised the situation in the years 2015–2020 as follows:

- Primary threat perception: U.S.
- Primary alliance pattern: Regional hegemon
- Military strategy: Strong-state strategy/ Blue-water fleet
- Internal events: Reunification with Taiwan?
- External events: Korean unification?/ Nuclear Japan?/More assertive India[30]

But Levin is arguing for a future threat from China and *Russia* acting together against the United States, while it would be difficult to imagine from the American point of view a more challenging threat than that of her historical (in the sense of communist) and current nemeses conjoined.

The threat is intensified by China's growing expertise in technological warfare, which harnessed to the loyalty and fanaticism of an elite unit of the Iranian Revolutionary Guard Corps like the 'Qods', of whom more later, would be disturbing beyond anything Osama Bin Laden could imagine.

Take the most advanced forms of cyber warfare, for example. China's growing expertise in computer technology and its ability to manipulate and exploit the Internet would already make it relatively easy to disable much of the Western world's technological infrastructure. In 2007 there were several incidents assumed to have been caused by Chinese government hackers in US government offices, military suppliers and think-tanks, in one case entering computers in the office of Defence Secretary Robert Gates in the Pentagon. Although such attempts are probably common on both sides, the Pentagon attack caused particular concern because it suggested that the PLA could disrupt American military systems at will. In the words of one official, it showed that they had the ability 'to conduct attacks that disable our system … and the ability in a conflict situation to re-enter and disrupt on a very large scale.'[31] Other reports spoke of detailed plans to disable America's aircraft carriers – obviously useful in the case of a strike against Taiwan – and of a detailed plan to achieve 'electronic dominance' over rivals such as the United States, Britain, Russia and South Korea by 2050.[32] That year, incidentally, has often been cited by President Hu Jintao as the year by which Taiwan re-enters the fold.

Then there is the spectre of electro-magnetic pulse (EMP) attacks. China is capable of delivering such an attack from an intercontinental ballistic missile, a submarine-launched ballistic missile, a long-range cruise missile, or an orbiting satellite armed with a nuclear or non-nuclear EMP warhead. American sources suggest the possibility of an electro-magnetic pulse attack against Taiwan. The fascinating if disturbing hypothesis is that of using a nuclear burst to generate a high-altitude electromagnetic pulse (HEMP). This would cause a change in the ionisation of the upper atmosphere, and lead to 'the degradation of important war fighting capabilities, such as key communication links, radar transmissions, and the full spectrum of electro-optic sensors.'[33] The attraction of this for China is that such an action might not be considered by the international community to be an all-out nuclear attack; thus Taiwan could effectively be disabled without the fear of nuclear retaliation. The problem is that the effects of such an action might also have an impact on Japan, the Philippines, commercial shipping and air routes, and even the Chinese mainland itself. Worse still, a single nuclear burst of one or more megatons four kilometres over one of the central states like Nebraska or Kansas could cover the entire continent with electro-magnetic pulses in less than a second. This would damage electrical grids, and immediately disable computers and all other devices containing microchips; the economy would grind to a halt as entire industries and all services shut down. One hesitates to think what Iran might do with such technology.

At present China has limited ability to project and sustain power at a distance, and faces what has been described as an 'ambition-capability gap', in terms of being able to 'secure its foreign energy investments' and 'defend critical sea lanes against disruption'. But the pace of development and level of expenditure suggest that this might not be the case for long. The latest *Report to Congress* on China's military power, published in the summer of 2008, argues that 'China's leaders may seek to close this gap by developing: extended-range power projection, including aircraft carrier development; expeditionary warfare; undersea warfare; anti-air warfare; long-range precision strike; maritime C4ISR; expeditionary logistics and forward basing; training and exercises, especially in open water; and a more activist military presence abroad.'[34] In other words, China is preparing to extend its 'defence' system far beyond its frontiers, and the main reason is to secure future energy supplies. The problem here is the PLA's definition of 'defence', since actions which other nations might define as an attack are often referred to as 'self-defence counter-attacks', such as those against India in 1962 and Vietnam in 1979. For one of their training manuals, the *Science of Campaigns*, asserts that 'the essence of [active defence] is to take the initiative and to annihilate the enemy … While strategically the guideline is active defence, [in military campaigns] the emphasis is placed on taking the initiative in active offence. Only in this way can the strategic objective of active defence be realized.'[35] Or, to express the same concept in simpler form: to defend means to attack. It does not require too great a leap of the imagination to foresee in a moment of crisis a future need to 'defend' oil supplies which would lead to a pre-emptive attack designed to 'annihilate' a country in Turkestan.

Some of the technologies discussed above are already within China's military capabilities; new and more advanced weapons and systems will soon be available. The real question is: what would it take for China to deploy such resources in ernest?

Military Power: Iran

One of the Middle East's most sophisticated military forces found itself in disarray after the Revolution in 1979, and the extenuating war with Iraq from 1980 to 1988, with many weapons – including advanced aircraft such as the F-14 fighter – of American origin for which spare parts and replacements were longer available as the result of embargoes and sanctions.

Since then, the Islamic Republic has again built up substantial forces, and now also produces its own equipment such as tanks, guided missiles, submarines and fighter aircraft. In 2007, military manpower in Iran was thought to number around 545,000 men, divided into two separate but overlapping command structures: the Islamic Republic of Iran Army and the Iranian Revolutionary Guard Corps (IRGC), the latter of which accounts for about one third of total personnel. The main body of the army is considered to be neither well-enough trained nor equipped to be a concern for high-tech and highly-trained forces like those of the United States or even powerful neighbours such as Pakistan and Turkey. It is likely however that it would be adequate against the armed forces of weaker neighbours such as Afghanistan, Azerbaijan and Turkmenistan. The IRGC, on the other hand, has specialised and elite troops. Both these forces have their own navy and air force.

According to American intelligence in the summer of 2008, the conventional land forces possess 1,693 tanks and 150 I-Hawk Surface-to-Air Missiles.[36] The air force has 280 combat aircraft, including twenty-five MIG 29s and thirty Su-24s, and also has anti-aircraft missile systems purchased from Ukraine and Russia, the most recent deriving from an agreement in December 2007 by which Russia will supply its advanced SA-20 air defence system, based on the American Patriot system. The navy is equipped with 200 ships, including ten Chinese-made Hudong fast missile-carrying boats equipped with HY-2 Silkworm missiles based at Larak Island and at Kuhestak on the Strait of Hormuz. It also has several other anti-ship cruise missiles which could be used in the same area. In addition, the navy has three frigates, and C-14 China Cat Class fast attack missile craft equipped with anti-ship missiles. It has also purchased three Russian-made 'Kilo' class submarines which are extremely quiet and can easily pass unnoticed in such a heavily used stretch of water as the Gulf. The latest version is 'considered to be to be one of the quietest diesel submarines in the world ... capable of detecting an enemy submarine at a range three to four times greater than it can be detected itself.'[37] Iran also owns some midget submarines, supplied by North Korea, and in late 2007 claimed to have produced its own small sub equipped with sonar-evading technology. It also has Chinese-made mines which could be tethered to the bottom of the Persian Gulf to reinforce a possible blockade.

The main function of the IRGC is to guarantee national security, which includes border security and duties usually carried out by law-enforcement agencies. But it is also responsible for the country's missile forces and comprises an elite unit of the IRGC known as the 'Qods' (*Niru e Qods* or 'Jerusalem Force'). This unit consists of an unknown number of specialised operatives anywhere between a few thousand and over 15,000 men who operate mainly outside Iran – and are thought to have been active in Afghanistan, Bosnia, Iraq and Lebanon. They engage in intelligence operations as well as providing financial support, training and weapons for other forces. In late 2008 they were thought to be using three main bases, two in the Kenesht Valley near Kermanshah for Iraqis affiliated to Qods, and one at Varamin, near Tehran, where more Iraqis have been trained in bomb-making and the use of rocket-propelled grenades, Russian-made Katyusha rockets and surface-to-surface and surface-to-air missiles.[38]

It is the role of the Qods which is most worrying for the Western powers, especially in Afghanistan, for this force can carry out a dual function of reinforcing the traditional position of Iran in a once-time province in which its own language is widely spoken, and at the same time deliver a blow to American hegemony by undermining its operations there. In fact a terrorism report prepared for the US State Department in 2007 accused the Qods of supplying ammunition and rockets to the Taliban and other militants in Afghanistan. Officers from NATO have on several occasions intercepted shipments of heavy weapons, explosives and so-called EFPs (explosively forced projectiles, or advanced roadside bombs) to terrorists in Afghanistan.[39]

In addition to these regular forces, there are the ten million or so *basiji*, members of the Basij religious militia which is directly under the command of the Revolutionary Guards. In peacetime, this forces acts as a paramilitary bulwark to revolutionary values by enforcing dress codes and moral behaviour throughout the country. But they also represent a dangerous and potentially devastating weapon in the event of future conflicts, as they were in Iraq. At a moment of rising tension between Iran and the United States in October 2007, Brigadier General Ali Fahdavi, deputy commander of the Revolutionary Guards' Navy, referred to the possibility of launching suicide attacks in the Straits of Hormuz by 'martyrdom-seeking' militia, meaning *basiji*. Fahdavi asserted in an interview at that time that they would be capable of disrupting oil flows through the Persian Gulf. Referring to their possible suicide attacks, he said that the key to the *basiji* threat lay not in their numbers but in the 'quality of their presence because each one of them can carry out big actions.'[40] Indeed small numbers of suicide bombers could wreak havoc in such a small area. Patrol boats are quite sufficient for operations in the Strait of Hormuz, usually placid and so narrow that the coast of Iran can be clearly seen from Oman – the distance is roughly the same as that from Dover to Calais, with fewer clouds.

There are also well-known, and much more sinister, weapons in Iran's contemporary arsenal. The United States remains convinced that 'Iran has conducted a clandestine uranium enrichment program for nearly two decades in violation of its International Atomic Energy Agency (IAEA)', and that although it 'probably has not yet [i.e. in 2006] produced or acquired the fissile material (weapons-grade nuclear fuel) needed to produce a nuclear weapon' it would be able to build home-made nuclear weapons 'sometime between the beginning of the next decade and the middle of the next decade'. Worse still, it was already believed in 2006 to have an offensive chemical weapons research and development capability for an offensive biological weapons program.[41] Even this cautious report suggests that Iran may be in a position to have a nuclear weapon by around 2015 – which is not so far off. If in the next ten to fifteen years it also achieves the objective of integrating these weapons with the ballistic missiles which it already possesses, this means that within our timeframe of 2030–2050 Iran could be a fully-fledged nuclear power of frightening potential.

In this, the Islamic Republic appears to follow the logic of the Shah. In fact one study found that Iran's leaders since 1979 have pursued nuclear weapons for the same basic strategic reasons that he built up conventional forces, especially the air force: to deter and, if deterrence fails, to defeat regional adversaries; to establish a regional leadership position in the Middle East; and to forestall intervention in Iranian or Middle Eastern affairs by a global superpower.[42] Dr Akbar Etemad, nuclear adviser to the Shah, claims that in the second half of the 1970s he was not interested in making nuclear bombs as he believed that his country's conventional army was already the most powerful in the region. However, Etemad also believes that if the Shah were still in power today, then 'he would have developed nuclear weapons because now Pakistan, India and Israel all have them.' He further argues that 'the way the west is isolating Iran leaves it no choice but to build nuclear weapons. Iran has nothing to lose and nothing to fear from sanctions any more. When Israel threatens to attack Iran, it dares to do so because it has nuclear weapons and Iran does not. The Iranian government may now see them as the only way they can defend themselves.' Dr Etemad adds with an assertion that is common amongst his countrymen today and echoes the sentiments of Dear Uncle: 'I, as an Iranian, feel insulted when countries talk about attacking Iran militarily. A military attack would not weaken the Iranian government, and it could not stop the nuclear programme.'[43] Such an attack, he believes, would only start a new regional crisis without a foreseeable end.

Then there are the other weapons, perhaps more terrifying. In terms of chemical weapons, American intelligence believes that Iran may possess stockpiles of blister, blood, choking and nerve agents, and also the artillery shells needed to deliver them. Moreover, although it possesses a limited capacity to 'weaponise' biological agents, this will also change in the next decade or so. Already in 2006, its Shahab-3 missile was capable of delivering conventional, chemical, biological or even nuclear warheads as far west as Israel and South-Eastern Europe; with the Shahab-4 this range will be extended to cover Germany, Italy and Moscow.[44] Yet in these estimates and conclusions, there is the usual emphasis on Iraq, Hezbollah and Israel, while it is already possible for Iran to strike American forces anywhere within Turkestan and the Middle East – currently in Afghanistan, Bahrain, Iraq, Kuwait, Kyrgyzstan, Oman, Pakistan, Qatar, Saudi Arabia, and the United Arab Emirates.[45] Longer term, the strategic implications of Iran's growing strength are more disturbing, especially if considered as an extension of China's military reach. In 2006, for example, Iran is believed to have received from North Korea a shipment of BM-25 missiles, based on an earlier Soviet missile and capable of carrying nuclear warheads. In fact, it is an ideal weapon for clandestine shipping; designed originally to be launched from a submarine, it can be transported in an ordinary shipping container. American analysts believe that Iran could develop an intercontinental ballistic missile (ICBM) with a range of up to 3,000 miles by 2015. Early in 2008 Iran claimed to have launched a probe into space, which suggests the ICBM might be much closer.[46] Certainly, like China, it will spare neither effort nor expense in order to enhance its role as a regional powerhouse.

One of the key points of Article 121 of the Five-Year-Plan states that the government should 'secure presence and deployment corresponding with the threats in the country's marine areas (the Persian Gulf, Oman Sea and Caspian Sea).' For Iran is well aware that its future wealth and security depend on defence of its oil and gas deposits, with an emphasis on maritime defence.

Population Growth

Global population is expected to grow from the present 6.5 billion to around 9.4 billion by 2050, with China's figure growing modestly from 1.3 billion to around 1.42 billion, and Iran more substantially from the current 70 million to around 82 million over the same period (compared with the 33 million or so during the Shah's last years of power).[47] That will make Iran, which already has the largest population in the Middle East, the twenty-first most populous country in the world, with India by then the first with 1.8 billion people.

In fact, each country has one interesting, and distinct feature. In Iran, there will be a predominance of youth and young adults, given a predicted twenty-five per cent increase in the population. Already in the 2000 political elections, as many as sixty per cent of the electorate was under the age of twenty-five, enough to suggest to one observer that this would bring about the 'end of Islamic ideology'[48] since these young people – just like their contemporaries in China – were quite uninterested in ideology and religion, and more inclined to worship football, fashion and music. One of the main social problems in Iran now and at least for the immediate future is youth unemployment.

From the early 1980s to 2001, the population growth rate declined from 3.7 percent to 1.4 percent, and in the same period the fertility rate fell from 6.8 to 2.6. Nonetheless, because of high rates in the 1980s, the labour force is still growing at close to four percent a year and approximately 700,000 additional new entrants join the job market every year.[49] In 2007 there was a slight increase in the growth rate, to 1.6 per cent, but the real problem is that nearly three-quarters of the inhabitants of Iran are less than thirty years old – which means nearly twenty million ambitious and often unsatisfied young males. This is a crucial fact according to the theories of the German academic Gunnar Heinsohn based on the concept of 'youth bulge'. For he argues that when over thirty per cent of the male population is aged between fifteen and twenty-nine there is a good chance that violence will follow, since this is what he calls the 'fighting age'. Heinsohn provides recent examples from Afghanistan and Palestine, and indeed Iran in 1978 was previously in the same situation. He calculates that there are currently sixty-seven countries in the world with this fighting-age bulge, and finds that in sixty of them there is indeed a high level of some form of violence, which might be expressed in war, terrorism, civil rebellion or criminal actions.[50] Compare, for example, the average age of males in Afghanistan and Iraq in 2006 (17.6 and 19.6 respectively), with those of the United States (35.1) and the antithesis of a warlike state like the Netherlands (38.9). In the two countries which interest us here, China and Iran, the average age of males in China in 2008 is 33.1, just beyond fighting age, while in 2006 in Iran it was 26, just below.[51] According to the latest Census, carried out in 2007 (the year 1385 in the Persian calendar), 25.1 per cent of the population is under fifteen years old.[52]

Heinsohn provides some interesting historical data concerning the number of males per thousand of fighting age. To illustrate our argument, here are a few examples extracted from his tables:

	Europe/USA	Islam
1914	350	95
2005	130	270
2020	120	290

In other words, the fact that there were so many males available in European and American families in 1914, often two or more from a single family, meant that they were quite literally superfluous, or expendable, without diminishing the long-term population. Although this sounds callous, it actually meant that in population terms Europe and America could *afford* a war, and was able to sustain the losses of such a massive conflict. In fact an interesting part of his argument concerns what he calls 'superfluous but well-brought up sons', who were in fact the classic second and third sons of the British upper and middle classes who learned their lessons on the 'playing fields of Eton' and similar schools. Given the absence of an estate for second sons and beyond in a society of primogeniture, or simply lack of land, they went off to war or to make their fortunes far from home. If necessary they were expendable in the cause of empire, although many prospered. In the eleventh century, second sons of the Norman nobility went to conquer southern Italy (King Roger I of Sicily was one of twelve sons); in seventeenth century Spain they were known more precisely as *secundones*; in the nineteenth century, 'superfluous' young men built the British Empire. Now and in future decades, it will be the Muslim countries which uniquely offer up *secundones* as martyrs to the cause of Islam, or, to paraphrase the expression of Gilles Keppel quoted above, to the much greater conflicts 'crystallised' in Islam. For according to Heinsohn's statistics, nearly one third of Muslim males will be of fighting age by 2020. In Iran, for example, this is likely to be the case as the population continues to increase exponentially. President Ahmadinejad is on record stating that he is 'against saying that two children are enough' and that Iran has the capacity to sustain a population of 120 million.[53]

Yet again, the problem in China is apparently the opposite, and in a sense complementary to that of Iran. For it is already evident that the 'one-child-policy', introduced in 1979 following other attempts to reduce population growth, has had and will continue to have devastating consequences.

One well-known consequence of the one-child policy is that there is and will be a predominance of the elderly, given the present extremely low birth rates. Indeed, China is expected to enter into a phase of declining population around 2030.[54] By that time there will be an increasing number of what are known as 4:2:1 families, in which there are four grandparents, two parents and one child – which in a country in which children are brought up expecting one day to care for the elderly means they might find themselves looking after six people. Another well-known consequence is an imbalance between the sexes. In 2007, according to the Chinese government's statistical review, there were 680 million males in the country compared to 640 million females. This imbalance can only worsen, and represents one of the demographic time-bombs of China's mid-term future: for millions of boys born in this decade who will then be of 'fighting age', which is roughly the same as marriageable age, there will be around 2030 a dramatic shortage of wives. Once again, in a society where the family is still central to the concept of being and the individual counts for little, this could have devastating effects. How will this energy be expended?

But there are two lesser-known consequences which are equally significant and extremely pertinent to our argument. First is the fact, not generally recognised in the West, that the one-child restriction does not apply to ethnic minorities. Thus is it common for Muslim families to have three or four children, with obvious long-term consequences on the balance between Han Chinese, who currently represent ninety per cent of the population, and Muslims. In fact the proportion of Muslims has grown from around six per cent of the total population at the inception of the People's Republic to around ten per cent today. More recently, between the census of 1990 and that of 2000, they accounted for as much as forty-two per cent of the net increase in the population. Today, partly as a result of the absence of a one-child policy and partly as the result of general ethnic revival, the fifty-five ethnic minorities present in the country are thought to be growing seven times faster than the Han Chinese. This clearly exacerbates the widespread problems of education and employment felt throughout the country. As the male youth segment continues to grow, it may find outlets to the west rather than to the east, in neighbouring and sympathetic Muslim nations rather than the more distant and hostile east coast of China.

The second lesser-known fact is that the one-child rules are more lax in rural areas than in the large cities. One of the problems for the urban family, that of legally registering a child in order to be able to benefit from state schooling and health care, are seen as less important in families with low literacy levels who may be more interested in having another pair of working hands. But this fact compounds the problem, given the propensity by state planners to consider the process of urbanisation as one means of alleviating poverty in remote rural areas. It forms a sub-set of one of the problems of lack of wives. For it is expected that in the coming two decades at least 400 million rural workers will move to live and find employment in the richer coastal conurbations. According to a research report based on hundreds of interviews with key officials, planners, academics and city managers and published by McKinsey in 2008, in the year 2025 there will be 221 cities in China with over a million inhabitants; 23 of these will have more than 5 million, while there will be 15 'super cities' with over 25 million inhabitants each (Chongqing is already there, and will be joined by Beijing, Shanghai, Tianjin, Shenzhen, Wuhan, Chengdu, Guangzhou and others). The total number of people living in urban centres could be as high as one billion.[55] For the most part the new arrivals will be male able-bodied migrant workers, the same disadvantaged and unmarried young men in their twenties who move to work on the construction sites of new housing developments and industrial infrastructure. These young, wifeless and sexually frustrated workers will be just as 'superfluous' as the second and third sons of the past. Few specialists doubt that over the next twenty years there will be an excess of twelve to fifteen per cent of young men in China.

The effects are already visible in a society in which marriage is a matter of social status and procreation a sacred duty, and in which a large proportion of the 'surplus' men belong to a rural underclass with very low levels of education. One academic study has shown that ninety-four per cent of all unmarried people aged from twenty-eight to forty-nine in China are male and that ninety-seven per cent of them have not completed high school. They are men, many of fighting/

marrying age, who are 'marginalized because of lack of family prospects and who have little outlet for sexual energy.' The authors of this report substantially agree with Heinsohn, although they do not cite him, that this will lead to increased levels of urban violence and will ultimately present a threat to the stability and security of China. Other studies show that migrant workers already 'account for 50 per cent of all criminal cases in the major receiving cities for migrants, with some cities reporting up to 80 per cent.'[56] In fact anecdotal evidence in the author's own community in Beijing suggests an increase in 'minor' crimes such as mugging and burglary as major national holidays approach and migrant workers seek extra funds for their trip home – perhaps for the journey itself, perhaps to impress when they arrive.

Paradoxically, therefore, in a country which most people see as facing a huge ageing problem, the real risk might be this time-bomb constituted by a large number of frustrated and disenfranchised young men of fighting age, many of whom are Muslim.

Now let us consider the outcome of such a youth bulge, or the presence of a significant number of *secundones*. According to Heinsohn, the male members of a youth bulge are influenced by four main factors: they are agitated by common adolescent irritation and idealism; they feel superfluous in not being able to inherit a social position or business activity; they may be unemployed or blocked in a job which offers little satisfaction or prospects of advancement; they may have no access to a legal sex life until they can establish themselves enough to sustain a family. In other words, the young man is stuck in a frustrating dead-end: desperate. But he can also see possible ways out:

1. Emigration, with high potential for violence if he is also blocked in his new destination;
2. Violent crime;
3. Rebellion by young men with access to military equipment;
4. Civil war, in which the young men on two sides kill each other;
5. Genocide, taking the power, wealth and status of those killed;
6. Conquest, or violent colonisation.

It is impossible to know with certainty which of these exit strategies will prevail when over thirty per cent of the Chinese male population falls into the range of Hensohn's 'fighting age', especially in the heavily populated eastern strip of China between Shenzhen and Tianjin. Perhaps emigration, as has always been the case from the south-east; perhaps violent crime. But in the extreme west, with growing religious sentiment, continuing resentment against the government in Beijing, a strong sense of Muslim identity, and the proximity of countries with a similar cultural identity, it is easy to imagine strategies (3) and (4) becoming attractive, and (6) an outlet into which Muslim males could be channelled.

There is a parallel population problem sitting between China and Iran, namely the increase of the Muslim population in Russia, which has a higher birth-rate than the Slav component. In terms of religious believers, there is already a degree of balance: according to the CIA *World Factbook*, fifteen to twenty per cent of the population is Russian Orthodox in faith and ten to fifteen per cent Muslim. But if present trends continue, by mid-century Russia could become a much more Muslim country than it is today, with as yet unimaginable effects on the country's foreign policy, which will be influenced by the geopolitics of the time and the impact of Islam on neighbours and strategic partners. But that is still far off. As one expert has observed, 'currently the Moslem population is not highly politicised' with no Muslim lobby and little Muslim influence outside the Northern Caucasus.[57] But a new imbalance in population could change this and bring further religious and racial tensions to the fore. For although, to take a fairly recent documented example, the population of Russia fell by 400,000 in the year 2005, this was mainly due to a decline in the number of Slav inhabitants. The population actually *increased* in fifteen regions including Muslim areas such as Chechnya, Dagestan and Ingushetia. According to one study, the birthrate in Dagestan is 1.8 children per woman compared to 1.3 for Russia as a whole.[58] Together with this increase in population, as in many other countries, there has been an Islamic revival in Russia in recent years, with a particular impulse following the break-up of the Soviet Union and the consequent spiritual void. While in 1968 there were 311 mosques and just one madrasah in the whole of the Soviet Union, by the turn of the century there were in the Russian Federation around 7,000 and 100 respectively.[59] This increase in numbers is accompanied by political pressure, for instance in calls for a Muslim vice-president, in demands that Christian symbols be removed from the Federation coat of arms, in the creation of a Islamic Heritage Society in 2005, and in the fact that the Russia became an observer at the Organisation of the Islamic Conference in the same year.[60] The current official Muslim population numbers around 25 million, including immigrants from Muslim areas which were once part of the Soviet Union. Unofficially, it is thought to be much higher, as is the case in China.

Russian Muslims are concentrated geographically in two regions. The first of these is the Volga-Urals region, including Tatarstan, Bashkortostan, Udmurtia, Chuvashia, Mari-El, and parts of Ulyanovsk, Samara, Astrakhan, Perm, Nizhniy Novgorod and Yekaterinburg. The second is the northern Caucasus, where several of the major ethnic conflicts since the break-up of the Soviet Union, such as those in Chechnya, have occurred.

Aleksei Malashenko, scholar-in-residence at the Moscow Carnegie Centre and author of several books on the problem of Islam in Russia, has said that while he does not expect Russia to become a Muslim society in the imminent future, 'perhaps in half a century we'll see something surprising'.[60] For although Russia has had a significant Muslim population for many centuries, without major religious tensions and terrorism, there are signs such as the Beslan incident of 2004, when Chechen terrorists held over a thousand people hostage in a school in this north Ossetian city, that this might not be the case in the future. Indeed, Russia has officially listed no fewer than seventeen Muslim banned terrorist organisations, including some well-known groups like Hizb ut-Tahrir and al-Qaida but many lesser known organisations.[62] If Muslims continue to increase in number in comparison with the Slav population and reach more than a fifth of the total, then there will very likely be a 'major political shift in the country' as Mark Smith expresses it.[63] Yet that is nothing compared to longer-term predictions, for it is believed that Muslims will become the *majority* of the population of Russia around 2050, and will be around a third of a global population of around nine billion.

For these and many other reasons, the results of a recent study sound both plausible and worrying: 'Many nations in North Africa, the Middle East, South and East Asia, and the former Soviet bloc – including China, Russia, Iran, and Pakistan – are now experiencing rapid or extreme demographic change that could push them either toward civil collapse or (in reaction) neo-authoritarianism.'[64] For these countries, China and Iran, with Russia and Pakistan revolving around that axis, have been the focus of our argument.

Oil

Into this simmering cauldron, we must pour oil. As technology and alternative sources of energy stand at present, and are likely to stand for the next quarter of a century, all the above scenarios depend in one way or another on the availability of oil. For most experts seem to agree that even if policies, finance and technologies were ready, which they are not, that is the minimum time needed to implement them to such an extent that alternative energy will be a viable substitute for oil. Now is the time to consider the notion of peak oil again, especially in view of the fact that even as supplies diminish world demand is likely to increase by something like fifty per cent over the period 2000–2020, compared to an increase of about thirty-four per cent from 1980 to 2000. Or, as Shell succinctly puts it in an industry scenario, 'by 2015, growth in the production of easily accessible oil and gas will not match the projected rate of demand growth.'[65]

As far as China is concerned, the largest oilfield actually in production, Daqing, in the north-eastern province of Heilongjiang, is already in decline. It is estimated that urban China will consume around one fifth of global energy by 2030 and account for as much as a quarter of growth in oil demand.[66] It is enough to think of the growing middle class and their aspirations to car ownership, since we know that when countries reach a per capita GDP of around $5,000, commercial and transportation usage become the main drivers of demand. Such levels are already visible in the wealthier coastal cities, and more will follow. Thus China can reasonably be expected to have nearly 400 million cars and lorries on the road by 2030, having started from a low base of a few million in the 1990s and progressed to around 37 million at present.[67] The question is, what will they run on?

This is one reason why Chinese exploration companies have been concentrating on oil under the East China Sea, and diplomatic efforts to resolve territorial disputes have been intensified. According to Schindler and Zittel, Chinese oil production overall is expected to 'peak before 2010 and then decline by around five per cent per year on average until 2030'; according to estimates by the International Energy Agency (IEA), it will peak just a little later at the beginning of the next decade.'[68] So let us look again at the numbers, especially those regarding China, Iran, and their major competitors in the world. One of China's key suppliers, Venezuela, is already in decline, having peaked in 2000, so that 'even with increased non-conventional oil production, [Venezuela] will not be able to maintain its present production rate.' All African oil will peak between 2010 and 2015, and then enter into sharp decline so that the continent's production in 2030 is likely to be around one third of that seen at time of writing. Looking at the global oil peak scenario, production is likely to decrease by around fifty per cent by 2030, which represents an annual decline of three per cent. But even this may be an optimistic scenario. Schindler and Zittel observe as follows:

> However, it must be noted that this is a moderate assumption as today a large fraction of the oil is produced offshore. Offshore fields are produced by very aggressive modern extraction methods, e.g. injection of water, gas, heat and surfactants – in order to increase the pressure and decrease the viscosity – and horizontal drilling – in order to extract the oil faster. These methods allow the faster extraction of the oil for a limited time. The horizontal wells allow to extract more oil per time, but as soon as the water level reaches the horizontal well, oil production switches to water production almost within several months. These production methods lead to decline rates after peak of 10 per cent per year or even more (e.g. 14 per cent per year in Cantarell (Mexico), 8–10 per cent in Alaska, UK and Norway, more than 10 per cent in Oman and possibly 10 per cent or more in Ghawar, the world's largest oil field in Saudi Arabia).[69]

None of this is very encouraging. As the oil geologist Colin Campbell has observed, whenever the point of global peak oil is reached, the decline will be remorseless: 'The transition to decline threatens to be a time of great international tension. Petroleum Man will be virtually extinct this Century, and Homo sapiens faces a major challenge in adapting to his loss.'[70] The problem is, that if there is truth in these predictions China's new economic power will be accelerating in mid-century exactly when Campbell's catastrophic predictions come to maturity. This in turn means that in future years China's foreign policy and network of alliances will be increasingly driven by the country's energy requirements.

Iran's *20-Year Vision* provides the objectives for the energy sector up to 2025, which are to maintain its position as the second largest producer in OPEC, with around seven per cent of global oil production, to become the world's third largest gas producer with around ten per cent of the global market, and to become the leading producer of petrochemicals in the Middle East.

Although it has itself entered into a second peak in oil production (having previously experienced a sharp decline in production at the time of Khomeini's revolution), Iran will experience a very gentle decline with fairly constant production up to 2030. But by that time, oil may no longer be the dominant source of energy for the world, having lost its place to natural gas – which a quarter of a century ago accounted for twenty per cent of total supply against thirty per cent for coal and fifty per cent for oil. It is true that there are large quantities of coal in the world, especially in China, and that the use of coal for producing energy is likely to double in the same period. Yet transport and pollution militate against greater use of coal, while the alternative sources of energy will be unable to substitute oil in the foreseeable future. Biofuels and nuclear energy make take up some of the slack, but will not be able to cope with demand. There is, as the Shell scenario quoted above puts it, 'no "silver bullet" that will completely resolve supply-demand tensions.' Already today gas has overtaken coal in the global energy mix, and many experts believe that it may also overtake oil by around 2025. Gas is now the abundant fuel, and 'in many respects, the rise of gas parallels that of oil half a century ago.'[71] Already, enormous investments are being made in infrastructure, shipping and pipelines for the future dominance of gas. Iran's importance as an oil producer will inevitably decline, as has already happened in Britain.

Yet, if anything, Iran will be *more* powerful, and the dominance of Turkestan more important than ever. For over half of all known gas in the world is located in Iran, Qatar, Russia and Turkmenistan, with Iran being second only to Russia in its reserves. The switch to a gas economy will replicate the geopolitical dynamic of oil, but more so. Already in late 2008, following an earlier suggestion by President Khamenei of Iran, the chairman of Gazprom, Alexey Miller, together with the oil ministers of Iran and Qatar, Gholamhossein Nozari and Abdullah Bin Hamad Al-Attiyah, announced in Tehran the creation of a 'Gas G3' on the model of OPEC. The agreement would, Miller said, involve 'joint projects embracing the entire value chain from geological exploration and production to transportation and joint marketing of gas' under the auspices of a tripartite 'Supreme Technical Committee'. [72] This represented an immediate challenge to China. For, to a great extent, the future success of China's ambitious plan to achieve in the second half of this century a standard of living in her major cities equivalent to that of the Western world today will depend on the country's ability to secure, transport and store natural gas. It is true that these needs might be satisfied by a closer relationship with Russia, as many commentators suggest, but the historical, ideological and frontier history with Russia create tensions and fears which the much smaller and more distant Iran will never generate. As Ilan Berman, vice president of the American Foreign Policy Council, observed with a stunning comparison hinting willy-nilly at the alliance we have been predicting, 'Iran has become the engineer of China's economic growth. It may not be like Saudi Arabia is to the U.S. economy, but it's close.'[73] For the factors described above will make a stronger future alliance with Iran, and closer ties with the other gas-producing nations of Turkestan, an imperative. A secure distribution system of gas, primarily through pipelines, will increasingly require alliances which protect the major supply routes.

That means land. It requires the kind of direct investment in production facilities in which China has recently been engaging in Iran. It will no longer be a matter of building ports, protecting sea-routes, or avoiding naval blockades, but of creating a *guaranteed physical corridor* which links the gas fields of Iran to the consumers of Shanghai.

Notes

1. Huntington, *Clash of Civilizations*, p. 258.
2. Philip Bobbitt, *The Shield of Achilles: War, Peace and the Course of History*, p. 819.
3. *Mapping the Gobal Future: Report of the National Intelligence Council's 2020 Project*, Based on consultations with nongovernmental experts around the world, Pittsburgh, PA: Government Printing Office, 2004, p. 8.
4. Fogel, 'Capitalism and Democracy in 2040', pp. 3–4.
5. Vladimir Paramonov and Aleksey Strokov, 'Russian-Chinese Relations: Past, Present & Future', Central Asia series, Defence Academy of the United Kingdom, September 2006, p. 13.
6. Background Note: Iran, March 2008, US Department of State, Bureau of Near Eastern Affairs; http://www.state.gov/r/pa/ei/bgn/5314.html.
7. http://www.mfa.gov.ir/cms/cms/Tehran/en/EconomicPart/EconomicKeyIndicators.html.
8. *Background Note: Iran*, March 2008, US Department of State.
9. *Law of the Fourth Economic, Social and Cultural Development Plan of the Islamic Republic of Iran 2004–2009*, Management and Planning Organization, Islamic Republic of Iran, 1st September 2004, Article 18.
10. This company, which describes itself as a 'Business Development Company' and seems to have only five employees in Toronto, and small offices in Tehran and Beijing, is alleged to be a money-laundering vehicle for the clerical establishment. One exile website, Iran-Resist, concludes that '*Solitac sera bientôt en possession d'importants bénéfices (21 per cent du chiffre d'affaires de la co-entreprise Solitac-Chery-Iran Khodro): Au moins 252 millions de dollars vont chaque année atterrir sur les comptes bancaires de cette société fântome … l'une des multiples interfaces du réseau de blanchiment et transferts de capitaux iraniens vers des destinations introuvables.*' http://www.iran-resist.org/article3776.

11. See the scant information available on the joint-venture at http://www.solitac.com/home.htm and http://www.cheryglobal.com/mtzx/text_detail.jsp?artId=11869668130001&columnId=11700520360001.
12. http://www.mvs.ir/Index.asp. In Farsi, without an English translation.
13. Ibid, Part One, passim.
14. Executive Summary, *Annual Report to Congress: The Military Power of the People's Republic of China,* 2005 (no page number, but before page i).
15. Executive Summary, *Annual Report to Congress: The Military Power of the People's Republic of China,* 2007, p. i.
16. Executive Summary, *Annual Report to Congress: The Military Power of the People's Republic of China,* 2008, p. i.
17. Outlined in the White Paper 'China's National Defence in 2006', Beijing: Information Office of the State Council of the People's Republic of China, 29 December 2006 (also available at http://english.people.com.cn/whitepaper/defense2006/defense2006.html.
18. According to analysts from Jane's Information Group, reported in 'China aims for military might', *Daily Telegraph*, 28 September 2008.
19. *Annual Report to Congress: The Military Power of the People's Republic of China,* 2008, p. 4.
20. Analysts from Jane's Information Group, reported in 'China aims for military might', *Daily Telegraph*, 28 September 2008.
21. The precise numbers of ships varies from report to report. These approximate figures are based on those in Howarth, *China's Rising Sea Power: The PLA Navy's Submarine Challenge*, p. 15, and the *Annual Report to Congress: 'The Military Power of the People's Republic of China*, the 2008 edition.
22. 2006 *Report to Congress of the U.S.-China Economic and Security Review Commission*, Washington: U.S. Government Printing Office, November 2006, p. 130.
23. According to analysts from Jane's Information Group, reported in 'China aims for military might', *Daily Telegraph*, 28 September 2008.
24. See the account by Tarique Niazi, 'Gwadar: China's Naval Outpost on the Indian Ocean', in *ChinaBrief* ,Volume V, Issue 4, 15 February 2005, Washington DC, Jamestown Foundation, pp. 7-8.
25. In Gwadarcorner.com, at http://www.gwadarcorner.com/index.php?action=future
26. For example, *India News Online*, at http://news.indiamart.com/news-analysis/gwadar-port-pakistan-12098.html.
27. Asian Development Bank; http://www.adb.org/Documents/CSPs/PAK/2004/csp0200.asp.
28. Bernard D. Cole, 'The Energy Factor in Chinese Maritime Strategy', in Collins et al., *China's Energy Strategy*, pp. 336–52, p. 345.
29. James R. Holmes, 'China's Naval Ambitions in the Indian Ocean', in Collins et al., *China's Energy Strategy*, pp. 117–42, p. 127.
30. Levin, *The Next Great Clash*, Table 4.2, p. 47 (this is the last of six columns, beginning with the 1950s and considering alliances and military strategies in each decade since).

31. See, for example, the article in the *Financial Times*, 3 September 2007, and many other newspapers and magazines.
32. *The Times*, 8 September 2007.
33. *Annual Report to Congress: The Military Power of the People's Republic of China*, 2005, p. 40.
34. *Annual Report to Congress: The Military Power of the People's Republic of China*, 2008, p. 13.
35. Ibid., p. 17.
36. Most of the data in this paragraph are taken from the CRS Report for Congress, *Iran: US Concerns and Policy Responses*, 6 May 2008, p. 16.
37. http://www.naval-technology.com/projects/kilo/.
38. 'Iran Qods Force infiltrates Iraq, *Middle East Times*, 22 September 2008; http://www.metimes.com/International/2008/02/08/iran_qods_force_infiltrates_iraq/4246/.
39. CRS Report for Congress, *Iran: US Concerns and Policy Responses*, 6 May 2008, p. 33.
40. Interview with *Fars* news agency, reported by *Reuters*, 30th october 2007; http://www.reuters.com/article/worldNews/idUSBLA96443220071030.
41. 'Recognizing Iran as a Strategic Threat: An Intelligence Challenge for the United States', Washington: Staff Report of the House Permanent Select Committee on Intelligence Subcommittee on Intelligence Policy, 23 August 2006, p. 4.
42. Quillen, 'Iranian Nuclear Weapons Policy', pp. 21–2.
43. Interview with Dr Etemad, 'The shah's plan was to build bombs', *New Statesman*, 11 September 2008; http://www.newstatesman.com/asia/2008/09/iran-nuclear-shah-west.
44. 'Recognizing Iran as a Strategic Threat', pp. 14–15.
45. Levin, *The Next Great Clash*, Table 3.1, pp. 30–31.
46. 'The Iranian Missile Threat', *Washington Times*, 9 November 2006, http://www.washtimes.com/news/2006/nov/09/20061109-082809-3991r/; see also 'Iran and North Korea's Military Relations', in *The Daily NK*, 5 February 2007, available at http://www.dailynk.com/english/read.php?cataId=nk00300&num=1638.
47. Figures are taken from the US Census Bureau's International Database, available at http://www.census.gov/ipc/www/idb/index.html.
48. See Dabashi, 'The End of Islamic Ideology', p. 475.
49. Iran: World Bank Country Brief, 2006; http://web.worldbank.org WBSITE/EXTERNAL/COUNTRIES/MENAEXT/IRANEXTN/0,,menuPK:312966~pagePK:141132~piPK:141107~theSitePK:312943,00.html.
50. Gunnar Heinsohn, *Söhne und Weltmacht* (Sons and World Power), Zurich: Orell Fuessli Verlag, 2006; these data are taken from a presentation given by Professor Heinsohn at the LUX centre in Nijmegen (Holland) on 2 April 2008; available at http://www.slideshare.net/LUXdebat/powerpoint-presentatie-gunnar-heinsohn/.
51. This come as no surprise, recalling the absurdly youthful faces that manned some of the road-blocks in Tehran and attacked me in southern Iran, to see that in 1978 the average age of males was only fifteen.
52. http://www.sci.org.ir/portal/faces/public/sci_en/sci_en.Glance/sci_en.generalinf.
53. On 23 October 2006, quoted in the Heinsohn presentation mentioned in n. 7.
54. Richard Jackson and Neil Howe, *The Graying of the Great Powers: Demography and*

Geopolitics in the 21st Century, Washington DC: Center for Strategic and International Studies, May 2008, p. 3.

55. *Preparing for China's Urban Billion: Summary of Findings*, McKinsey Global Institute, March 2008, pp. 9–10; available at http://www.mckinsey.com/mgi/publications/china_urban_summary_of_findings.asp.

56. Therese Hesketh and Zhu Wei Xing, 'Abnormal sex ratios in human populations: Causes and consequences', *Proceedings of the National Academy of Sciences of the United States of America*, September 5, 2006, Vol. 103, No. 36, pp. 13271–13275; p. 13273.

57. Mark A. Smith, 'Islam in the Russian Federation', Conflict Studies Research Centre, Russian Series, Defence Academy of the United Kingdom, November 2006.

58. Smith, 'Islam in the Russian Federation', p. 1.

59. Algis Prazauskas, 'Russia and Islam', p. 6; available at www.sipa.columbia.edu/ece/research/intermarium/vol8no3/russia-and-islam.pdf.

60. Smith, 'Islam in the Russian Federation', pp. 1–2.

61. Quoted in Smith, 'Islam in the Russian Federation', p. 2.

62. The full list is as follows (from *Rossiyskaya Gazeta*, 28 July 2006):

1. Supreme Military Majlis ul Shura of the Joint Forces of Mujaheddin in the Caucasus
2. Congress of the People of Ichkeria and Dagestan
3. The Base (Al-Qa'idah)
4. Asbat al-Ansar [also Isbat al-Ansar]
5. Holy War (Al-Jihad or Egyptian Islamic Jihad)
6. Islamic Group (Al-Jama'ah al-Islamiyyah)
7. Moslem Brotherhood (Al-Ikhwan al-Moslemun)
8. Islamic Liberation Party (Hizb ut-Tahrir al-Islami)
9. Lashkar-e-Taiba
10. Islamic Assembly (Jamaat-e-Islami)
11. Taleban
12. Islamic Party of Turkestan (former Islamic Movement of Uzbekistan)
13. Social Reform Society (Jama'ah al-Islah al-Ijtima'i)
14. Islamic Heritage Revival Society (Jama'ah Ihya ul-Turath al-Islamia)
15. House of The Two Sacred Mosques (Al-Haramayn)
16. Islamic Jihad - Jamaat Mujaheddin
17. Jund ash-Sham

Quoted in Smith, 'Islam in the Russian Federation', Appendix 5.

63. Smith, 'Islam in the Russian Federation', p. 9.

64. Jackson and Howe, The Graying of the Great Powers, p. 11.

65. *Shell Energy Scenarios to 2050*, Shell International, 2008, p. 8; available at http://www.shell.com/home/content/aboutshell/our_strategy/shell_global_scenarios/dir_global_scenarios_07112006.html.

66. *Preparing for China's Urban Billion*: Summary of Findings, McKinsey Global Institute, March 2008, pp. 16.

67. Daniel H. Rosen and Trevor Houser, *China Energy: A Guide for the Perplexed, China Balance Sheet*, a Joint Project by the Center for Strategic and International Studies and the Peterson Institute for International Economics, May 2007, p. 14.

68. Schindler and Zittel, 'Crude Oil', p. 64.

69. Ibid., p. 68.

70. http://www.peakoil.net/about-peak-oil.

71. Roberts, *The End of Oil*, p. 167.

72. See the Gazprom press release at http://www.gazprom.com/eng/news/2008/10/31681.shtml.

73. Quoted in *The Washington Post*, 18 November 2007, http://www.washingtonpost.com/wp-dyn/content/article/2007/11/17/AR2007111701680.html.

Chapter 9

Scenarios

Now we are in a position to consider five scenarios in which China and Iran will be intimately involved. At present, it might seem to be an unbalanced relationship, when some pundits write about China as the future – indulging in hyperbolic phrases such as 'the Chinese century' – while others dismiss Iran as little more than an international pariah. But, as we have shown in the preceding chapters, in the ineluctable energy crunch which lies ahead Iran holds one of the strongest hands.

Two things we can be absolutely certain about are that the world in 2030, and even more so in 2050, will be a very different place from the world we live in today, and that the speed of change will accelerate between now and both those dates. China itself will be a very different place as it moves towards the First World, and its international ambitions will increase with increasing economic and military power. Throughout the leadership of Deng Xiao Ping, Jiang Zemin and Hu Jintao, the emphasis in foreign policy has been on biding time, concealing capabilities and avoiding confrontation, at least partly because as a developing country China could not realistically compete with its advanced industrial rivals. This, Avery Goldstein asserts in a survey of China's Grand Strategy, 'is likely to continue well into the twenty-first century.'[1] Yet 2050, or even the period 2030–50, *will be* well into the century. A still-weak China, without a blue-water fleet and lacking long-distance air capability without aircraft carriers or overseas bases, cannot contemplate a more assertive role. But when these assets are in place?

Not long ago, prophets of the 'Singularity', a future time in which social, scientific and economic change is so rapid that we cannot even imagine what will happen next (or, pushed to its *reductio ad absurdum*, in which events occur before they *can* occur), predicted the year 2030 (Vernor Vinge) or 2045 (Ray Kurzweil) as its moment of realisation. Both years fall within our time frame. To understand such levels of change it is enough to think back to 1960, when we still lived in a grey post-war world, with no colour television, no personal computers, no Internet, no music CDs, when very few people had credit cards and travel was immensely more complicated and slower; no one then imagined the collapse of the Soviet Union, the rise of China as an economic power, or the Seven Sisters' loss of control over the oil market. Now think forwards, where there will be, in Kurzweil's view, a rate of change in the order of several magnitudes greater.[2]

Let us then move to our scenarios. We will call them the *Diplomatic/Political Scenario*, the *Commercial Scenario*, the *Religious Scenario*, the *Demographic Scenario*, and the *Military Scenario*. Each of these consists of a brief outline of the scenario concerning China and Iran, today and at undefined year between 2030 and 2050, followed by a series of events which could bring the two countries closer together in a future alliance. They will be complemented by the summary of scenario for a future war between China and the United States sketched by Samuel P. Huntington in 1996.

The Diplomatic/Political Scenario:

Today

As we saw above, the two new republican governments of China and Iran established diplomatic relations in 1922, after 2,000 years in which occasional diplomatic missions had met. The People's Republic of China first began trade relations with Iran in 1950, and then the two countries established formal diplomatic relations on 16 August 1971. The relationship intensified after 1989, and by the mid-1990s amounted to a *de facto* but understated alliance, especially concerning sales of military equipment.

It has always been conditional and pragmatic, and major differences have been contained: for example, Iran's implicit support for the Uyghurs and requests for official visits to Kashgar when religious/political leaders travel east; or China's support in the past for Tudeh, the communist party of Iran, which led to offering asylum to banned leaders. But each country has refrained from openly criticising or attacking the other. In 1979, for example, in spite of American entreaties China abstained from voting to impose sanctions on Iran in the United Nations Security Council after the hostage crisis. Although, in the 1990s, it then bowed to American pressure by blocking the export of cruise missiles to Iran, more recently China has again rejected calls for sanctions, this time over the nuclear issue, and has supported Iran's right to access nuclear technology. Conversely, Iran's militancy, for example in its stance towards Israel, which the leadership in Beijing has considered a 'friend' since diplomatic relations were established in 1992, endangers China's attempt to portray itself as a peace-loving stakeholder in the institutions of global governance – especially, in the view of Israel, when China also maintains good relations with sworn enemies like Iran and Syria.

But suppose this pragmatic attitude were allowed to blossom into a true marriage of interests in spite of ideological differences? Suppose the fifth or sixth generation of Chinese leadership (as they take full power in the Politburo in 2012 and 2022 respectively) takes a different view in changed geopolitical circumstances? China, like most countries with an eye on survival, has always been willing to change tack, as no political leader has ever done so dramatically and effectively than Deng Xiao Ping. Where will the next Deng lead his country?

China needs to think about alternatives, because the 'alternatives' are thinking about her.

Tomorrow

Iran is the key member of the Turkestan Federation of Islamic Republics, popularly known as the 'Silk Road Union' on the model of the European Union. The headquarters building, financed by the Chinese Federation, is located in Tehran. Regional offices have been established in Sverdlovsk (Capital of the Muslim Russian Federation, situated east of the Urals; formerly Yekaterinburg, returned to its Bolshevik name to cancel associations with the Christian saint), in Astana (capital of the Kazakh Islamic Republic), and in Kashgar (capital of the United Muslim Autonomous Province of East Turkestan, part of the Chinese Federation). There is also a large representative office in Beijing. Other member countries are the North Afghanistan Republic, the Muslim Republic of Pakistan, Tajikistan, Turkmenistan and Uzbekistan. The recognised observers are India, Iraq, Oman, Qatar and the United Arab Emirates. The Chinese Federation and the Turkestan Federation of Islamic Republics overlap in economic and diplomatic matters and maintain a common Regional Defence Force (TFRDF), but each maintains independence in internal matters and social policy (the TFIR within traditional Chinese territory is regarded as an autonomous region, without frontiers).

The Turkestan Federation and Chinese Federation together control eighty per cent of the world's manufacturing capability, fifty per cent of the world's oil, fifty per cent of the world's gas, and thirty-five per cent of global population, with economic, diplomatic and political leverage far superior to those of the old Soviet Union or the United States.

Events which could push China and Iran closer

– A dramatic global increase in oil and gas prices, and a pressing need for the Chinese Federation to guarantee supplies;
– Attempts to dominate Turkestan by Russia or the emergence of a new nuclear power like Kazakhstan;

– Attempts to create a Hizb ut-Tahrir inspired Islamic Turkestan based on Uzbekistan;
– The resurgence of a more assertive Japan with renewed ambition to become a Great Power;
– The North Afghanistan Republic sees explosive growth after peace enables large reserves of copper, gold and other minerals discovered in the 1960s and 1970s to be developed, together with new discoveries, with the help of the Chinese Federation, and larger reserves of oil and natural gas than are now known are discovered in the Tajik area of the Republic under the Tethys Ocean.[3]

The Commercial Scenario:

Today

In 2008, China became for the first time the major exporter to Iran, overtaking Germany – which had held this position since the time of the Shah, and whose exports to Iran dropped a massive twenty per cent in compared to the previous year. One sign of increased export activity was the presence of over 1,000 traders and importers from Iran at the China Import and Export Fair (better known as the Canton Fair) in Guangzhou in October 2008.[4] But this is not merely a question of one country selling goods and services to another, for present agreements and partnerships suggest a much closer relationship developing over the next few decades. China already has a formidable industrial presence, facilitated, it should be said, by sanctions which alienate American multinationals, from engineering contracts on the Tehran subway and electric railway system won by China North Industries Corp (Norinco[5]) to the widespread availability of consumer goods from major Chinese manufacturers like Haier, which manufactures washing machines in Iran, and Lenovo. Norinco built the first Tehran Metro line between 1996 and 1999 (actually Line 5 of seven planned, but the first to be inaugurated), and in 2008 was awarded what it describes as 'China's biggest international project contract' to date', worth $836 million and entirely financed by Norinco, to build a further subway line, Line 4.[6] Tellingly, on the bid for this project the main competitor was Germany's Siemens.

In 2007, Iran was China's sixteenth largest trading partner, with exports totalling $7.3 billion and imports $13.3 billion, representing a year-on-year increase of sixty-two per cent and thirty-four per cent respectively. Most of the imports from Iran were crude oil, about eighty-seven per cent of the total, while China's main exports to Iran were iron and steel, machinery and vehicles and parts, which together accounted for half of the imports.[7]

Tomorrow

The Chinese Federation is Iran's largest trading partner, both its largest export market and its primary source of imports. Iran supplies over thirty per cent of China's energy needs, mainly natural gas, through a wholly-owned pipeline which links the two countries through North Afghanistan and Tajikistan.

Iran is the major manufacturing hub in the Middle East, producing with its Chinese partners motor vehicles, railway rolling-stock and heavy machinery for the markets of the Middle East and Africa, and through Turkey to its fellow EU countries. It is also a major computer manufacturer, and assembles Chinese wide-bodied jets for Western markets. On the coast near Bandar Abbas, on the Strait of Hormuz, is the largest commercial and exhibition centre in the world, known as the *Persian Dragon*, built over the *Global Hub*. This innovative tax-free hub comprises the 'New International Trading Port' and the 'International Airport of Bandar Abbas', and is considered the most sophisticated transport hub in the world. The airport is the main base of Iran-Emirates Airlines. The port and airport are directly linked by the high-speed Trans-Turkestan RailNet to Tehran, Istanbul, Karachi, Islamabad and Tianjin, via the 'Trans-Iraq-Link' to Baghdad, Amman and Cairo, and via the 'Trans-Turkestan-Link' to Ashgabat, Tashkent, Bishkek and Astana.

Just outside the Strait, on the Gulf of Oman, is the Chinese Federation's largest overseas military base, with its own airport and a deep-sea port run by the PLA in conjunction with the TFRDF.

Events Which Could Push China and Iran Closer

– Renewed sanctions imposed by the United States and extended to all its trading partners, such as the European Union;
– the formation of a new East Asian trading group, based on the re-united Koreas and Japan, pushes China's interests further West;
– China fails to sustain its growth rate and seeks other ways to expand its economy;
– China and Iran partition Afghanistan into horizontal spheres of interest as Britain and Russia did in horizontal spheres in Persia;
– A shift in vision from Iran as a Middle East power to Iran as a Turkestan power.

The Religious Scenario:

Today

The clerics in Iran feel a sense of religious duty towards the Shi'a minorities in predominantly Sunni countries such as Afghanistan (where about twenty per cent of the population are Shi'a), Pakistan (twenty per cent) and Saudi Arabia (an often forgotten ten to fifteen per cent) which can often influence their policies. They also feel an intense dislike for the most extreme forms of Sunni militancy found in countries like Pakistan and Saudi Arabia. This is why Iran supported the so-called Northern Alliance (more correctly, the Islamic United Front) against the fanatically Sunni guerrillas of the mainly Pushtun-speaking Taliban from the southern part of the country. The ethnic Tajiks in Afghanistan already make up around twenty-seven per cent of that country's population, and were a key part of the Northern Alliance. In addition, half of the Afghans speak Farsi, and around twenty per cent are Shi'a Muslims, living mainly in the north. It would require a minimum of desire on the part of Tajikistan to make a new alliance work, but several factors could easily combine to make this desirable. In particular, new or extended discoveries – or indeed adequate exploitation of what is already discovered – of oil and gas deposits along the 750 mile frontier between Tajikstan and north-eastern Afghanistan. But even without them, the common culture works in favour of such alliances.

Lest this seem exaggerated, we should note that in October 2008 the Afghan Deputy Minister of Culture and Information, Din Mohammad Rashedi Mobarez, announced that in the following spring high-ranking officials of the three Persian-speaking countries of Iran, Tajikistan, and Afghanistan would celebrate Noruz (the Persian New Year) together in Balkh. He also announced the creation of a joint Persian-language television network, stating that 'compiling and editing the joint cultural programs through this network can help develop and strengthen ties between the people of Afghanistan, Iran, and Tajikistan.'[8] Such a network can only promote further integration.

This small, symbolic decision illustrates the success of Iran's deployment of 'soft power' in the region, which is mainly based on the diffusion and acceptance of Farsi and its derivative languages, the strong Persian cultural tradition through literature and music, and a network based on the shared values of Shi-ism. Just as solidarity and a sense of Muslim identity were increased by regional and political conflicts such as that in Chechnya, so other hot-beds will emerge in Turkestan and could be guided by a strong Iran. As Huntington expressed it in 1996, 'the dynamism of Islam is the ongoing source of many relatively small fault line wars; the rise of China is the potential source of a big intercivilizations war of core states.'[9] And if they came together?

Tomorrow

Under the auspices of the Turkestan Federation of Islamic Republics, a Shi'a Pilgrimage Corridor has been created, with guaranteed personal safety and controlled prices in government-owned Pilgrim Inns. The Corridor runs from Najaf, Karbala and Samarra in Iraq, to Qom and Mashad in Iran, across the frontier into Herat in Afghanistan, and thence to Dushanbe in Tajikistan, ending in Kashgar.

As part of its recent alliance negotiations with Iran, the Chinese Federation has granted the Muslim majority the right to establish an entirely Islamic province in the southern half of Xinjiang, with its capital in Kashgar. The province remains an integral part of China, but maintains an open frontier on the west as part of the Free Economic Trading Area to which all members of the Turkestan Federation belong. Large numbers of new theological schools are under construction, with a focus on vocational training for young, unemployed and disaffected males.

The continuing resurgence of Islam, and corresponding increase in the Muslim sense of identity, has spawned new radical ideologies throughout Turkestan. New theological schools are tapping into the long radical traditions of Sufism and Ismailism. Personal communication tools facilitate what used to be called distance learning, and can spread new ideas and radical projects instantly to millions of young co-religionists. Spontaneous support against any perceived slight can be instantly rallied into organised protest.

Events which could push China and Iran closer

– A nuclear attack by a non-Islamic power against an Islamic country which shares a frontier with China, say against Pakistan, which is eighty per cent Sunni but twenty per cent Shi'a and would therefore appeal to the resentment and fury of both sects;
– A partitioning of Afghanistan into two horizontal areas, a Pushtun southern part naturally linked through tribal loyalties, religion and economy with Pakistan, and a northern Shi'a-based part linked via Tajikistan to China in the east and directly to Iran in the west;
– A radical Islamic coup in a country between China and Iran (Uzbekistan?) could inspire young Muslims in neighbouring countries to new fervour and political activism;
– The arrival of a new inspirational and unifying leader (a Khomeini?) who detracts from their geopolitical importance;
– A break-up of existing nation states which are allies to China: Pakistan could break up into two religious entities, one Shi'a and one Sunni (just as west Pakistan itself broke away from India in 1947 on religious grounds), or even smaller units; Kazakhstan could also break up into two states, one Muslim projected towards

the east and south and one Russian Orthodox projected towards the west. This would reinforce the idea of a strong Muslim corridor.

The Demographic Scenario:

Today

In two or three decades, around a quarter of the population of China will be over sixty-five years old and there will be a shortage of people of working age. In most countries, the most natural response to these two needs would be immigration. But China has been historically hostile to immigration, and is one of the most difficult countries in the world in which to obtain citizenship. Historically it *was* possible to become Chinese, but in any case the barrier was high, since it required being able to read Chinese characters, living in a city administered by officials appointed by the emperor, and being recorded in the emperor's census register. More recently, citizenship was defined in terms of common blood and language; hence the importance given to the word *hanren*, '*han* people'. Today, the number of adopted citizens of non-Chinese origin in particular may be counted on the fingers of one hand. One rare example is the distinguished translator Sidney Shapiro, now ninety-three and married to his Chinese wife for over half a century. He went to China in 1947, is a long-serving member of the Communist Party of China, and became a citizen in 1963. Neither easy nor fast!

How will the shortfall be made up? There is already a lack of some 40 million females in China, and this can only get worse. How can *that* problem be resolved? Then, there is the future problem of fighting age Muslims and disaffected urban migrant youths in the large conurbations.

Tomorrow

The one-child policy was revoked by the 2017 National Congress, with a consequent doubling of the birth rate in the next few years. But this did not resolve the problem of an ageing population dependent on an insufficient workforce. Neither did it prevent the explosion in female trafficking and smuggling into a multi-billion dollar illegal business ($8 billion in 2020). Thus new rules for immigration were introduced at the 2022 National Congress. The Chinese Federation has become a more open society, with a massive influx of young women from neighbouring countries: from Vietnam, Laos and Cambodia in the south, from Uzbekistan and Kazakhstan in the north-west, and from Japan in the north-east.

In the mega-cities of the east coast, large numbers of youth gangs terrorise the elderly population, who are forced to live in heavily-guarded compounds. Micro-

criminality is driven by unemployed migrant youths from the central provinces, while drug-related crimes are mainly carried out by Muslim gangs operating through their urban network of mosques and madrasah – in spite of attempts by their elders and the Muslim Federation to prevent such activities. The average age of gang-members is seventeen.
--There are widespread fears for mid-century, when children born during the baby boom of 2018–2025 reach fighting age and increasing youth unemployment is expected. Politicians are pressing for the re-introduction of the soldier-farmer border militia which guarded the frontier with Russia from the 1950s to the 1970s. In the north-east, they will be given license to expand into the new colonies acquired in Siberia beyond the Chinese cities of Erkhüü, Boli and Haishenwei (formerly known as Irkutsk, Khabarovsk and Vladivostock). In the north-west, they will inducted into the Roving Anti-Terrorist Forces (RATForce) of the Turkestan Federation of Islamic Republics.

Events Which Could Push China and Iran Closer

– Demographic imbalance necessitates deeper cooperation: young versus old; male versus female;
– A dramatic increase in global warming raises the sea-level off the East coast of China, submerging cities with huge populations like Shanghai and Tianjin (in 2030 *c.*40 million together) and large areas of the Pearl River Delta (*c.*90 million) forcing both a population shift to the west and a need for new transport nodes for international trade;
– A huge increase in the 'youth bulge' of China after one-child policies are revoked, resulting in millions of 'superfluous' fighting-age men in both China and Iran between 2030 and 2050.

The Military Scenario:

Today

Already in the mid-1970s, some Chinese journalists suggested that Iran might use its military power to counter threats by the United States against other militant oil-producing countries: 'Reporting on US speculations about possible military action against militant OPEC countries, *Peking Review* quoted Iranian commentary to the effect that "the Shah has said that nobody could dictate to us or shake his fists at us because we could do the same".'[10] Iran could also exploit its territorial advantage, as was suggested in early 2008 after irritating – to her – visits to the Persian Gulf by Presidents Bush and Sarkozy. Why not, it was argued, balance the American presence in permanent bases and naval forces by granting the use of an existing port on the Indian Ocean or in the Gulf to China, or indeed allow the building of a new port on one of the islands in the Gulf by the Chinese navy?[11]

Since the United States already imports about seventy-five per cent of its oil needs, and a quarter of that comes from the Persian Gulf, blocking or mining the Strait of Hormuz could be an effective short-term tactic for Iran. We saw above the willingness of the *basiji*, or religious militia, to carry out suicide attacks in the Strait in order to block oil flows, while missiles could easily be launched against ships within and beyond Hormuz. But such a blockade would have an impact on China as well as on the United States – especially if, in the ultimate irony, Chinese-made missiles fired from Chinese-made patrol boats were to destroy Chinese oil tankers.

These considerations, far from bringing China into conflict with Iran or entering into anti-Iran coalitions, are more likely to nudge China towards a deeper partnership because the two countries' mutual interests would thus be protected. This is sometimes difficult to appreciate from the American point of view, which tends to take a high moral stance and use phrases like 'morality gap' and 'responsible stakeholder' when discussing Beijing. Here is an example, from a report to the U.S.-China Economic and Security Review Commission:

> Indeed, so long as Beijing pursues commercial interactions without regard to the odious behaviour of its foreign partners, it will be perceived in some quarters as defying international moral standards and contributing to instability and lawlessness … Nowhere is this issue now more apparent than in relations between China and Iran.'[12]

Other regional factors in Asia could also push China westward, such as the resurgent Japan mentioned above, or a more confident and militarily assertive India which becomes a direct rival for Middle East energy supplies.

Tomorrow

Historically three major issues concern the Chinese Federation and the Turkestan Federation of Islamic Republics: Taiwan, nuclear warfare, and the Persian Gulf.

Now Taiwan is fully integrated into China, and is therefore no longer a military problem. The PLA and 2nd Artillery Division which once confronted the island from Fujian and Jiangxi provinces have now been redeployed (just as they were from the north after the collapse of the Soviet Union).

Nuclear warfare remains a threat. The Turkestan Federation of Islamic Republics sees itself as a vast sporting arena, with the neighbouring countries ranged around it. Most of the world's nuclear powers, those with the capacity to build and launch nuclear weapons past, present and future, may be found among the spectators: the Chinese Federation and Iran sit at opposite ends, with the

Russian and Kazakhstan Islamic Republics on one side and India and Pakistan on the other; the United States is implicitly a spectator with bases and naval vessels within striking range, while Israel watches the action on a mega-screen situated outside the main arena, monitoring activities which could have an impact on her own existence. In addition, there are the 'New-Nukes', which as soon as Iran developed its own nuclear warheads in 2012 considered acquiring the same firepower a defensive necessity: Saudi Arabia, Unified Korea, and Turkey, all of which have interests in Turkestan. Only Britain and France are absent from this dangerous version of the Great Game, although they too have the capability to operate in this arena. There is constant jockeying and bluffing to get a good ringside seat at the arena. Moreover, there are rumours of two separate terrorist groups now in possession of nuclear weapons: Revolutionary Hizb ut-Tahrir in Uzbekistan, and New al-Qaida in southern Afghanistan.

In the Persian Gulf there is a state of crisis. The United States has started building a new naval base on a man-made island off the coast of a new Saudi enclave on the Arabian Sea, between Raysut in Oman and Al Ghaydah in Yemen. Known as the 'American Aden' this new base will house the headquarters of the U.S. Naval Forces Central Command and the Fifth Fleet, which will be transferred from Naval Support Activity Bahrain (NSA Bahrain). Unlike the old days, in 2008, when a blockade by Iran of the Strait of Hormuz was described as 'Iranian Suicide' by the Saudi Arabian newspaper *Al-Watan*, the Turkestan Federation of Islamic Republics is now contemplating such an action in retaliation for the new base. Its political leaders argue that it would be better to prevent completion of the base.

Plans are being drawn up by the Federation to begin with a diplomatic offensive, and if that fails to enforce a blockade as a counter-threat to the United States - which would have the double advantage of cutting off supplies to America and also to its Asian allies Japan and Korea. The new military port east of Bandar Abbas, Donggang, and its secondary base in Gwadar, supervises all shipping through the Strait of Hormuz. Chinese aircraft carriers stand off Jask, just outside the Strait, and nuclear submarines patrol in blue water outside territorial waters. On the Chinese Mainland, reserves of oil and gas have been extended from ninety to 120 days, and alternative plans have been made to deliver extra supplies by pipeline and railway using part of the quotas usually available to other member states of the Turkestan Federation.

Historians and older journalists compare the situation to the stand-off between the United States and the Soviet Union off the coast of Cuba in 1962.

Events which could push China and Iran closer

– An American blockade of the Strait of Malacca or the Persian Gulf;
– A Chinese/Iranian blockade of the Persian Gulf;

– An American attack against Russia;
– An American pre-emptive attack on a regional nuclear power (Kazakhstan?);
– Japan adds nuclear capability to a rapidly growing military arsenal;
– North and South Korea reunify, and the new country becomes a nuclear power with regional ambitions;
– An act of terrorism with non-nuclear weapons of mass destruction;
– A catastrophic event in a country within Turkestan directly or indirectly related to the United States and perceived to be both anti-Muslim and anti-Chinese makes it imperative for the two sides to contain the explosion within.

Another War Scenario

At the end of his influential book *The Clash of Civilizations*, Huntington tries to imagine how a war between the United States and China might start and evolve.[13] It is true that he placed this hypothetical war in 2010 (imagined in 1996), which seems rather implausible today, but the basic circumstances that he imagined – that American troops have left Korea, that the two Koreas have reunified, that Taiwan has reached agreement with China by remaining independent but recognising Beijing's suzerainty and has been admitted to the UN – might still happen a little further off than he thought. Say, around 2030–50. As we have hypothesised above, the real dispute here concerns oil.

The key problem in this scenario is Vietnam. The specific issue is a dispute over oil reserves under the South China Sea, or more precisely under the Paracel Islands, which consist of fifteen islets and a dozen or so reefs and banks, roughly equidistant from Hainan Island in the north and Vietnam to the west.

In fact, Chinese maps of the thirteenth century already show these islands, and China claims that they have been used in navigation for over 2,000 years.[14] But the claim has long been disputed by Vietnam, although in the past France also claimed sovereignty and Taiwan has more recently done so. The dispute is therefore long-standing, and merges into the history of other disputes and wars: France annexed the islands in 1932 and set up a meteorological station which passed to Vietnam in 1954, when France, defeated by the Viet Minh, retreated from Asia. In 1974, China took a South Vietnamese garrison holding the western islands and has held them since then; it maintains a token military force there, and in 1997 announced plans to develop tourism on the islands.[15] In this case, after a detailed historical and legal review, Greg Austin, an Australian international affairs expert who has written a detailed study of China's 'Ocean Frontier', comes down in favour of China, although careful phrases such as 'would appear to suggest'[16] show that his opinions are not definitive. In fact, Vietnam, with over 2,000 miles of coastline stretching along the main shipping lanes, is the biggest obstacle to Chinese control of this vital area of sea. In a sense, conflict is inevitable in the long run.

So Huntington's hypotheses meld into a well-known dispute. To turn back to his scenario, China announces that it will exercise control over the entire area, Vietnam resists, and warships of the two countries enter into conflict. Vietnam is supported by the United States, while Japan is concerned about future territorial claims over islands further north if she acquiesces to Chinese demands. Chinese submarines and land-based forces attack US forces from both Taiwan and the mainland, while the PLA enters Hanoi and occupies most of Vietnam. A stand-off situation rapidly develops between two nuclear powers, China and the United States, but many frightened Americans begin to wonder whether it is worth all the trouble to go to war – and nuclear war – over such a distant bit of sea. In view of the demographic section above, it is interesting to note that Huntington refers to the Hispanic population of the south-west as the doubters. But what will be the reaction of a *majority* of non-whites in 2050, when according to the US Census Bureau 30 per cent of Americans will be Hispanic, 15 per cent black, 9.2 per cent Asian and 2 per cent American Indian and Alaska natives?[17]

The situation rapidly spirals out of American control. For when India realises that China is blocked by these new circumstances in the South China Sea, it sees an opportunity to attack Pakistan without fear of Chinese retaliation and reduce its cantankerous neighbour's nuclear and conventional forces – thus removing a future threat to itself. This leads to intervention by Iran, and appeals by Pakistan to its Arab neighbours, and 'India becomes bogged down fighting Iranian troops and Pakistani guerrillas from several different ethnic groups'. The effect spreads west with anti-Western protests in Muslim countries, and results in the overthrow of the Turkish government by Islamic extremists and a massive Arab attack against Israel. In the East, Japan gradually becomes involved and sides with China, one of the consequences of which is the occupation of remaining American military bases in Japan – which America counters by creating a naval blockade of Japan. When Russia, fearing encroachment of its own territory by the conflict, sends reinforcements of troops to Siberia, China retaliates by occupying Vladivostok and the lands of the Amur Valley which were once its own.

A nightmare situation is developing as the Muslim oil producers, now dominated by militants, cut off supplies to Western nations, which means that they must turn to Russia and Central Asia to keep the military machine in motion. It also becomes essential for the United States to seek European support, which further antagonises China. In order to intimidate the European powers, China supplies 'intermediate-range nuclear-capable missiles' secretly to Bosnia and Algeria. The scenario degenerates in a breathless series of actions which defy summary:

> 'Serbia, wishing to reclaim its historic role as the defender of Christianity against the Turks, invades Bosnia. Croatia joins in and the two other countries occupy and partition Bosnia, capture the missiles, and proceed with efforts to complete the ethnic cleansing which they had been forced to stop in the 1990s. Albania and Turkey

attempt to help the Bosnians; Greece and Bulgaria launch invasions of European Turkey and panic erupts in Istanbul as Turks flee across the Bosporus. Meanwhile, a missile with a nuclear warhead, launched from Algeria, explodes outside Marseilles, and NATO retaliates with devastating air attacks against North African targets.'[18]

The whole scenario obviously reflects the contemporary context in which he was writing, for example the Serbs attacking Bosnia, but is all the same disturbing in the plausibility of the domino effects going askew as ancient rivalries and resentments emerge. It is worth recalling that these events are sketched by an ivy league-educated distinguished professor at Harvard University's Department of Government, and not by an extreme religious fanatic.

In an escalating sequence eerily reminiscent of events post-Sarajevo in 1914, to which, ironically, Huntington returns us by implicating the Bosnian capital once again in his future scenario, a squabble over a handful of barren islands and reefs in a remote stretch of ocean - albeit with rich fishing rights and oil deposits beneath - has led to a global war with the United States, Europe, Russia and India on one side pitted against China, Japan, and many Islamic nations on the other. He himself describes the scenario as perhaps 'a wildly implausible fantasy'. Yet the underlying assumption that the United States would seek to frame the issue in terms of international maritime law, while China, and of course Iran, would perceive the American action as a fresh example of imperial arrogance, is perfectly plausible. The real question is another: can we feel totally confident that this or some other sequence will not occur when the tensions we have observed above collide like massive tectonic plates and, in Hardy's phrase, 'consummation comes'?

Notes

1. Goldstein, *Rising to the Challenge*, p. 198.

2. Kurzweil outlines the future rate of change in these terms: '...we won't experience one hundred years of technological advance in the twenty-first century; we will witness in the order of twenty thousand years of progress... or about one thousand years greater than what was achieved in the twentieth century.' Ray Kurweil, *The Singularity Is Near: When Humans Transcend Biology*, New York: Viking, 2005, p. 11. This makes virtually any hypothesis or scenario plausible.

3. A US Geological Survey report, *Assessment of Undiscovered Petroleum Resources of Northern Afghanistan* (2006), found known reserves to be much large than previously thought; it can be downloaded from http://pubs.usgs.gov/fs/2006/3031/. See also the website of the Afghanistan Geological Survey, founded in 1955, for details of geological exploration before the recent wars, at http://www.bgs.ac.uk/AfghanMinerals/geology.htm.

4. *Tehran Times*, 9 October 2008; http://www.tehrantimes.com/Index_view.asp?code=179654. In 2008 I encountered for the first time in five years in western Beijing

two businessmen from Tehran, who I was able to help in a local shop. They were, for reasons not completely clear to me, on a one-night stopover in a hotel on their way from Tehran to Guangzhou for the Canton Fair.

5. Norinco is a typically ambiguous Chinese company, which while branding itself here as an international engineering contracting firm is actually a huge conglomerate with the defence industry as its core business area – and products like precision strike systems, amphibious assault weapons and equipment, long-range suppression weapon systems, anti-aircraft and anti-missile systems, information and night vision products, high-effect destruction systems, anti-terrorism and anti-riot products, and small arms (list of products taken from http://www.norinco.com/c1024/english/aboutnorinco/index.html/.

6. http://www.norinco.com/c1024/english/newscenter/press_08.html; see also http://www.tehranmetro.com/about/facts/history.asp.

7. Wayne M. Morrison, 'China's Economic Conditions', Washington DC: *CRS Report for Congress*, 11 March 2008, pp. 19-20; available at http://digitalcommons.ilr.cornell.edu/key.

8. Quoted in the *Tehran Times*, 9 October 2008; http://www.tehrantimes.com/index_View.asp?code=179658.

9. Huntington, *Clash of Civilizations*, p. 209.

10. Garver, *China and Iran*, p. 38.

11. Kaveh L. Afrasiabi, 'A China base in Iran?' Asiatimesonline, 29 January 2008, http://www.atimes.com/atimes/Middle_East/JA29Ak03.html.

12. John Keefer Douglas, Matthew B. Nelson, Kevin Schwartz, 'Fueling the Dragon's Flame: How China's Energy Demands Affect its Relationships in the Middle East', presented to the
U.S.-China Economic and Security Review Commission, 14 September 2006, p. 2; available at http://www.uscc.gov/researchpapers/comm_research_archive.php.

13. The following summary is based on his account in *Clash of Civilizations*, pp. 313-6.

14. Austin, *China's Ocean Frontier: International Law, Military Force and National Development*, pp. 98–99.

15. https://www.cia.gov/cia/publications/factbook/geos/pf.html.

16. Austin, *China's Ocean Frontier*, p. 130.

17. U.S. Census Bureau News, Press Release, 14 August 2008, available at http://www.census.gov/Press-Release/www/releases/archives/population/012496.html.

18. Huntington, *Clash of Civilizations*, p. 315.

Epilogue

None of the above scenarios is more outlandish, and none of the events within them inherently more unlikely, than the assassination of Archduke Franz Ferdinand in Sarajevo. Indeed, experts in many fields believe that future combinations of military arrogance, a technological error, a major outburst of terrorism, a demographic explosion, global warming, religious confrontation, regional nuclear warfare, or just sheer madness on the part of a single individual with sophisticated weaponry at his or her disposal, will eventually and ineluctably lead to catastrophe. Yet no one can foresee with any degree of certainty what the consequences might be. As the old building blocks of world order, the nation states and the international institutions in which they participate, are replaced and undermined by networks which do not accept the dictates of their treaties and non-proliferation agreements, catastrophe seems a more and more plausible outcome of political and religious disputes. And disputes seem likely when we consider the crucial role of energy and its producers today, and recall the disruptions which radical and extremist oil-state presidents such as Muammar al-Gadaffi and Saddam Hussein have caused in the recent past. To quote the Shell scenario for 2050 once again, 'When all three of the most powerful drivers of our current energy world – demand, supply, and effects on the environment – are set to undergo significant change, we are facing an era of revolutionary transitions and considerable turbulence.'[1]

At the same time, however, the demise of nation states, prophesized in works like Philip Bobbitt's *Shield of Achilles*, is in some ways nothing but a return to the past. Bobbitt himself has a chapter describing the shift from 'state-nations' to 'nation-states' from 1776 to 1914, from what he defines as a 'state that mobilizes a nation – a national, ethnocultural group – to act on behalf of the State' to a state which is created 'in order to benefit the nation it governs' with a constitution, political legitimacy and popular ideals.[2] Those were the days when British surveyors drew straight lines across vast swathes of Turkestan and declared them borders, creating everlasting problems by dividing proud and bellicose peoples between nations which meant little to them, such as the Kurds and the Baluchis. Some, such as the border between Iran and Pakistan, in Baluchistan, running through one of the most hostile environments on earth in the Makran, are virtually indefensible and wide open to the passage of drugs and weapons between East and West; others, like the mountainous frontier between northern Pakistan and Afghanistan, are useless barriers against operations like those of al-Qaida. For, above all else, the loyalty of the people who lived in the deserts and mountains of Turkestan was always in the past and is still today to the family, the clan, the tribe, and – in the case of Muslims – to the *ummah* and to the sect to which they belong. That is why the conflict in Chechnya was not merely a war between Russians and Chechens: 'Political and clan factions were just as capable of fighting each other, and some Chechens chose to collaborate with the Russians to bring the conflict to a conclusion.'[3] Clan and ethnic violence also occurred within the Afghanistan and Tajikistan civil wars, and during the Karabakh conflict, and in the past also in Xinjiang. In Iran, Ayatollah Khomeini was at least in part successful because he rose above the nation state of the Shah, and nationalism, to propagate a world view in which loyalty to Islam trumped loyalty to a temporal state. These examples help us to understand why the tribal and religious loyalties in the crescent which joins China and Iran must always be laid over the modern states which are marked on the conventional map.

For in times of extreme difficulty blood runs thick, and we have seen in Part I of this book how profoundly deep are the similarities between China and Iran, and how influential the resentment and humiliation caused by imperial occupation turn out to be on detailed examination. Should these two countries seek to create a deeper partnership or alliance, it could revolutionise the global order, especially if other oil-and-gas rich states of Turkestan become their partners. In terms of sheer strength, manufacturing dominance, militant Islam, demographic imbalance and domination of the largest oil and gas reserves in the world, this would be a truly formidable alliance.

The above scenarios tally extremely well with those for 2020 elaborated by the National Intelligence Council. Yet these latter are extremely US-focused and tend to ignore Iran in terms of future economic power, with a constant and very American emphasis on 'arriviste' powers such as China, India, Brazil and perhaps Indonesia; Iran is seen more in terms of an 'axis of evil' nemesis, an irrelevance as a conventional threat. These are the scenarios sketched out by the NIC:

> *Davos World*: an illustration of how robust economic growth, led by China and India, over the next fifteen years could reshape the globalisation process and give it a more non-Western face (in the detailed scenario, Davos in 2020 has itself moved to China – not merely the local version in Dalian);

New Caliphate: a global movement fueled by radical religious identity politics could constitute a challenge to Western norms and values;

Pax Americana: US predominance survives radical changes to the global political landscape and serves to fashion a new and inclusive global order;

Cycle of Fear: concerns about proliferation increase to the point that large-scale intrusive security measures are taken to prevent outbreaks of deadly attacks, possibly introducing an Orwellian world.[4]

What, then, is needed, from the point of view of China and Iran, to shift what is now a vague spirit of anti-hegemonic cooperation into a stronger partnership, and eventually into a full-blooded alliance which brings about a China-led 'Davos World' existing in harmony with an Iran-led 'New Caliphate' and eliminate the others, the first of which seems unlikely and the last inauspicable?

Not much. Any *one* of the above events able to 'push China and Iran closer' could be enough, within any variant of the hypothetical scenarios, for something as yet unimaginable to occur – a single drop which causes the cup to overflow. The future we have tried to outline will imply paradigm shifts in technology, economic dominance, power alignments and global governance which no one can predict with certainty, but the historical associations, current mutual interests and future matching needs of China and Iran, which we have described in earlier chapters, all point to closer integration.

That it will happen seems, on balance, given known tensions and the dire threats gathering on the horizon, more likely than unlikely.

Notes

1. Shell Energy Scenarios to 2050, p. 10.
2. Bobbitt, *Shield of Achilles*, Chapter 8, pp. 146 and 201–4.
3. Johnson, *Oil, Islam and Conflict*, p. 241.
4. *Mapping the Global Future*, p. 16.

Bibliography

Abidi, Aqil Hyder Hasan, *China, Iran and the Persian Gulf*, Atlantic Highlands (NJ): Humanities Press, 1982 (New Delhi: Radiant Publishers, 1982)

Abru, Hafiz, *A Persian Embassy to China, Being an Extract from Zubdatu't Tawarikh, Trs. K.M. Maitra* (Reprint of 1934 Lahore edition), New York: Paragon Book Reprint Corp, 1970

Adib-Moghaddam, Arshin, *Iran in World Politics: The Question of the Islamic Republic*, New York: Columbia University Press, 2008

Ahrari, M. Ehsan, 'Iran, China, and Russia: The Emerging Anti-US Nexus?', *Security Dialogue*, Vol. 32, No. 4 (2001), pp. 453-466

Aisin-Goro Pu Yi, *From Emperor to Citizen: The Autobiography of Aisin-Goro Pu Yi*, Translated by W.J.F. Jenner, Beijing: Foreign Languages Press, 1989

Allsen, Thomas, 'The rise of the Mongolian empire and Mongolian rule in North China', in Herbert Franke and Denis Twitchett (Eds), *The Cambridge History of China*, Vol. 6, Cambridge: CUP, 1994, pp. 321-413

Alterman, Jon B. and Garver, John W., *The Vital Triangle: China, the United States, and the Middle East*, Washington, DC: Center for Strategic & International Studies, 2008

Amitai-Press, Reuvan, and Biran, Michal (Eds), *Mongols, Turks, and Others: Eurasian Nomads and the Sedentary World*, Leiden: Brill, 2003

Amitai-Preiss, Reuvan & David O. Morgan (Eds), *The Mongol Empire & Its Legacy*, Leiden: Brill, 2000

Andreeva, Elena, *Russia and Iran in the Great Game: Travelogues and Orientalism*, London: Routledge, 2007

Ansari, Ali, *Iran*, New York: Routledge, 2004

Arberry, A.J., *Sufism: An Account of the Mystics of Islam*, London: George Allen & Unwin, 1950
The Legacy of Persia, Oxford: Clarendon Press, 1953

Arfa, General Hassan, *Under Five Shahs*, London: John Murray, 1964

Asia Research Centre (Ed), *The Great Cultural Revolution in China*, Rutland, VT: Charles E. Tuttle, 1968

Austin, Greg, *China's Ocean Frontier: International Law, Military Force and National Development*, Canberra: Allen & Unwin, 1998

Avery, Peter, *Modern Iran*, London: Ernest Benn, 1965

Azimi, Fakhreddin, *The Quest for Democracy in Iran: A Century of Struggle against Authoritarian Rule*, Cambridge, MA: Harvard University Press, 2008

Bate, Gill, and Oresman, Matthew, *China's New Journey to the West: China's Emergence in Central Asia and Implications for U.S. Interests*, Washington DC: The Center for Strategic and International Studies, 2003

Banani, Amin, *The Modernization of Iran 1921–1941*, Stanford: Stanford University Press, 1961

Baranovitch, Nimrod, *China's New Voices: Popular Music, Ethnicity, Gender, and Politics*, 1978–1998, Berkeley: University of California Press, 2003

Bharier, Julian, *Economic Development in Iran 1900–1970*, Oxford: OUP, 1971

Barnett, A. Doak, *China's Far West: Four Decades of Change*, Boulder (CO): Westview Press, 1993

Barfield, Thomas J., *The Perilous Frontier: Nomadic Empires and China, 221 BC to AD 1757*, Cambridge, MA: Blackwell, 1989

Bayly, C.A., *The Birth of the Modern World 1780–1914*, Oxford: Blackwell, 2004

Bergière, Marie-Claire, *Sun Yat-sen*, Stanford: Stanford University Press, 1994

Berman, Ilan, *Tehran Rising: Iran's Challenge to the United States*, Lanham, MD: Rowman & Littlefield, 2005

—— 'The Logic behind Sino-Iranian Cooperation', *China and Eurasia Forum Quarterly*, Volume 4, No. 4 (2006), pp. 15-23

Biran, Michal, *The Empire of the Qara Khitai in Eurasian History: Between China and the Islamic World*, Cambridge: CUP, 2005

Blasko, Dennis J., *The Chinese Army Today: Tradition and Transformation for the 21st Century*, London: Routledge, 2006

Blücher, Wipert von, *Zeitenwende in Iran. Erlebnisse und Beobachtungen*, Berlin: Biberach, Koehler & Voigtländer, 1949.

Blum, Susan D., and Jensen, Lionel M. (Eds), *China off Center: Mapping the Margins of the Middle Kingdom*, Honolulu: University of Hawai'i Press, 2002

Blumenthal, Dan, 'Providing Arms: China and the Middle East', *Middle East Quarterly*, Spring 2005, pp. 11-19.

Bobbitt, Philip, *The Shield of Achilles: War, Peace and the Course of History*, London: Allen Lane, 2002

—— *Terror and Consent: The Wars for the Twenty-First Century*, New York: Alfred A. Knopf, 2008

Boulger, Demetrius Charles, *The Life of Yakoob Beg; Athalik Ghazi, and Badaulet, Ameer of Kashgar*, London: W.H. Allen, 1878

Boyle, J.A., *The History of the World Conqueror*, Manchester: University of Manchester Press, 1958 (2 vols)

Bretschneider, E., *On the Knowledge Possessed by the Ancient Chinese of the Arabs and Arabian Colonies, and Other Western Countries, Mentioned in Chinese Books*, London: Trübner & Co, 1871

—— *Notes on Chinese Mediæval Travellers to the West*, Shanghai: American Presbyterian Mission Press, 1875

—— *Medieval Researches from Eastern Asiatic Sources: Fragments Towards the Knowledge of the Geography and History of Central and Western Asia from the 13th to the 17th Century*, London: Trübner & Co, 1888, 2 vols

Broomhall, Marshall, *Islam in China: A Neglected Problem*, London: Morgan & Scott, 1910

Brown Lester R., *Plan B 2.0: Rescuing a Planet Under Stress and a Civilization in Trouble*, New York: W.W. Norton, 2006

Browne, Edward G., *A Literary History of Persia, From the Earliest Times until Firdawsí*, London: T. Fisher Unwin, 1902

—— *A Literary History of Persia, Volume II: From Firdawsí to Sa'dí*, London: T. Fisher Unwin, 1906

—— *The Persian Revolution of 1905–1909*, Cambridge: Cambridge University Press, 1910

—— *The Persian Crisis of December, 1911; How It Arose and Whither It May Lead Us*, Cambridge: Privately Printed at the University Press, 1912

Brysac, Shareen Blair, 'A Very British Coup: How Reza Shah Won and Lost His Throne,' *World Policy Journal*, Summer 2007, Vol. 24, No. 2, pp. 90–103.

Brzezinski, Zbigniew, *The Grand Chessboard: American Primacy and its Geostrategic Imperative*, New York: Basic Books, 1997

Burman, Edward, *The Assassins: Holy Killers of Islam*, Wellingborough: Crucible, 1987

—— *The World Before Columbus 1100–1492*, London: W.H. Allen, 1989

—— *Stealth Empire*, Stroud: Sutton, 2008

Bush, Richard C., and O'Hanlon, Michael E., *A War Like No Other: The Truth about China's Challenge to America*, Hoboken, NJ: John Wiley, 2007

Byman, Daniel L., Cliff, Roger, *China's Arms Sales: Motivations and Implications*, Washington DC: Rand, 1999

Byron, Robert, *The Road to Oxiana*, London: John Lehmann, 1950

Calabrese, John, 'China and Iran: Mismatched Partners', *Occasional Papers*, Washington: The Jamestown Foundation, August 2006; available at www.jamestown.org

—— Testimony in *China's Proliferation to North Korea and Iran, and its Role in Addressing the Nuclear and Missile Situations in both Nations*, Washington: US-China Economic and Security Commission, 14 September 2006, pp. 40–9

Cantlie, James, and Sheridan Jones, C., *Sun Yat Sen and the Awakening of China*, New York: Fleming H. Revell, 1912

Chen, Jack, *The Sinkiang Story*, New York: Macmillan, 1977

Cheng, Kevin C., 'Economic Implication of China's Demographics in the 21st Century', *Washington: International Monetary Fund* (WP/03/29), 2003.

Ch'en, Yuan, *Western and Central Asians in China Under the Mongols: Their transformation into Chinese*, Los Angeles: Monumenta Serica at the University of California, 1966

Chung, Jae Ho (Ed), *Charting China's Future: Political, Social, and International Dimensions*, Lanham, MD: Rowman & Littlefield, 2006

Cole, Juan, *Sacred Space and Holy War: The Politics, Culture and History of Shi'ite Islam*, London: IB Tauris, 2002

Collins, Gabriel B., Erickson, Andrew S., Goldstein, Lyle J., and Murray, William S. (Eds), *China's Energy Strategy: The Impact on Beijing's Maritime Politics*, Annapolis, MD, Naval Institute Press, 2008

Cottam, Richard W., *Nationalism in Iran*, Pittsburgh: University of Pittsburg Press, 1964

Cresson, W.P., Persia: *The Awakening East, Phildelphia & London*: J. B. Lippincott, 1908

Cronin, Stephanie, *The Making of Modern Iran: State and Society Under Riza Shah*, London: Routledge Curzon, 2003

Crossley, Pamela Kyle, *A Translucent Mirror: History and Identity in Qing Imperial Ideology*, Berkley: University of California Press, 1999

Crossley, Pamela Kyle & Siu, Helen F. & Sutton, Donald S., *Empire at the Margins: Culture, Ethnicity, and Frontier in Early Modern China*, Berkley: University of California Press, 2006

Curzon, George N., *Russia in Central Asia in 1889 and the Anglo-Russian Question*, London: Longmans, Green, and Co., 1889

Dabashi, Hamid, *Iran: A People Interrupted*, New York: New Press, 2007

—— 'The End of Islamic Ideology,' *Social Research*, Vol. 67, Number 2, Summer 2000, pp. 475–518

Daftari, Maryam, 'Sino-Iranian Relations and "Encounters": Past and Present', *Iranian Journal of International Affairs*, Vol. 7, No. 4 (Winter 1996), pp. 854–76

De Groot, Joanna, *Religion, Culture and Politics in Iran: From the Qajars to Khomeini*, London: I.B. Tauris, 2007

De Filippi, Filippo, *Storia della Spedizione Scientifica Italiana nel Himàlaia Caracorlim e Turchestàn Cinese (1913–1914), con capitoli aggiuntivi di Giotto Dainelli e J.A. Spranger*, Bologna: Nicola Zanichelli Editore, 1923

Dillon, Michael, *China's Muslim Hui Community*, Richmond (Surrey): Curzon, 1999

Dittmer, Lowell and Kim, Samuel S. (Eds), *China's Quest for National Identity*, Ithaca: Cornell University Press, 1993

Douglas, John Keefer, Nelson, Matthew B., and Schwartz, Kevin, 'Fueling the Dragon's Flame: How China's Energy Demands Affect its Relationships in the Middle East', Washington: *U.S.-China Economic and Security Review Commission*, 14 September, 2006; available at www.uscc.gov/researchpapers/2006/China_ME_FINAL.pdf

Dreyfuss, Robert, *Hostage to Khomeini*, New York: New Benjamin Franklin House, 1980

Elwell-Sutton, L.P., *Modern Iran*, London: Routledge, 1941

Esposito, John L. (Ed.), *The Iranian Revolution: Its Global Impact*, New York: Oxford University Press, 2001

Evans, Richard, *Deng Xiaoping and the Making of Modern China*, New York: Viking, 1993

Fairbank, John King, (Ed), *The Chinese World Order: Traditional China's Foreign Relations*, Cambridge, MA: Harvard University Press, 1970

Fairbank, John King., *The United States and China*, Cambridge, MA: Harvard University Press, 1983

Fenby, Jonathan, *Generalissimo Chiang Kai-Shek and the China He Lost*, London: The Free Press, 2003

Fleming, Peter, *News From Tartary: A Journey from Peking to Kashmir*, London: Futura, 1980

Floor, Willem, 'Industrialization in Iran 1900–1941', *CMEIS Occasional Paper Series* No. 23, University of Durham, Centre for Middle Eastern and Islamic Studies, 1984; available at http://eprints.dur.ac.uk/archive/00000187/

Fogel, Robert W., 'Capitalism and Democracy in 2040: Forecasts and Speculations', *Working Paper 13184*, Cambridge (Mass.): National Bureau of Economic Research, June 2007

Forsyth, T.D. (Ed), *Report of a Mission to Yarkund in 1873 under command of Sir T.D. Forsyth with historical and geographical information regarding the possessions of the ameer of Yarkund*, Calcutta: Foreign Department Press, 1875

Fuller, Graham E., and Starr, S. Frederick, *The Xinjiang Problem*, Baltimore: Central Asia-Caucasus Institute, John Hopkins University, 2005

Fung, Edmund S.K., *The Military Dimension of the Chinese Revolution: The New Army and its Role in the Revolution of 1911*, Vancouver: University of British Columbia Press, 1908

Gardner, Charles S., *Chinese Traditional Historiography*, Cambridge, MA*f*: Harvard University Press, 1983

Garver, John W., *Protracted Contest; Sino-Indian Rivalry in the Twentieth Century*, Seattle, WA: University of Washington Press, 2001

—— *China and Iran: Ancient Partners in a Post-Imperial World*, Seattle, WA: University of Washington Press, 2007

Gentry, J. Brandon, 'The Dragon and the Magi: Burgeoning Sino-Iranian Relations in the 21st Century', *China and Eurasia Forum Quarterly*, Vol. 3, No. 3 (2005), pp. 111–25

Gill, Bates, 'Chinese Arms Exports to Iran', *Middle East Review of International Affairs*, Vol. 2, No. 2 (May 1998, pp. 55–70

—— *Rising Star: China's New Security Diplomacy*, Washington D.C.: Brookings Institution Press, 2007

Gillette, Maris Boyd, *Between Mecca and Beijing: Modernization and Consumption Among Young Urban Chinese Muslims*, Stanford: Stanford University Press, 2000

Giustozzi, Antonio, *Koran, Kalashnikov, and Laptop: The Neo-Taliban Insurgency in Afghanistan*, New York: Columbia University Press, 2008

Gladney, Dru, *Muslim Chinese: Ethnic Nationalism in the People's Republic*, Cambridge, MA: Harvard University Press, 1996

—— *Ethnic Identity in China: The Making of a Muslim Minority Nationality*, New York: Harcourt Brace College Publishers, 1998

—— 'Whither the Uighur?' *Harvard Asia Pacific Review*, Winter 1998–99, Vol. 3, No 1, pp. 11–16

—— 'Central Asia and China: Transnationalization, Islamization, and Ethnicization', in John L. Esposito (Ed), *The Oxford History of Islam*, Oxford and New York: Oxford University Press, 1999, pp. 432-73

—— *Dislocating China: Muslims, Minorities, and Other Subaltern Subjects*, Chicago: University of Chicago Press, 2004

—— 'The Chinese Program of Development and Control, 1978–2001', in S. Frederick Starr (Ed), *Xinjiang: China's Muslim Borderland*, Armonk, NY: M.E. Sharpe, 2004, pp. 101-19

Goldstein, Avery, *Rising to the Challenge: China's Grand Strategy and International Security*, Stanford: Stanford University Press, 2005

—— 'The Diplomatic Face of China's Grand Strategy: A Rising Power's Emerging Choice', *The China Quarterly*, No. 168 (December 2001), pp. 835–64

Gries, Peter Hays, *China's New Nationalism: Pride, Politics, and Diplomacy*, Berkeley: University of California Press, 2004

—— 'China Eyes the Hegemon', *Orbis: A Journal of World Affairs*, Summer 2005, pp.401-412

—— 'Forecasting US-China Relations, 2015', *Asian Security*, Vol. 2, No. 2, June 2006, pp.1–23

Haas, William S., *Iran*, New York: Columbia University Press, 1946

Hahn, Gordon M., *Russia's Islamic Threat*, New Haven: Yale University Press, 2007

Hancock, Kathleen J., 'Escaping Russia, Looking to China: Turkmenistan Pins Hopes on China's Thirst for Natural Gas', *China and Eurasia Forum Quarterly*, Volume 4, No. 3 (2006), pp. 67–87

Hannas, William C., *The Writing on the Wall: How Asian Orthography Curbs Creativity*, Philadelphia: University of Pennsylvania Press, 2003

Harding, Harry, *China's Second Revolution: Reform After Mao*, Washington: The Brookings Institution, 1987

Heinson, Gunnar, *Söhne und Weltmacht*, Zürich: Orell Fuessli Verlag, 2006

Hirsch, Robert L., 'Peaking of World Oil Production: Impacts, Mitigation, & Risk Management', Washington: Science Applications International Corporation (for the US Department of Energy), February 2006; available at www.netl.doe.gov/publications/others/pdf/Oil_Peaking_NETL.pdf

Hitti, Philip K., *History of the Arabs from the Earliest Times to the Present*, London: Macmillan, 1970 (10th edition)

Hopkirk, Peter, *The Great Game: On Secret Service in High Asia*, Oxford: OUP, 1991

Hoveyda, Fereydoun, *The Fall of the Shah: The Inside Story by the Shah's Former Ambassador to the United Nations*, London: Weidenfeld and Nicholson, 1979

Howard, Roger, *Iran Oil: The New Middle East Challenge to America*, London: I.B. Tauris, 2007

Howarth, Peter, *China's Rising Sea Power: The PLA Navy's Submarine Challenge*, London: Routledge, 2006

Hsüeh, Chün-tu, *The Chinese Revolution of 1911: New Perspectives*, Hong Kong: Joint Publishing Co., 1986

Huff, Toby E., *Rise of Early Modern Science: Islam, China, and the West*, Cambridge: CUP, 1993

Huntington, Samuel P., 'The Clash of Civilizations?' *Foreign Affairs*, Summer 1993, Vol. 72, Number 3, pp. 22-49

—— *The Clash of Civilizations? The Debate*, New York: Council on Foreign Relations, 1996

—— *The Clash of Civilizations and the Remaking of World Order*, New York: Simon & Schuster, 1996

Isaacs, Harold R., *Scratches on our Minds: American Views of China and India*, Armonk, NY: M.E. Sharpe, 1980

Johnson, Rob, *Oil, Islam and Conflict: Central Asia Since 1945*, London: Reaktion Books, 2007

Johnson, Robert, *Spying for Empire: The Great Game in Central and South Asia, 1757–1947*, London: Greenhill, 2006

Juvaini, *Ala-ad-Din 'Ata-Malik, The History of the World Conqueror, Translated From the Text of Mirza Muhammad Qazvini* by John Andrew Boyle, Manchester: Manchester Unievrsity Press, 1958, 2 vols.

Kagan, Robert, *The Return of History and the End of Dreams*, New York: Knopf, 2008

Kaltman, Blaine, *Under the Heel of the Dragon: Islam, Racism, Crime, and the Uighur in China*, Athens, OH: Ohio University Press, 2007

Katouzian, Homa & Shahidi, Hossein (Eds), *Iran in the 21st Century: Politics, Economics & Conflict*, London: Routledge, 2008

Karl, Rebecca E., *Staging the World: Chinese Nationalism at the Turn of the Twentieth Century*, Durham and London: Duke University Press, 2002

Khanna, Parag, *The Second World: Empires and Influence in the New World Order*, New York: Random House, 2008

Kim, Hodong, *Holy War in China: The Muslim Rebellion and State in Chinese Central Asia, 1864–1877*, Stanford: Stanford University Press, 2004

Kuropatkin, A.N., *Kashgaria (Eastern or Chinese Turkistan): Historical and Geographical Sketch of the Country; its Military Strength, Industries and Trade*, Calcutta: Thacker, Spink and Co, 1882 (facsimile reprint by Elibron Classics in 2003)

Laing, Margaret, *The Shah*, London: Sidgwick & Jackson, 1977

Lattimore, Owen, *The Desert Road to Turkestan*, New York: Little, Brown, 1929

—— *Pivot of Asia: Sinkiang and the Inner Asian Frontiers of China and Russia*, Boston: Little, Brown, 1950

—— *Inner Asian Frontiers of China*, American Geographical Society, Research Series, No.21, Irving-on-Hudson, NY: Capitol Publishing, 1951

—— *Studies in Frontier History: Collected Papers 1928–1958*, London: OUP, 1962

Laufer, Berthold, 'Sino-Iranica: Chinese contributions to the history of civilization in ancient Iran, with special reference to the history of cultivated plants and products', *Publication 201, Anthropological Series*, Chicago: Field Museum of Natural History, 1919, Vol. XV, No. 3, pp. 185–630

Lenczowski, George, *Russia and the West in Iran, 1918–1927*, New York: Cornell University Press, 1949

Levenson, Joseph R., *Liang Ch'i-Ch'ao and the Mind of Modern China*, Berkeley: University of California Press, 1967

Levin, Michael L., *The Next Great Clash: China and Russia vs. the United States*, Westport, CT: Praeger Security International, 2008

Lewis, Jeffrey G., *The Minimum Means of Reprisal: China's Search for Security in the Nuclear Age*, Cambridge (Mass): MIT Press, 2007

Li, Lillian M., Dray-Novey. Alison J., and Kong, Haili, *Beijing: From Imperial Capital to Olympic City*, London: Palgrave Macmillan, 2007

Liu, Lydia H., *The Clash of Empires: The Invention of China in Modern World Making*, Cambridge, MA: Harvard University Press, 2004

Longhurst, Henry, *Adventure in Oil: The Story of British Petroleum*, London: Sidgwick and Jackson, 1959

Longrigg, Stephen Hemsley, *Oil in the Middle East: Its Discovery and Development*, Oxford: OUP, 1954

Mackerras, Colin, *The Uighur Empire, According to the T'ang Dynastic Histories*, Canberra: Australian National University Press, 1972

Mackinder, Halford J., 'The geographical pivot of history', *The Geographical Journal*, Vol. XXIII, No. 4. (1904), pp. 421–44

—— *Democratic Ideals and Reality*, London: Constable, 1942

Mahan, Alfred Thayer, *The Influence of Sea Power Upon History*, London: Sampson Low, 1890

Majd, Mohammad G., *Great Britain and Reza Shah: The Plunder of Iran*, 1921–1941. Miami: University Press of Florida, 2001

Marashi, Afshin, *Nationalizing Iran: Culture, Power, and the State*, 1870–1940, Seattle: University of Washington Press, 2008

Martin, *The Meaning of the 21st Century: A Vital Blueprint or Ensuring Our Future*, London: Eden Project Books, 2006

Mason, Isaac, 'A Chinese Life of Mohammed', *Journal of the North-China Branch of the Royal Asiatic Society*, Vol. LI (1920), pp. 159–160

—— 'Notes on Chinese Mohammedan Literature', *Journal of the North-China Branch of the Royal Asiatic Society*, Vol. LV (1924), pp. 172–215

—— *When and How Muhammadanism Entered China*, London: China Society, 1932

Melman, Yossi and Javedanfar, Meir, *The Nuclear Sphinx of Tehran: Mahmud Ahmadinejad and the State of Iran*, New York: Carroll & Graf, 2007

Mi, Shoujiang and You, Jia, *Islam in China*, Beijing: Intercontinental Press, 2004

Millward, James A., *Beyond the Pass: Economy, Ethnicity and Empire in Qing Central Asia, 1759–1864*, Stanford: Stanford University Press, 1998

—— *Eurasian Crossroads: A History of Xinjiang*, New York: Columbia University Press, 2007

Minosrksy, V., 'Tamim ibn Bahr's Journey to the Uyghurs', *Bulletin of the School of Oriental and African Studies*, University of London, Vol. 12, No. 2 (1948), pp. 275-305

Mitter, Rana, *Bitter Revolution: China's Struggle With the Modern World*, Oxford: OUP, 2004

Morgan, David, *The Mongols*, Oxford: Blackwell, 1986

Mote, F.W., *Imperial China 900–1800*, Cambridge, MA: Harvard University Press, 1999

Mott, William H., and Kim Jae Chang, *The Philosophy of Chinese Military Culture: Shih vs. Li*, New York: Palgrave Macmillan, 2006

Nasr, Vali, *The Shia Revival: How Conflicts Within Islam Will Shape the Future*, New York: Norton, 2006

Navarro, Peter, *The Coming China Wars: Where They Will Be Fought and How They Can Be Won*, Upper Saddle River, NJ: FT Press, 2007

Newby, L.J., *The Empire and the Khanate: A Political History of Qing Relations with Khoqand c.1760–1860*, Leiden: Brill, 2005

Ng, Ka Po, *Interpreting China's Military Power: Doctrine Makes Readiness*, London: Frank Cass, 2005

Nyíri, Pál, and Breidenbach, Joana, *China Inside Out: Contemporary Chinese Nationalism and Transnationalism*, Budapest: Central European University Press, 2005

Olmstead, A.T., *History of the Persian Empire*, Chicago: Chicago University Press, 1970

Pahlavi, Mohammed Reza Shah, *Mission for My Country*, London: Hutchinson, 1960

Paine, S.C.M., *Imperial Rivals: China, Russia, and Their Disputed Frontier*, Armonk, NY: M.E. Sharpe, 1996

Pakravan, Emineh, *Vieux Teheran*, Tehran: La Banque Melli-e Iran, 1962

Perdue, Peter C., *China Marches West: The Qing Conquest of Central Eurasia*, Cambridge, MA: Belknap Press, 2005

Perlin, Ross, 'Where Four Worlds Meet" Russians, Kazakhs, Uighurs, and Han Chinese in the PRC-Kazakhstan Border Zone', *Journal of the China-Eurasia Forum*, October 2004, pp. 22-7

Pezeshkzad, Iraj, *My Uncle Napoleon: A Novel*, New York: The Modern Library, 2006

Pollack, Jonathan D. (Ed), *Strategic Surprise? U.S.–China Relations in the Early Twenty-first Century*, Newport (RI): Naval War College Press, 2003

Pottinger, Henry, *Travels in Beloochistan and Sinde; Accompanied by a Geographical and Historical Account of Those Countries*, London: Longman, Hurst, Rees, Orme, and Brown, 1816

Prasenjit, Duara, *Rescuing History from the Nation: Questioning Narratives of Modern China*, Chicago: University of Chicago Press, 1997

Pulleyblank, Edwin G., 'Chinese-Iranian Relations in Pre-Islamic Times', *Encyclopaedia Iranica*, Ehsan Yarshater (Ed), Vol.5, fascicle 4, pp. 424–431

Quillen, Chris, 'Iranian Nuclear Weapons Policy: Past, Present and Possible Future', *Middle East Review of International Affairs*, Vol. 6, No. 2 (2002), pp. 17–24.

Rashid, A., *Jihad: The Rise of Militant Islam in Central Asia*, New Haven: Yale University Press, 2002

Rasgotra, M. K. (Ed), *The New Asian Power Dynamic*, New Delhi: Sage Publications, 2007

Ramazani, Rouhollah K., *The Foreign Policy of Iran: A Developing Nation in Foreign Affairs 1500-1941*, Charlottesville: University Press of Virginia, 1966

Redhouse, James W. (Ed. & Trs), *The Diary of H.M. the Shah of Persia, during his tour through Europe in A.D. 1873*, London: John Murray, 1874

Rezun, Miron, *The Soviet Union and Iran: Soviet Policy in Iran from the Beginnings of the Pahlavi Dynasty Until the Soviet Invasion in 1941*, Boulder, CO: Westview Press, 1980

—— 'Reza Shah's Court Minister: Teymourtash', *International Journal of Middle East Studies*, Vol. 12, No. 2 (September 1980), pp. 119–137

Rittenberg, Sidney, *The Man Who Stayed Behind*, Durham, NC: Duke University Press, 2001

Roberts, Paul, *The End of Oil: the Decline of the Petroleum Economy and the Rise of a New Energy Order*, London: Bloomsbury, 2004

Robertson, Jacquelin T., 'Shahestan Pahlavi: Steps Toward a New Iranian Centre', in Renata Holod (Ed), *Toward an Architecture in the Spirit of Islam*, Philadelphia: The Aga Khan Award for Architecture, 1978, pp. 44–51

Rossabi, Morris, *Khubilai Khan: His Life and Times*, Berkeley: University of California Press, 1988

—— 'The reign of Khubilai Khan', in Herbert Franke and Denis Twitchett (Eds), *The Cambridge History of China*, Vol. 6, Cambridge: CUP, 1994, pp. 414–89

—— *China and Inner Asia: From 1368 to the Present Day*, London: Thames and Hudson, 1975

Rowland, John, and Basil, Second Baron Cadman, *Ambassador for Oil: The Life of John, First Baron Cadman*, London: Herbert Jenkins, 1960

Said, Edward W., *Orientalism*, New York: Vintage, 1979

—— *Culture and Imperialism*, New York: Vintage, 1994

Sanghvi, Ramesh, *Aryamehr: The Shah of Iran, A Political Biography*, London: Macmillan, 1968

Schiffrin, Harold Z., *Sun Yat-sen and the Origins of the Chinese Revolution*, Berkeley: University of California Press, 1970

Schwarcz, Vera, *The Chinese Enlightenment: Intellectuals and the Legacy of the May Fourth Movement*, Berkeley: University of California Press, 1986

Schwartz, Benjamin, *In Search of Wealth and Power: Yen Fu and the West*, Cambridge, MA: Harvard University Press, 1964

Scobell, Andrew, *China's Use of Military Force: Beyond the Great Wall and the Long March*, Cambridge: CUP, 2003

Seagrave, Sterling, *Lords of the Rim: The Invisible Empire of the Overseas Chinese*, New York: G.P Putnam's Sons, 1995

Shambaugh, David, *Modernizing China's Military: Progress, Problems, and Prospects*, Berkeley: University of California Press, 2002

Shen, Fuwei, *Cultural Flow Between China and Outside World Throughout History*, Beijing: Foreign Languages Press, 1996

Shichor, Yitzhak, *The Middle East in China's Foreign Policy 1949–1977*, Cambridge: CUP, 1979

Shih, Chih-Yu, *Navigating Sovereignty: World Politics Lost in China*, New York: Palgrave Macmillan, 2003

Skinner, Anthony, 'Fuelling the People's Republic', *The Middle East*, January 2008

Soucek, Svat, *A History of Inner Asia*, Cambridge: CUP, 2000

Spence, Jonathan, *The Chan's Great Continent: China in Western Minds*, New York: Norton, 1998

—— *The Search for Modern China*, 2nd Edition, New York: Norton, 1999

Starr, S. Frederick (Ed), *Xinjiang: China's Muslim Borderland*, Armonk (NY): M.E. Sharpe, 2004

Stevens, Roger, *The Land of the Great Sophy*, London: Methuen, 1962

Su, Xiaokang, and Wang, Luxiang, *Deathsong of the River: A Reader's Guide to the Chinese TV Series Heshang*, Ithaca: East Asia Program, Cornell University, 1991

Sun Tzu, *The Art of War*, Trs. Lionel Giles, London: Luzac & Co, 1910

Sun, Yat-sen, *The International Development of China*, London: Hutchinson, 1922

—— *San Min Chu I: The Three Principles of the People*, Taipei: China Cultural Service, 1953

Sykes, Christopher, *Four Studies in Loyalty*, London: Collins, 1946

Teng, Ssu-yü and Fairbank, John K., *China's Response to the West: a documentary survey 1839–1923*, Cambridge, MA: Harvard University Press, 1961

Terrill, Ross, *The New Chinese Empire, and What it Means for the United States*, New York: Basic Books, 2003

Tu, Wei-ming, 'Cultural China: the periphery as the center', *Daedalus*, Volume 134, Number 4, Fall 2005, pp. 145–167

Upton, Joseph M., *The History of Modern Iran: An Interpretation*, Cambridge, MA: Harvard University Press, 1968

Waley-Cohen, Joanna, *Exile in Mid-Qing China: Banishment to Xinjiang, 1758–1820*, New Haven: Yale University Press, 1991

Wang, Q. Edward, *Inventing China Through History: The May Fourth Approach to Historiography*, Albany, MA: State University of New York Press, 2001

Waterfield, Gordon, *Professional Diplomat: Sir Percy Loraine of Kirkharle Bt. 1880–1961*, London: John Murray, 1973

Watson, Francis, *The Frontiers of China*, New York: Frederick A. Praeger, 1966

Wayne, Martin I., *China's War on Terrorism: Counter-insurgency, Politics and Internal Security*, London: Routledge, 2008

Weale, B.L. Putnam, *The Fight for the Republic in China*, London: Hurst & Blackett, 1918

Weidenbaum, Murray L and Hughes, Samuel, *The Bamboo Network: How Expatriate Chinese Entrepreneurs Are Creating a New Economic Superpower in Asia*, New York: Free Press, 1996

Wickens, G.M., 'Persian Literature as an Affirmation of National Identity', in *Review of National Literatures*, Volume II, Number 1, Spring 1971, pp. 29–60

Wilson, Sir Arnold, *S.W. Persia: Letters and Diary of a Young Political Officer 1907–1914*, London: Readers Union Limited, 1942

Whitlock, Eugene (Ed), *Iran and Its Neighbours: Diverging Views on a Strategic Region*, Berlin: Stiftung Wissenschaft und Politik (German Institute for International and Security Affairs), 2003

Wright, David, 'Yan Fu and the Tasks of the Translator', in Michael Lackner, Iwo Amelung and Joachim Kurtz (Eds), *New Terms for New Ideas. Western Knowledge and Lexical Change in Late Imperial China*, Leiden: Brill, 2001, pp. 235–256

Wright, Dennis, *The English Amongst the Persians, During the Qajar Period 1787–1921*, London: Heinemann, 1977

Wright, Robin, *The Last Great Revolution: Turmoil and Transformation in Iran*, New York: Vintage Books, 2000

Wynn, Antony, 'Abul Ghassem Khan Gharagozlou, Nasser ul-Molk: The First Persian at Balliol', *Balliol College Record*, 2006, pp. 18-21

Yeh, Wen-hsin (Ed), *Becoming Chinese: Passages to Modernity and Beyond*, Berkeley: University of California Press, 2000

Yemelianova, Galina M., 'The Rise of Islam in Muslim Eurasia: Internal Determinants and Potential Consequences', *China and Eurasia Forum Quarterly*, Vol. 5, No. 2 (2007), pp. 73–91

Young, T. Cuyler, 'The Problem of Westernization in Modern Iran', *The Middle East Journal*, Vol. 2, No. 1 (1948), pp. 47-59

Zhang, Xinxin and Sang, Ye, *Chinese Profiles*, Beijing: Panda Books, 1986

Zhang, Yongjin and Austin, Greg (Eds), *Power and Responsibility in Chinese Foreign Policy*, Canberra: Asia Pacific Press

Zirinsky, Michael P., 'Imperial Power and Dictatorship: Britain and the Rise of Reza Shah, 1921–1926', *International Journal of Middle East Studies*, Vol. 24 (1992), pp. 639–663

Zonis, Marvin, *The Political Elite of Iran*, Princeton University Press: Princeton, 1971

Index

NB: Since the events in the final chapter of scenarios are hypothetical, reference is not made to countries or places cited in that chapter.